TOEFL

托福
词组必备

俞敏洪 ◦ 编著

浙江教育出版社·杭州

图书在版编目(CIP)数据

托福词组必备 / 俞敏洪编著. —杭州：浙江教育
出版社，2012（2013.4 重印）

ISBN 978-7-5338-9537-2

Ⅰ．①托… Ⅱ．①俞… Ⅲ．①TOEFL—词汇—自学参
考资料 Ⅳ．①H313

中国版本图书馆 CIP 数据核字（2012）第 003687 号

托福词组必备

编　　著	俞敏洪
责任编辑	孔令宇　张　茜
责任校对	黄英妮
责任印务	陆　江
封面设计	大愚设计
出版发行	浙江教育出版社
	（杭州市天目山路 40 号　　邮编：310013）
印　　刷	北京鑫海达印刷有限公司
开　　本	880×1230　1/32
印　　张	8
字　　数	242 000
版　　次	2012 年 2 月第 1 版
印　　次	2013 年 4 月第 3 次印刷
标准书号	ISBN 978-7-5338-9537-2
定　　价	22.00 元
联系电话	0571－85170300－80928
电子邮箱	bj62605588@163.com
网　　址	www. zjeph. com

新东方图书策划委员会

主任　俞敏洪

委员　（按姓氏笔画为序）

王　强　　包凡一

仲晓红　　沙云龙

陈向东　　张洪伟

邱政政　　汪海涛

周成刚　　徐小平

谢　琴　　窦中川

前　言

　　对于许多中国考生而言，托福听力、口语一直以来都是弱项，这两部分难就难在发音不适应、语速跟不上、词汇量上不去，以及一些用法不熟悉。很多考生往往因为一两个单词、词组没听明白而丢分，令人扼腕叹息。在托福听力和口语考试中有许多词组，其用法是不容忽视的部分。先来看看下面这几个托福考试中的常用词组：

come what may	cut in
drive sb. up the wall	finishing touch

　　这些词组中的单词本身都不难，但组合在一起后却让很多考生感到陌生。在考试中，如果没掌握这些词组的意思，就会给理解文章造成障碍，影响做题，从而影响最终的分数。它们的意思分别是："不管怎样"、"（汽车）超车抢档"、"把某人逼到绝境"、"收尾；最后润色"。从上述例子可以看出，有时单单掌握了词组中的每个单词并不保证就能理解整个词组的意思与用法，而这正是许多考生徒有丰富的词汇量却无法在考试中取得高分的症结所在。托福听力和口语材料模拟真实的交流语境，包含大量生动的习语和词组，对考生的词汇量更是提出了一个高要求。因此，本书通过深入分析和研究托福考试的历次机经和真题，全面收录考试中的常用词组，为考生打造一条更从容的应试之路。

本书特色

1. 紧扣真题，选词科学

　　本书在严格分析托福考试特点的基础上，结合中国考生的弱项，从历次托福机经的听力原文与口语考试材料中精选大量词组，保证了词组的常考性与实用性，帮助考生学习原汁原味的托福常考词组，更加高效地备考。

2. 例句经典，原汁原味

　　本书精选大量托福听力和口语真题例句，为记忆词组提供准确语境，加深理解记忆。同时力求再现真实考试场景，帮助考生更好地熟悉考试难度，了解考查要点。其中，部分例句在书中重复出现，让考生反复记忆，掌握经典。

3. 同义词组，扩充词汇量

熟悉托福听力考试的考生会发现，将听力材料和题目对应起来是托福听力的难点之一，这要求考生掌握大量的同义单词和词组，如用 finish with 代替 end up with。口语考试中考生也应尽量丰富自己的语言，采用不同表达，给考官留下词汇量丰富的印象，从而获得高分。针对这一特点，本书针对重点词组选取了大量同/近义词组，帮助考生扩充词汇量，使表达更加多样化。

4. 要点提示，有力补充

本书总结听力、口语中的重点难点，如单词音变、连读、用法区别等相关知识，帮助考生掌握考试技巧，克服发音、用法上的障碍。归纳大量与主词组相关的表达，方便考生进行词群记忆，扩充词汇量。同时，为主词组补充必要的背景知识，丰富有趣，加深记忆。如：in contest，该词组中 contest(比赛)这个单词还有两个常考的同义词 race 和 match，本书对三个单词所出现的语境做了详细的总结和区别。再如：opportunity cost，该词组的中文释义是"机会成本"，是一个经济学概念，本书对其进行了清晰明了的解释。

5. 幽默插图，巧妙助记

本书为词组配备约 100 幅生动有趣的插图，变抽象记忆为形象记忆，为考生营造一个愉悦的学习氛围，高效学习词组。

本书旨在为考生解决托福考试中的词组难题，衷心希望它能帮助广大考生在托福考试中取得优异的成绩！

新东方教育科技集团董事长兼总裁

目 录

Unit 1

10% discount　10%的折扣，九折

☞ There is a *10% discount* for the new flavor in the ice cream parlor. 在这家冰激凌店购买新口味的冰激凌会打九折。

50% off　半价

☞ I went shopping today and got this necklace for *50% off*. 我今天逛街以半价买下了这条项链。

☞ half price

a balance of nature　自然平衡

☞ The conservationists are trying their best to maintain *a balance of nature*. 环保主义者正在尽全力维持生态平衡。

a beach person　常去海滩的人

☞ A: Jennifer is going to the shore again this weekend.

　 B: Well, she's always been *a beach person*.

　 A：珍妮弗这周末又要去海滩了。

　 B：嗯，她一直都是个经常去海滩的人。

a bunch of　一群；一束

☞ A: *A bunch of* us are getting together to go to the basketball game on Saturday afternoon. You want to come?

　 B: Oh, I'd love to, but I have to work.

　 A：我们一群人要在周六下午一起去看篮球赛，你想去吗？

　 B：哦，我很想去，但是我得工作。

☞ A: Hey Neal, now that the midterms are over, *a bunch of* us are getting away for the weekend to go canoeing; wanna come along?

　 B: Well, it'd be great to get away, but I've never done it before.

　 A: None of the others have either except for me. I went once last fall. But there'll be an instructor in each canoe the first day.

　 A：嗨，尼尔，现在期中考试结束了，我们一群人准备周末去划船，你想一起去吗？

　 B：嗯，一定很好玩，但是我从来没划过啊。

　 A：除了我之外，其他人也都没玩过。去年秋天我玩过一次。第一天，每条船上都会有一个教练。

☞ a group of

a chunk of 一大块；一大部分

☞ We have completed *a* fairly great *chunk of* the term paper. 我们已经完成了学期论文的一大部分。

☞ a block of

a complicated question 复杂的问题

☞ The group of people are working on *a complicated question*. 这些人正在研究一个复杂的问题。

a couple of 两个；几个

☞ A: I kept looking for Mary at the seminar but never did see her. I can't imagine she forgot about it. She'd be talking about it for weeks.

B: Oh she didn't. It's just that she caught a really bad cold *a couple of* days ago.

A：研讨会上我一直在找玛丽，但始终没看见她。我无法想象她竟忘了这事。她谈论这次研讨会有好几周了。

B：哦，她没有忘，她只是几天前得了重感冒。

☞ A: Excuse me, I heard that there were *a couple of* jobs available in the library. So I'd like to apply for one of them. Can I fill out the application form at home and bring it back next week?

B: Sure, but you should know that we're about to start looking at the applications, and we hope to make some job offers in a few days.

A：打扰了，我听说图书馆有几个职位空缺，我想申请一个。我能回家填写申请表然后下周带过来吗？

B：可以，但是你应该了解，我们就要开始看这些申请表了，并且希望在这几天内就招到人。

☞ a few, several

> 🔍 couple of 在口语中经常连读成 coupla，在听的过程中要注意。

a flash of （强光）一闪

☞ Many people who have synesthesia experience intense colors when they hear specific words. For example, they might see *a flash of* pink every time they hear the word "jump". 许多有"联觉"的人在听到某些特殊词的时候都会看到强烈的颜色。例如，每次他们听到"跳"这个字的时候都会看见一抹粉色。

a foot of 1英尺厚的…

☞ A: Did you hear the weather report says we are going to get at least *a foot of* snow tomorrow?

B: That much! That's incredible. I can't wait to get outside and play in it.

A：你听天气预报了吗？明天积雪将达到至少 1 英尺厚。

B：那么大的雪！太不可思议了。我已经等不及要出去玩雪了。

☞ A: Do you ever get as much as *a foot of* snow here?

B: Hardly ever.

A：你们这里下过 1 英尺厚的雪吗?

B：几乎没有。

---

a group of 一群；一组

☞ I just get so embarrassed and nervous whenever I have to speak in front of *a group of* people. 我只要在人群面前讲话就会感到窘迫和紧张。

☞ A: What's the problem, Paul? You really look panicked.

B: I am speaking to *a group of* high school students about engineering this afternoon. But I have no idea how I am going to simplify some of the concepts for them.

A：怎么了，保罗? 你看起来很惊慌。

B：我今天下午要给一群中学生讲工程学。但是我还没想好怎么把一些概念简化，再讲给他们听。

🔍 注意 group 和 of 的连读。

---

a heavy line 厚衬里

☞ A: That's a really nice raincoat, Lisa.

B: Thanks. I like it too. If only it had *a heavy line* in it before I can wear it in winter too.

A：莉萨，这件雨衣真好。

B：谢谢，我也喜欢它。要是它有个厚的衬里就好了，我在冬天也可以穿。

🔍 heavy 和 line 这两个词的词义都很多，这里列举一些它们在托福听力中常见的词义和用法:

heavy: heavy schedule 安排很紧的日程　　heavy traffic 拥挤的交通
heavy smog 浓雾

line: 台词: The lines are too long. 台词太长了。

队，列: the line at the auto inspection center 汽车监测中心的队伍

诗句: write a few lines of poetry 写几句诗

轮廓线: shore line 海岸线

电话线: Your line's always busy. 你的电话总是占线。

（另外，line drawing 的含义为"线条描绘"，也就是"素描"。）

---

a heavy schedule 安排很紧的日程

☞ A: This is the second time this month that my boss's asked me to work extra hours. I am glad to get a bigger paycheck, but I just don't want her to give me such *a heavy schedule*.

B: Better watch your step. A lot of people would like to trade places with you.

A：在这个月里，这是老板第二次让我加班了。我很高兴可以得到更多的报酬，但是我不想将我的工作日程安排得这么紧张。

B：你最好小心行事。很多人想跟你换位子呢。

☞ a busy schedule

a herd of / herds of　一群／成群，大量

☞ One duty of the cowboys was to guide *herds of* cattle from grassy ranges into towns around the railroad lines where the cows were loaded on the trains. 牛仔的一个职责就是把牛群从绵延的草原上赶到铁路沿线的城镇里去，在那里牛会被装运到火车上。

a lack of　缺少

☞ It usually takes more than just *a lack of* water to turn productive land into a desert. 缺水通常并不是导致耕地变成沙漠的唯一原因。

a matter of time　时间问题

☞ It's only *a matter of time* before my car breaks down again. 我的车会再坏的，这只是个时间问题。

a money order　汇款单

☞ A: The application instructions say to enclose a check or *a money order* for twenty dollars. But I don't have a checking account.

B: You can just get a money order at the post office.

A：申请说明上说要在信封中装入 20 美元的支票或者汇款单。但是我没有活期存款账户。

B：你可以在邮局得到汇款单。

a pay raise　提高报酬

☞ A: Have you gotten *a pay raise* in the time you taught here?

B: I'm due for my first next year.

A：你在这里教学期间涨工资了吗？

B：我明年应该第一次涨工资。

☞ a wage increase

a phone call away　随叫随到

☞ A: You were right about the puzzle you lent me last week. It really is a challenge. I want to try to get it myself though. So I'm going to work on it a little longer.

B: Well, if you get really stuck, remember I'm only *a phone call away*.

A：你说得对，上周你借给我的拼图真是一个挑战。我想自己试着拼出来。因此我打算多花一点时间研究一下。

B：好的，如果你真的想不出的话，记着我会随叫随到哦。

a (...) portion of 一(…)部分

☞ A: How did you do on the math quiz?

B: Well, I am lucky that only counts for *a* small *portion of* our final grade for the course.

A：你数学测验考得怎么样？

B：嗯，很幸运，测试的分数只占我们期末成绩的一小部分。

☞ a (...) part of

a range of 一系列的

☞ Opportunities are available in *a* wide *range of* fields including publishing, public administration, health care and finance. 在很多领域都有机会，包括出版、公共管理、卫生保健和金融。

☞ *A* narrow *range of* popular edible fish, such as carp, has been introduced to many lakes and ponds all over the world. 一小部分受人喜爱的可食用鱼，像鲤鱼，已经被引进到了世界各地的湖泊和鱼池中。

☞ a series of

a series of 一连串的，一系列的

☞ As you know, we hold *a series of* events during the school year on various culture topics. I am happy there's such a large crowd of both students and professors. 就如你们所知道的，我们在这一学年中，就不同的文化主题举办了一系列活动。我很高兴很多学生和教授都参加了这些活动。

☞ For the second consecutive summer, the community center will be offering American Sign Language and the Performing Arts *a series of* classes, seminars, and workshops. 在接下来的夏季学期，社团中心将会为美国手语专业和表演艺术专业提供一系列的课程、研讨会和专题研究小组。

a train/flight schedule 火车／航班时刻（表）

a train schedule

☞ Please check your *flight schedule* in the morning. 请在早晨查看一下你们的航班时刻表。

☞ A: I thought you were going to call me last night about the *train schedule*.

B: Sorry. I should have. But Harry and Jack stopped by and stayed past midnight.

A：我原以为你昨晚会打电话告诉我列车时刻的事情。

B：对不起，我本来应该打。但是哈里和杰克来找我，一直待到深夜。

a vertical line 垂直线

☞ Draw *a vertical line* down the central part of the paper and write down your name and contact number on the left side. 在纸的中央画一条垂直线，并在左侧写下你的姓名和联系电话。

a waste of 浪费

☞ I really felt the movie was **a waste of** money. 我真的觉得看这部电影是浪费钱。

☞ When we move ahead a few decades into the 1980's, we see teachers and administrators and even parents telling us that teaching penmanship is **a waste of** time. 我们向前几十年来到 20 世纪 80 年代，看到教师和管理者，甚至是父母，都在告诉我们教授书法是在浪费时间。

a while back 刚才；不久以前

☞ A: Sam won't be able to play in the basketball game this week.
B: Yeah, he hurt his knee pretty badly **a while back**. I don't know why he didn't quit right away.
A：萨姆这周都不能参加篮球比赛了。
B：是啊，他刚才伤到了膝盖，而且很严重。我不知道他当时为什么不马上退出呢。

☞ not long ago

abnormal behavior 反常行为

☞ The problem of defining **abnormal behavior** via establishing just what is meant by normal behavior has proved extremely difficult. 经证明，通过确定什么是"正常行为"来定义"异常行为"是极其困难的。

🔍反义词组：normal behavior

above all 首先

☞ You all the students should learn **above all** how to adapt to the new environment. 你们所有学生首先应该学会如何去适应新环境。

☞ in the first place, firstly

🔍和 all 有关的短语：
in all 总的来说，总之；合计，总共
all over 到处，遍及
all of 所有；实足
and all 以及其他一切，等等

absolute advantages 绝对优势

☞ The football team won the match at an **absolute advantages**. 这支足球队以绝对的优势赢得比赛。

🔍相对优势：relative advantages

academic advisor 学术顾问

☞ Peter worked as an **academic advisor** at Harvard. 彼得在哈佛大学做学术顾问。

6

academic calendar 校历

☞ A: I just called the travel agent. It's all set. On June the first, I'm heading for the mountains for an entire week.

B: Have you checked the **academic calendar**? Because my classes aren't over till seventh.

A：我刚刚给旅行社打了电话，所有事宜都定好了。6 月 1 号，我将会去山里待整整一周。

B：你看过校历了吗？我的课得到 7 号才结束呢。

academic schedule 教学安排

☞ The **academic shedule** provides the brief information concerning admission, fees and a listing of course offerings. 这份教学安排提供了有关入学、费用及课程设置的简要信息。

🔍 学年：academic year

access to 接近／进入…的方法／使用或见到…的机会，权利

☞ The college students should have **access to** more practical knowledge. 大学生需要接触更多实用的知识。

according to 依照

☞ A: I washed this sweater **according to** the directions on the label. Look, what happened to it!

B: It could be a manufactures' defect. We'll exchange it for a new one.

A：我按标签上的说明洗了这件毛衣，看看，现在它成什么样了！

B：这可能是生产厂家的问题，我们给您换一件。

☞ **According to** the vitalist, the laws of physics and chemistry alone can not explain the processes of life. 根据活力论者的观点，只用物理或化学规律无法解释生命过程。

account for 解释，说明(原因等)；(指数量等)占…

☞ You should **account for** your absence from the tutorial. 你应该解释一下你为什么没去上辅导课。

acquaint...with 使认识，使了解，使熟悉

☞ The better way for students to become **acquainted with** a new subject is to look through its outline. 学生熟悉一个新学科的较好方法是浏览其纲要。

adapt to 适应

☞ You just have to be the kind of person who is receptive to new ways of looking at things and willing to **adapt to** a new life style. 你只需做一个能以新视角看问题并愿意适应新的生活方式的人。

adapt...for 改造；改编，改写

☞ Those old trains have been specially *adapted for* the temporary use in the disastrous area. 那些旧火车进行特殊改造后被临时用在了受灾地区。

advance in 在…方面的进展

☞ Scientists wanted to make a more precise measurement, using a new method that takes advantage of recent *advances in* technology. 科学家们想利用一种来自最新科技成果的方法做一个更为精确的测量。

advanced degree 高等学位

☞ My boss says the company will pay for any college costs if I can take the *advanced degree*. 我的老板说如果我能取得高等学位，公司就会为我支付任何一所大学的学费。

adverse aspect 弊端，不利方面

☞ The new headlights on cars cancel out the *adverse aspects* of sodium lighting and the colors appear more natural. 新式的车前灯抵消了钠光灯的弊端，而且灯光的颜色看起来也更自然了。

☞ disadvantage, unfavorable aspect

Advertising Topic 广告学概论

☞ Joe decided to take *Advertising Topic* next semester. 乔决定下学期选广告学概论这门课。

afford to (do) 经受得住；负担得起（费用）

☞ A: Are you sure this is the right way to the M auditorium? I can't *afford to* be late.
  B: Oh, that won't happen; we'll be there in no time.
  A：你确定这是去 M 礼堂的路吗？我可不能迟到啊。
  B：哦，不会迟到的，我们很快就到了。

☞ After living a couple of months, I am wondering if I can *afford to* stay in the apartment. 住了几个月后，现在我怀疑自己是否能继续住得起这个公寓。

🔍 afford 常和否定词 can't, couldn't 连用，后面接动词不定式，注意与 to 连读的时候 d 的发音要弱化。

after all 毕竟，终究

☞ A: We still haven't decided on the time for lunch tomorrow.
  B: Oh, I forgot to tell you. I won't be able to make it *after all*.
  A：我们还没有定下来明天吃午饭的时间。
  B：哦，我忘了告诉你了，我终究还是去不了。

☞ A: Mark didn't win that science award *after all*?
  B: Can you believe it? I thought for sure he would.
  A：马克终究没有赢得那个科学奖是吗？
  B：你能相信吗？我以为他稳拿了呢。

ahead of schedule 提前

☞ Let's finish the work within this week so that our group can fulfill our plan *ahead of schedule*. 让我们在这周结束工作吧，这样我们组就能提前完成任务了。

☞ ahead of time, in advance

air currents 气流

☞ Altitude, *air currents* and humidity can affect the local temperature. 海拔、气流和湿度都可以影响当地温度。

air currents

air pressure 大气压

☞ Without space suit it will not be possible for us to survive in the space. For example, outer space is a vacuum. There's no gravity or *air pressure*. Without protection, a body would explode. 没有太空服，我们就不能在太空空间中存活。举例来说，太空是真空的，没有重力也没有气压。如果没有保护的话，人的身体会爆炸。

☞ atmospheric pressure

🔍 相关表达：

high pressure 高气压	lightning 闪电
fog 雾	frost 霜
thunder 雷	hail 冰雹

all along 一直

☞ A: The dean just announced that Dr. Jeff was going to take over as Chairperson of the English Department.

B: I knew it *all along*. He was the obvious choice.

A：院长刚刚宣布杰夫博士要接管英语系主任一职。

B：我就知道会这样，很显然会选他。

☞ all the while

all the way 一直

☞ By the 1890s railroads reached *all the way* to Texas. 19 世纪 90 年代，铁路一直通到得克萨斯州。

all year around 一年到头

☞ A: I spent my summer vacation at north in Montana. The views of the mountain were so beautiful. I think it would be great to live there *all year around*.

B: You've got to be kidding. I'm from there and believe me, in the winter time, it's so cold out that you could care less about the scenery.

A：我在蒙大拿北部度过了暑假，那里的山景很漂亮。我想全年住在那里一定会非常好。

B：你一定是在开玩笑。我家住在那里，相信我，冬天的时候，那儿的室外冷得让你无心欣赏景色。

☞ all year long, throughout the year

along with　连同…一起

☞ The President has ten days to veto the bill by returning the bill to Congress, **along with** the message explaining why it's being rejected. 总统有 10 天的时间否决此议案，将议案连同否决的理由一起返回给议会。

☞ together with

alternative fuel　替代燃料

☞ A: Dr. Collin says DME is more efficient than other **alternative fuels**.

B: When will it replace diesel fuel?

A: Not for a while. It's not economical to mass-produce.

A：科林博士说二甲醚比其他替代燃料效率更高。

B：它什么时候才能取代柴油燃料呢？

A：还要一段时间。现在大批量生产造价还很高。

alternative theory　可供选择的理论

☞ A: Well, did the geologist have an **alternative theory** to explain where ocean water came from?

B: Yeah, he said the more traditional view is that the ocean water came from volcanoes.

A：嗯，那位地理学家有其他理论可以解释海水是从哪里来的吗？

B：有，他说更为传统的观点是海水来自火山。

☞ optional theory

an answer to　…的答案；…的回答

☞ We still don't know the **answer to** the question about why a certain group of turtles go to Ascension Island. 我们还是不清楚为什么那一群海龟要去阿森松岛。

☞ a reply to

an epidemic of　…的传播，…的流行

☞ **An epidemic of** flu was spreading rapidly on campus over the past two weeks. 在过去的两周里，感冒在校园里快速地传播。

an extra day's time　额外花一天的时间

☞ A: Do you think it'll be able to get this ink stain out of my pants?

B: It won't be a problem but I'll need to send them over to the main cleaning facility. That's **an extra day's time**.

A：你觉得我裤子上的墨迹能洗掉吗？

B：这没问题，但是我要把它送到洗衣总店去。这还要额外花一天的时间。

analyze the data　分析数据

☞ A: We finally finish this experiment. Let's go and have a cup of coffee.

B: Well, did you forget that we also need to *analyze the data* and make a conclusion?

A：终于做完试验了，一起去喝杯咖啡吧。

B：唔，你是不是忘了我们还要分析数据并做出结论呢？

ancient city　古城

☞ We could know more about this *ancient city* by studying the murals. 我们可以通过研究这些壁画来加深对这座古城的了解。

🔍 托福考试中，在涉及该词组时通常会谈论的话题是关于 the ancient Greece（古希腊），Maya（玛雅），Inca（印加）等相关文化，考生可以读一些相关文章，扩大词汇量。

ancient times　古代

☞ In *ancient times*, many people believed the earth was a flat disc. 在古代，许多人认为地球是一个扁平的圆盘。

ancient times

🔍 该词组出现的场景中可能还会出现其他相关的词：
archeologist 考古学家　　medieval times 中古时代
stone axe 石斧　　mammoth 猛犸象（古代巨象）

animated cartoon　卡通片

☞ The *animated cartoons* first thought about by Walt Disney overwhelmed the world, no matter the elder or the youth. 由沃尔特·迪斯尼最先构思的卡通片征服了全世界，无论老人还是年轻人。

🔍 沃尔特·迪斯尼是美国动画片制作家、演出主持人和电影制片人，以创作卡通人物米老鼠（Mickey Mouse）和唐老鸭（Donald Duck）而闻名。他制作的世界上第一部动画长片《白雪公主》（Snow White）到现在仍然被人们所喜爱。

anything but　决不，一点也不

☞ Susan can't think about *anything but* studying. 苏珊只考虑学习的问题。

🔍 注意和 nothing but "除了…之外都不" 相区别。

appeal to　对…有吸引力；呼吁，请求

☞ Nylon brushes *appeal to* many people, because they are inexpensive and produce acceptable effect on paper. 尼龙画笔吸引了很多人，因为它们便宜，而且写在纸上的效果还不错。

application form　申请表

☞ A: What do I need to do now?

B: Complete this *application form* and bring it back to me. Then I'll schedule you for another interview.

A：我现在需要做什么？

B：把这个申请表填好后交给我。然后我会给你安排另一次面试时间。

☞ A: I'm having trouble filling out this *application form*.

B: Take it line by line, and it won't seem so hard.

A：我填这个申请表有点困难。

B：一行一行地填，就不是很难了。

apply for　申请

☞ A: I would like to *apply for* one of the security guard positions you advertised in the local paper.

B: Good. May I ask you a few questions first?

A: Certainly.

A：我要申请你们在地方报纸上刊登的保安职位。

B：好的，我能先问您几个问题吗？

A：当然。

☞ Because he brought the wrong documents, my cousin couldn't *apply for* his driver's license. 我表弟由于拿错了文件，不能申请驾驶证了。

☞ put in for

apply to　向…申请

☞ A: I've decided to *apply to* graduate school in engineering for next year.

B: More school? I'm going into business for myself.

A：我决定申请明年读工程学研究生。

B：还上学？我要自己做生意了。

apply to customs　报关

☞ A: I'm a green hand. Could you tell me the process of *applying to customs*?

B: OK. But wait a minute, please. I'm getting a finish touch to my report.

A：我是个新手，您能给我讲下报关的程序吗？

B：好的，但是请等一下，我的报告马上就写完了。

☞ declare at customs

aquatic environment 水生环境

☞ The chemicals left in the treated water get into the *aquatic environment*; that is into the rivers and streams where plants or fish and other animals live. 残留在被处理过的水中的化学物质会进入水生环境，即植物或鱼以及其他动物生存的河流和小溪中。

NOTES

Unit 2

arbitrary character　反复无常的性格

☞ My new roommate is really a bad girl with **arbitrary character**. 我的新室友真的是一个性格反复无常的坏女孩。

☞ changeable personality

arbitrary decision　武断的决定

☞ The reconstruction of the library is really a **arbitrary decision**. 重建图书馆真的是一个武断的决定。

arms trade　军火交易

☞ The country has long been the group's main source in legitimate **arms trade**. 该国长期以来一直是这个组织的合法军火交易的主要货源国。

army of volunteers　志愿者队伍；志愿军

☞ During the Olympic Games, the **army of volunteers** is sensitive to the needs of visitors and acts in the nicest possible way. 在奥运会期间，志愿者们细心留意参观者的需求，举止尽可能地友善可亲。

arouse...from　把…叫醒

☞ Lily, every morning, is **aroused from** a sound sleep by her mother. 每天早晨，莉莉都被她母亲从酣睡中叫醒。

☞ wake up from

arouse one's anxiety/curiosity/interest
引起不安/好奇/兴趣

arouse... from

☞ A good teacher could **arouse** students' **interest** in studying, but not just cram the knowledge to them. 一名好教师可以引起学生对学习的兴趣，而不仅仅是填鸭式地灌输知识。

art exhibit　艺术展览

☞ A: I was just about to go to the **art exhibit**; would you like to go over there with me?
B: I made plans with Susan to go tomorrow afternoon.
A：我正好要去参观艺术品展览，你愿意和我一起去那儿吗？
B：我和苏珊打算明天下午去。

☞ A: I'm really sorry I missed the pop *art exhibit* at the museum.

B: You might try to catch it when it opens in New York next month.

A：我错过了在博物馆举办的流行艺术展览，感觉真的很遗憾。

B：下个月在纽约举办时你看看能不能赶上。

☞ A: I saw some of your paintings at the student *art exhibit*. They are great.

B: Thanks. I feel as though I've come a long way.

A：我在学生艺术展览上看到了你的一些画。它们棒极了。

B：谢谢。我觉得我好像进步了很多。

artesian spring 自流泉

☞ Some natural springs geographers are interested in *artesian spring*. 一些研究天然泉水的地理学家对自流泉感兴趣。

artesian well 自流井

☞ How *artesian wells* are drilled? 自流井是如何钻出来的？

> 🔍 相关词组：
>
> pressure water 承压水   evaporate 蒸发
>
> low water level 低水位   groundwater level 地下水位

artificial bone tissue 人造骨组织

☞ The exact figure of *artificial bone tissue* could be provided to the patient by using the new equipment. 通过使用新仪器，可以为患者提供精确的人造骨组织。

artificial light 人造光

☞ A: Doctor, I haven't been able to get to sleep lately, and I'm too tired to concentrate during classes.

B: Well, you know spending too much time indoors with all that *artificial light* can do that to you. Your body loses track of whether it's day or night.

A：医生，我最近都睡不着觉，而且感觉很累，在课上都无法集中精神。

B：嗯，你要知道，在室内日光灯（人造光）下待时间长了就会这样。你的身体会分辨不清是白天还是夜晚。

> 🔍 人造光源包括：白炽灯（incandescent lamp），霓虹灯（neon lamp），广告灯（advertising lamp）等。

artificial organs 人造器官

☞ With the development of science and technology, some diseases could be cured by using *artificial organs*. 随着科技的发展，一些疾病可以使用人造器官来治愈。

artificial satellite 人造卫星

☞ Many **artificial satellites** were launched into space to detect the environment of the moon. 许多人造卫星被发射到太空中探测月球环境。

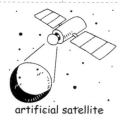

artificial satellite

🔍 在太阳系(Solar System)中，太阳(Sun)是恒星(fixed star)，环绕太阳运转的有八大行星(planet)，包括：水星(Mercury)，金星(Venus)，地球（Earth），火星（Mars），木星（Jupiter），土星（Saturn），天王星（Uranus），海王星(Neptune)。这些行星中除了水星和金星外都有自己的天然卫星(satellite)，地球的卫星就是月亮(Moon)。

---

artistic works 艺术作品

☞ At the historical society exhibit next week, we'll see many **artistic works** depicting the major events of Poke Hunters' life. 在下周的历史社会展览上，我们将看到许多艺术作品，这些作品描述了普克·亨特斯一生中的重要事件。

---

as a matter of fact 事实上

☞ A: Excuse me, did anybody find a black umbrella after the last show? I left it under my chair.

B: **As a matter of fact**, we did. Check it at the ticket counter. That's where we turn in the lost-and-found items.

A：劳驾，请问上次演出结束后，有没有人捡到一把黑色雨伞？我把它落在椅子下面了。

B：我们确实捡到了一把伞。你去售票处看一下。我们把失物招领的东西都放到那里。

☞ in fact, actually

---

as a result 结果

☞ The disease is caused by a fungus. When that fungus infects the tree, it blocks the circulation of water inside the tree. **As a result**, the tree cells don't receive water and without water, of course they can't survive. 这种疾病是由一种菌类引起的。当这种菌感染树的时候，它会阻碍树内部的水循环。结果，树的细胞就无法吸收水，没有水这些树当然也不能存活了。

---

as far as I am concerned 在我看来

☞ A: I need a new bicycle, and I just can't decide which one to get. There are just too many different kinds to choose from.

B: Don't ask me. **As far as I am concerned**, a bike is a bike; it's just transportation.

A：我需要一辆新自行车，我决定不了买哪一辆。可供选择的类型太多了。

B：别问我。在我看来，自行车就是自行车，它就是一个交通工具而已。

☞ in my opinion, personally, from my point of view

as far as I know　就我所知

☞ **As far as I know**, they haven't registered for camp yet. 据我所知，他们还没报名参加野营。

as good as　和…几乎一样，实际上等于

☞ A: When's a good time to get together to discuss our history project?

B: Other than this Wednesday. One day's **as good as** the next.

A：什么时间一起讨论我们的历史项目好呢？

B：除了这周三。早一天晚一天没有关系。

☞ A: Excuse me, could you tell me how to get to the post office?

B: Your guess is **as good as** mine. I'm new around here.

A：打扰一下，您可以告诉我怎么去邮局吗？

B：我也想知道。我也是刚到这里。

☞ the same to

as hard/tough as nails　铁石心肠的，冷酷无情的

☞ Cinderella's step-mother is **as hard as nails** and let her do all the housework at home without giving her enough food. 灰姑娘的继母冷酷无情，她让灰姑娘做所有的家务，却不给她足够的食物。

🔍 这个词组要引起注意，考生不要受汉语影响认为是"坚强如铁"的含义，那就大错特错了。

ask for permission　要求同意

☞ We should **ask for permission** from the professor to use his material at special hours. 我们应该向教授申请在特殊时间使用他的材料。

assign to　分配给；指派，选派；把…归因于；把(财产、权利等)让与…

☞ A: This is incredible! Only the first day of our Modern American History course and we've already been **assigned to** read three chapters by the next time we meet.

B: If that surprises you, then obviously you never had a class before with Prof. Smith.

A：太不可思议了！这只是我们的第一堂现代美国历史课，而我们的作业就已经是在下一次上课前要读完三个章节。

B：如果你对此感到惊讶，很明显你以前没有上过史密斯教授的课。

assigned books 指定书目

☞ A: Where is Jennifer? Didn't she know our homework?

B: She has already read most of the *assigned books*.

A：詹妮弗去哪了？她难道不知道我们的作业吗？

B：她已经读完了大部分指定书目了。

associate professor 副教授

☞ My brother was finally qualified an *Associate Professor* Certificate. 我哥哥终于被授予了副教授资格。

🔍 几种"副"的说法：

vice-president 副总统   by-product 副产品

side effect 副作用

associate with 把…和…联系起来

☞ This is a good place to start because it is home to many plants and animals typically *associated with* the Everglade. 从这个地方开始很好，因为它是很多与美国南部大沼泽地相关的动植物的家园。

☞ These are genes that are *associated with* particular nerve-cell receptors in the brain. 这些基因与大脑中特殊神经细胞接收器相关联。

assume obligation 承担责任

☞ The obligor should also *assume* the incidental *obligation* associated with the main obligation. 责任人同样也要承担与主要责任相关的连带责任。

☞ undertake an obligation

asteroid explosion 小行星爆炸

☞ The video is about astronomy, showing you the *asteroid explosion*. 这段视频是有关天文学的，展示小行星爆炸的场面。

astronomical object 天体

☞ The natural colors of *astronomical objects* can be captured. 我们可以观察到天体的自然色彩。

☞ Most *astronomical objects* are so remote that the light we receive from them is rather feeble. 大多数天体都离我们很远，我们所能看到的它们发出的光都很暗淡。

astronomical observatory

astronomical observatory 天文观测台

☞ *Astronomical observatory* is a place for making astronomical observations. 天文观测台是进行天文观测的地方。

National Radio Astronomy Observatory(NRAO)美国国家射电天文台是美国国家科学基金会资助的从事射电天文研究的机构, 总部位于弗吉尼亚大学。

astronomy class　天文学课程

☞ A: How did you like yesterday's *astronomy class*?

　B: It was interesting. But the point the professor was trying to make seemed a little far-fetched.

　A：你觉得昨天的天文学课怎么样?

　B：很有趣, 但是教授所讲解的知识点有些牵强。

astronomy society　天文学会

☞ Let's welcome Doctor Cole tell us about what he and his colleagues discussed at the annual *astronomy society* meeting last month. 我们欢迎科尔博士给我们讲一下他和他的同事在上个月的年度天文学会会议上所探讨的内容。

at a discount　打折的, 减价的

☞ People could always buy things *at a discount* during the festival. 在节日期间, 人们通常都能买到打折的商品。

☞ with some discount, on sale

at any rate　无论如何

☞ *At any rate*, these supplies should reach the earthquake-stricken area by this weekend. 无论如何, 这些物资在这周末前都要到达地震灾区。

☞ whatever, on every account, in any sort

与 rate 相关的短语还有:
at this / that rate 这样 / 那样的话　　　at an easy rate 廉价地; 容易地
discount rate 折扣率

at home with　对…很熟悉

☞ I certainly hope that most of you will soon feel right *at home with* our group. 我真的希望不久以后你们中的大部分人会和我们熟悉起来。

at least　至少

☞ A: There is a powerful new telescope being built in Arizona. Will that help the scientists see these planets?

　B: They should be able to see them *at least* in the form of small spots of light.

　A：亚利桑那州正在建一个新的有强大功能的天文望远镜。它会帮助科学家看到这些行星吗?

　B：至少能看到它们是一个个小亮点。

☞ no less than

反义词组: at most (至多)

at regular intervals 每隔一段时间，定期地

☞ It's good for people to examine the body *at regular intervals*. 定期体检对人们的健康有好处。

at sb.'s service 愿为某人服务

☞ A: Phil, could you give me a hand with this file cabinet? It belongs against the wall, next to the bulletin board.

B: *At your service*.

A：菲尔，你能帮我搬一下这个文件柜吗？它应该靠墙，挨着那个公告板。

B：愿意为你效劳。

at the age of 在…岁

☞ A: Look, Jessica is really a good dancer.

B: Yeah, she began to dance *at the age of* 4.

A：看，杰茜卡跳舞跳得可真好。

B：是啊，她从四岁就开始跳舞了。

☞ ... years old, ...-year-old

🔍 age 除了有年龄的意思外，在托福中还常考"时期；时代"的含义，如 the age of adolescence 意为"青春期"。

at the end of 在…结束时

☞ The auto inspection center will be closed *at the end of* the month. 自动检测中心在月底前将关闭。

☞ A: I've been taking four courses, but I think I'll drop one of them *at the end of* this term.

B: That may be for the best.

A：我修了四门课，但是我在这学期期末可能会放弃其中一门。

B：这可能是最好的选择。

🔍 注意区分相似词组：

in the end 最后，终于   to the end 到底，直到最后

at the head of 在…的上部；居…的首位

☞ A: I'm going to send this letter to Henry. Do you have anything to tell him?

B: I just want to tell you not to forget to put your address *at the head of* the letter.

A：我要把信寄给亨利了，你还有什么要跟他说的吗？

B：我只想告诉你别忘了把你的地址写在信头。

at the rate of　以…速度

☞ A: **At the rate of** its being used, the copier is not going to make it through the rest of the year.

B: The year? It's supposed to be good for five.

A：按照复印机当前的使用频率，估计用不到今年年底。

B：今年？我还想着能用五年呢。

🔍 注意 rate 和 of 的连读，可能会读成 rata。

at the request of　应…要求；应…邀请

☞ **At the request of** the audience, the famous singer sang an extra song. 应观众的请求，那个著名歌唱家又唱了一首歌。

☞ at sb.'s request

at this rate　照此速度；照这样看来，这样的话

☞ A: I've been working on this report all day. And I've still got 12 pages to write. **At this rate**, I'll never get it done by tomorrow.

B: Oh, that's right. You weren't in class today, so you probably haven't heard that the deadline has been extended a week.

A：我一天都在做这个报告。现在还有 12 页呢。照这个速度，我明天肯定完不成。

B：哦，对了，你今天没去上课，所以你可能还不知道，报告提交的截止日期已经延后了一周。

☞ A: This looks like Sweety Susan's house, but I don't know. I wish I read down the directions.

B: **At this rate**, we are lucky to get there in time for desert.

A：这儿看起来很像"甜蜜苏珊"屋，但是我不确定，真希望我看了地图。

B：这样的话，我们就可以幸运地赶上吃甜品了。

at work　在工作，忙于

☞ A: I know I promised to drive you to the airport next Tuesday. But I am afraid that something has come up. And they've called a special meeting **at work**.

B: No big deal. Karen said she was available as a backup.

A：我知道我答应下周二开车送你去机场。但是现在恐怕有点事，他们要开一个特别工作会议。

B：不要紧。卡伦说她可做后备。

☞ (be) tied up with, (be) busy with

atom of　…的原子

☞ A molecule of water is made up of two atoms of hydrogen and one **atom of** oxygen. 一个水分子是由两个氢原子和一个氧原子组成的。

🔍 注意 not an atom of 是"一点也没有"的意思。

attend the conference 参加会议

☞ A: Are we going to **attend the conference** this
     afternoon?
   B: You may get a wrong schedule.
   A：我们是不是今天下午要去参加会议？
   B：你可能拿错时间表了。

attend the conference

☞ attend the meeting, be at the meeting, be in the conference

attend the tournament 参加锦标赛

☞ Alan wants his brother to **attend the tournament** with him. 艾伦想让他的哥哥和他
   一起参加锦标赛。

attribute to 归因于；归功于

☞ The increased popularity of winter cycling can be **attributed to** the creation of
   mountain bike and its subsequent imitations. 冬季骑车兜风的日益流行应该归因
   于山地车以及随之而来的仿制品的发明。

☞ ascribe to

🔍 注意连读时，attribute 的最后一个 t 会出现吞音。

await trial 等候审讯

☞ These criminals are **awaiting trial** at the next court. 这些罪犯正在等候下次开庭的
   审讯。

☞ wait for trial

🔍 await 后面通常跟抽象名词，如 await announcement（等待公告），await decision
（等待决定）。

award ceremony 颁奖典礼

☞ Ruth helped plan the **award ceremony**. 露丝帮助策划了颁奖典礼。

🔍 相关词汇：
scholarship 奖学金   bonus 分红
welfare 福利   Academy Award 奥斯卡奖

back on one's feet 恢复健康

☞ Being taken care by her mother, Mary is finally **back on her feet** in a short time after
   the operation. 在母亲的照顾下，玛丽手术后很快就恢复了健康。

back out (of) 退出；放弃

☞ A: Remember when I said I might have to **back out of** the concert if I didn't have
     my history paper done yet? Well, guess what?
   B: That's okay. Do you know anyone else who enjoys Jazz?

A：记得我说过如果我没有完成历史论文，就不能去听音乐会吗？猜猜现在怎么了？

B：没关系，你知道谁还喜欢爵士乐吗？

☞ A: Thank goodness, spring break starts next week. Are you doing anything special?

B: I have been planning to go to Florida with a friend of mine. But since she's ***backed out***, everything's sort of on hold.

A：谢天谢地，春季假期下周就开始了。你有什么特别的事情要做吗？

B：我原打算和一位朋友去佛罗里达的。但是她不去了，所以一切就搁置了下来。

---

bacteria infection 细菌感染

☞ People should pay more attention to the ***bacteria infection***, since it could cause a lot of diseases. 人们应该更多地注意细菌感染，因为它能引起很多疾病。

🔍 相关词汇：

virus 病毒	parasite 寄生物
penicillin 青霉素	immunity 免疫

---

baggage counter 行李寄存处

☞ A: I'm sorry, sir. But you're allowed only one piece of luggage on the plane. You'll have to check one of your suitcases at the ***baggage counter***.

B: Actually, one of these belongs to the woman up ahead. I'm just giving her a hand.

A：对不起，先生，您只能带一件行李登机。您必须把其中一件行李放在行李寄存处。

B：事实上，其中一件行李是前面那位女士的，我只是帮她拿着。

---

balance one's budget 平衡预算

☞ It's more important to ***balance our budget*** especially under the economy crisis. 平衡预算很重要，尤其是在经济危机的时候。

---

balance oneself 保持自身平衡

☞ A: Why are you outside? The party is really exciting.

B: Well, I couldn't ***balance myself*** on one foot for a long time.

A：你为什么在外面？舞会真的令人兴奋。

B：嗯，我不能长时间单脚站立，无法保持平衡。

balance oneself

---

barter with sb. for sth. 与某人交换某物

☞ The slaves wanted to ***barter with*** their owner ***for*** their freedom. 奴隶们想和奴隶主换取自由。

☞ exchange sth. for sth.

base on/upon　基于

☞ A: Do you remember what the new theory that ocean water came from comets was **based on**?

B: Some recent satellite photos, I think.

A：你记不记得"海水来自彗星"这个新理论的基础是什么？

B：我想可能是最近的一些卫星照片吧。

☞ A: Joe, I thought your article on the school newspaper was right on target. You certainly convinced me anyway.

B: Thanks Mary. Unfortunately, **based on** the general response, you and I are definitely in the minority.

A：乔，我认为你在校报上的文章写得正中要害。你绝对说服了我。

B：谢谢你，玛丽。不幸的是，基于大众的反应，我跟你肯定是少数派。

☞ I'm sure you are aware that one third of your final grade is **based on** your lab work.
我确信你知道期末考试分数的三分之一是基于你的实验室工作。

basic element　基本元素

☞ Water is one of the **basic elements** for the existence of live creatures. 水是生物生存的基本元素之一。

basic rights　基本权利

☞ While the citizens could enjoy their **basic rights**, they should also fulfill their obligations. 公民在享有基本权利的同时也要履行义务。

be absent from　缺席

☞ A: Excuse me, Professor Jones. I **was absent from** the first class and I heard that's when you handed out the course outline. Would you have an extra copy?

B: I don't have anyone with me. There are a few left in my office. Why don't you stop by after class?

A：打扰一下，琼斯教授。我第一堂课缺席了，听说您发了课程大纲。您还有多余的吗？

B：我没带在身上。办公室里还有一些剩余的。你可以在课后过去一趟。

be abundant in　富于

☞ China **is abundant in** natural resources. 中国自然资源丰富。

☞ be full of, be rich in

be adequate for　足够的，充足的；适用于，适合

☞ A: I thought Betty's knowledge of computer **is adequate for** the job.

B: Actually they need a more professional employee.

A：我原以为贝蒂的电脑知识足够应对这个工作了。

B：事实上他们需要一个更专业的人员。

☞ be sufficient for

24

be allergic to   对…过敏

☞ A: Oh, man! Something in this room is making my eyes itch. I must *be allergic to* something.

B: Hmm. I wonder what it is.

A：哦，伙计，这屋子里有什么东西让我的眼睛很痒，我肯定是对什么东西过敏了。

B：嗯，我想知道是什么东西。

be attracted to   被…所吸引

☞ The baby turtles *are attracted to* light. 海龟宝宝会被亮光所吸引。

NOTES

Unit 3

---

be authorized to 被授权做，有权做

☞ A: Hi, I know Doctor Wilson's out of town at a conference, but I was wondering...
um...since she won't be back till next week, if you...if you could check in your
computer records and find out how I did on her mid-term exam?

B: I'm sorry, Miss. But I'***m*** not ***authorized to*** give out that kind of information.

A：嗨，我知道威尔逊博士出城开会去了，但是我在想…嗯…因为她下周才会
回来，你能不能…能不能看看你的电脑记录，看看我在她那门课的期中考
试中考得怎么样？

B：对不起，小姐，我无权告诉你这些信息。

be available to 可找到的；有空的；可获得的

☞ Prof. Jameson ***was*** always ***available to*** help me if I had any questions. 如果我有任
何问题，詹姆士教授随时都会帮助我。

☞ The writer will ***be available to*** answer any individual questions at the reception
immediately following the talk. 谈话之后，该作者会在接待处回答任何个人问题。

---

be away from 离开，远离

☞ A: Do you feel like watching the evening news?

B: You ought to ***be away from*** me. I have a bad cold and wouldn't want you to
catch it.

A：你想看晚间新闻吗？

B：你应该离我远点。我得重感冒了，不想传染给你。

☞ stay/get away from

---

be composed of 由…组成

☞ The moon and earth ***are composed of*** essentially the same minerals, a similarity not
shared with any other planet or moon in our solar system. 月亮和地球基本上是由
同样的矿物质构成的，这是太阳系中其他任何行星及其卫星所不具备的。

☞ In fact, some people say that such a poet never existed at all, that neither *the Iliad* nor
the Odyssey was written by a single poet, but rather each poem ***is composed of*** the
writings of several people. 事实上，一些人说这样的诗人根本不存在，无论《伊利
亚特》还是《奥德赛》都不是由一个诗人写出来的，而是由几个人共同创作的。

🔍 注意区分 compose 和 constitute，两个词的用法是：A is composed of B and C; B
and C constitute A。

26

be concerned about 关注，关心，挂念

☞ The main factors to **be** particularly **concerned about** in writing are the structure of essays and collection of written material. 写作中尤其需要关注的因素是文章的结构以及书面材料的收集。

be

concerned

about

be cut out for 适合于

☞ A: I admire your dedication. I could never finish that long laboratory experiment by myself.

B: I felt that I **was cut out for** that kind of work.

A：我佩服你的奉献精神，我自己绝对不可能做完那么长的试验。

B：我觉得自己天生适合做那种工作。

be dedicated to (doing) sth. 致力于某事

☞ Helen feels that her brother **is dedicated to** his work, so she decided to move by herself. 海伦觉得她哥哥在忙工作，所以她决定自己搬家。

☞ be devoted to do

be depleted of 被耗尽

☞ When there are no more insects to be fed to the young spiders, they attach themselves to the mother's leg joints and draw nourishment by sucking the nutrient-rich blood. After several weeks, the mother **is depleted of** all nutrients and she dies. 当小蜘蛛没有足够的昆虫吃时，它们就靠在蜘蛛妈妈的腿关节处通过吮吸富含营养的血液来摄取营养。几个星期后，蜘蛛妈妈就会因为耗尽营养而死去。

be different from 与…不同

☞ If green turtles always return to the place where they were hatched, then the turtles that have been going to the Ascension Island to nest would've been genetically isolated long enough to have DNA that **was** very **different from** the green turtles that nest elsewhere. 如果绿海龟总是返回它们出生的地方，那么去阿森松岛筑巢的海龟就会因为在遗传方面隔离太久，使得它们的 DNA 和在其他地方筑巢的绿海龟非常不同。

☞ differ from

be distracted by 被…打扰，被…搞得心烦意乱

☞ A: Did you catch what I said?

B: Well, I **was distracted by** the strange sound in the yard.

A：你听到我刚刚说什么了吗？

B：呃，我被院子里奇怪的声音弄得分了心。

be due 到期

☞ Since your lab notebooks for the semester *are due* on Thursday, the first three nights of this week will be your last opportunity to make up incomplete work. 因为你这学期的实验记录要在这周四上交，所以这周的前三天晚上将是你补全作业的最后机会。

☞ fall due, reach the appointed date

be effective from 对…是有效的；自…起生效

☞ A: This prescription is supposed to *be effective from* paining, but it's maybe too strong for me. I took it when I woke up in pain in the middle of the night, and now I feel nauseous.

B: You should read the label first. It says right here on the bottom to be taken with meals only.

A：这个药方应该对治疗疼痛很有效，但是对我来说可能药性太强了。我在半夜疼醒时吃的药，现在觉得恶心。

B：你应该先读标签，就在瓶底，标签上说这药只能饭后服用。

be eligible for 有条件，有资格

☞ Because of his careless reading of the introduction, the man thought he*'s eligible for* low cost housing. 由于没有认真读说明，那个男人还以为他有资格购买低价房。

☞ Barbara discovered she *was eligible for* the song contest. 芭芭拉发现她有资格参加歌唱比赛。

be eligible to do sth. 有资格做

☞ Every student with bachelor *is eligible to* apply for the position. 每个获得学士学位的学生都有资格申请这个职位。

☞ be entitled to, qualify for

be equivalent to 与…相等；相当于

☞ A: I'm going to talk to my boss about giving me a raise.

B: Well, actually yours *is equivalent to* my three months' salary.

A：我要跟老板谈谈给我涨工资的事。

B：嗯，事实上，你的工资都相当于我三个月的工资了。

☞ be equal to

be expected to 被期望

☞ The grasses and trees and shrubs of this area *are expected to* feed more animals than they reasonably can. 人们对该地区的草场和林木所能饲养动物量的期望值已经超出了其正常的能力。

be extracted from 从…中提炼

☞ Today we'd talk about how minerals *are extracted from* rock. 我们今天要讲矿物质是如何从石头中提炼出来的。

be familiar to　为…所熟悉的

☞ The hip-hop style clothes *is* quickly *familiar to* the youth because of its fashion elements. 由于嘻哈风格衣服中的流行元素，它很快就被年轻人所熟悉了。

be familiar with　对…熟悉

☞ A: I need to find a dermatologist. You*'re familiar with* Dr. Smith. Do you recommend him?

　 B: Well, I've been seen by him a few times. And the best I can say for him is he has interesting magazines in his waiting room.

　 A：我需要找一位皮肤科医生，你和史密斯大夫很熟，你觉得他怎么样呢？

　 B：嗯，我去他那里看过几次，而我所能说的就是他的候诊室里的杂志很有意思。

🔍 注意区分 be familiar to 和 be familiar with，前者表示"被某人所熟悉"，后者表示"熟悉某人或某物"，"熟悉"的主体和客体位置相反。

be free from　免于…；不受…影响

☞ An early printer named James Franklin, took a courageous step by starting an independent newspaper. Franklin, who owned his own printing press, wanted to *be free from* outside control. 一位叫詹姆斯·富兰克林的早期印刷工，大胆地开办了一家独立的报纸。拥有属于自己的出版社的富兰克林想摆脱外界的控制。

be full of remorse / be filled with remorse　充满自责 / 懊悔

☞ The mother *is full of remorse* after abandoning her son. 那个母亲遗弃自己的儿子后，心中充满懊悔。

🔍 without remorse 意为"无情地；坚持不懈地；不间断地"。

be head and shoulders above　好许多，远远超过

☞ In computer programming, Susan *is head and shoulders above* the rest of us. 苏珊在计算机程序设计方面远远超过我们其他人。

be identical to/with　与…相同，与…保持一致

☞ The director wanted the songs in the Broadway version to *be identical to* the songs in the film. 导演希望百老汇版的歌曲和电影版歌曲保持一致。

be in blossom　开花

☞ The apple trees *are in blossom*. 苹果树开花了。

be in cooperation with　与…合作

☞ If you want to play the bridge well, you should try to play *in cooperation with* your partner. 如果你想打好桥牌，就要试着与你的伙伴合作。

be in blossom

be in the dark　被蒙在鼓里，完全不知道

☞ A: Do you have any idea what his notice is about?

B: I'm as *in the dark* as you are.

A：你知道他通知的内容吗？

B：我和你一样被蒙在鼓里。

be kidding　开玩笑

☞ A: What do you think of this gallery space? They offered to let me exhibit some of my paintings here.

B: *Are* you *kidding*? Any art student I know would die to have an exhibition here.

A：你觉得这个画廊怎么样？他们提出让我在这里展览一些我的画。

B：你在开玩笑吗？任何一名艺术生都非常渴望在这里办画展。

☞ A: I think our baseball team's got a good chance of winning the championship this year.

B: What? *Are* you *kidding*? Have you seen them play recently?

A：我觉得今年我们的棒球队有很好的机会可以赢得冠军赛。

B：什么？你在开玩笑吗？你最近看他们比赛了吗？

🔍 在口语中通常用 Are you kidding?（你在开玩笑吗？）或 No kidding.（别开玩笑了。）表示对对方所说的话感到惊讶或不相信。

be made of　由…制成

☞ The ropes *are made of* elastic fabrics. 那些绳子是由弹性织物制成的。

☞ We have an old standard weight that we used to use. It had to be replaced because it was imprecise. You see it *was made of* poor quality metal that was too porous. 我们有一个旧的称重标准，是我们过去用的。因为它不精确，所以得换掉了。你看它是用低质量的金属制成的，上面都有小孔了。

🔍 be made in 后面加地点，表示在某地被制造；be made of 表示制作该物品的原材料是可以看出来的；而 be made from 的含义也是"由…制造"，但是表示制作该物品的原材料是不能被看出来的。

be notorious for　因…而臭名昭著

☞ Hitler *is notorious for* his dictatorship. 希特勒因其独裁统治而臭名昭著。

🔍 电影《美人计》(Notorious)是已故英籍大导演希区柯克的名作。本片是希区柯克最出色的间谍影片，爱情与家国的矛盾冲突融合悬念惊险，两大特色相得益彰。

be objective about 客观看待

☞ A: Why is Sally the winner? I don't think she sings better than my sister.

B: Well, if you ask me, I could just say you should **be objective about** it.

A：为什么萨莉是冠军？我觉得她没有我妹妹唱得好。

B：嗯，如果你问我的话，我只能说你应该客观一点看待这个问题。

be off 离开

☞ The professor's report **is off** the subject. 教授的报告跑题了。

☞ A: Fred **is off** to the golf course again.

B: You would think he was practicing for the championship.

A：弗雷德又去高尔夫球场了。

B：你可以想成他是为锦标赛去练习了。

☞ A: Every single book I need for my report **is off** the shelves.

B: Tough luck.

A：我作报告要用的书在书架上一本都没有。

B：太不幸了。

be on medication (for sth.) 接受药物治疗

☞ A: How is Steven now?

B: The doctor suggested him to **be on medication for** his allergies for another two weeks.

A：史蒂文现在怎么样了？

B：医生建议针对他的过敏再接受两个星期的药物治疗。

☞ have treatment

be out of condition 健康状况不好

☞ A: Hi, George, how are you doing? I heard you had an operation over the spring break.

B: Yes, thanks for asking. I **was** pretty much **out of condition** for a few weeks. But I'm fine now.

A：嗨，乔治，你怎么样？我听说你在春季假期时做手术了。

B：是的，谢谢关心。我有几个星期健康状况一直很不好，但是现在已经恢复了。

be out of condition

☞ be in bad condition

be out of focus 模糊的；不聚焦的

☞ A: I am just writing Mary about our vacation. Why don't I enclose this picture of us in front of the Grand Canyon?

B: Don't you think it**'s** a little **out of focus**?

A：我正在给玛丽写信告诉她关于我们假期的事情，为什么不把我们在大峡谷前照的这张照片也附上呢？

B：你不觉得那照片有点模糊吗？

🔍 反义词组：be in focus（清晰；焦点对准）

be prepared for　为…做好准备

☞ I hope you've all finished reading the assigned chapter on insurance, so that you*'re prepared for* our discussion today. 我希望你们都已经读完我布置的关于保险的章节了，这样你们就为今天的讨论做好准备了。

🔍 prepare for 意为"为…做准备"，for 后面的宾语是准备的目的，即所要应付的情况。be prepared for 强调准备好的状态。

be pumped out　被抽出；累得上气不接下气

☞ A large quantities of underground water *are pumped out*, so the surface of this area subsides a lot. 地下水被大量抽出，所以这个地区的地面下陷很严重。

🔍 注意 pumped 与 out 之间的连读。

be puzzled by　被…迷惑

☞ The audience *are puzzled by* the sudden pause of the performance. 观众对于突然暂停表演感到很迷惑。

🔍 be confused with 也表示"迷惑"，但是更强调的是由于两者的混淆而造成的迷惑，这个词组也是托福中常考到的。

be related to　与…有关；与…有亲缘关系

☞ The new pose stresses the relationship between dinosaurs and modern birds and supports the theory that dinosaurs *are* actually more closely *related to* birds than to any other existing creature. 这个新观点强调了恐龙与现代鸟类之间的关系，并且支持了一个理论，即恐龙与鸟类的联系实际上比与其他任何现存物种都要紧密。

☞ be in connection with

be relieved to　安心，欣慰

☞ A: To me, your presentation sounded really natural and well prepared.

　　B: Oh, I*'m relieved to* hear you say that. It took me over a month to put that presentation together.

A：在我看来，你的演讲听起来真的很自然，并且是经过精心准备的。

B：噢，听你这样说我真的很欣慰。我用了一个多月的时间才把它整理好。

☞ be delighted to

be resistant to 对…有抵抗力

☞ Many insects *are resistant to* DDT. 许多昆虫都对 DDT 有了抵抗力。

be responsible for 对…负有责任

☞ Our professor said that the exam will be comprehensive, which means we'll *be responsible for* all of the subject matter we've covered in class. 我们的教授说考试范围很广，也就是说课上所讲过的内容我们都要复习。

☞ In the economic sense, laisser faire meant that while the government should *be responsible for* things like maintaining peace and protecting property rights, it should not interfere with private business. 从经济意义上讲，自由主义是指政府对于维护和平与保护产权负有责任，但不应该干涉私人事务。

🔍 其他相关词语：liability 责任；obligation 义务；right 权利，这些词也是托福中经常会考到的。

be reviewed as 被看做

☞ The temple was built to honor the ruler and according to ancient Egyptian, the ruler *was reviewed as* god after the death. 这所庙宇是用来纪念那个统治者的，而且根据古埃及人的传说，那个统治者在死后被人们视作神灵。

be scanned into digital files 被扫描成数字文件

☞ These documents could *be scanned into digital files* by using the new machine and kept in the computer. 使用那台新机器可以把这些文件扫描成数字文件，保存在电脑中。

be scheduled for 预定在某时（进行）

☞ A: The seminar *is* originally *scheduled for* today, but it has been cancelled.

B: Too bad, but it's still on for next week, isn't it?

A：原定于今天的研讨会被取消了。

B：太糟糕了，但是下周还会有的，是吗？

be secure from 免受…侵害

☞ During the war, people will first find a safe place for the old and children to make sure they could *be secure from* the attack. 战争中，人们首先要为老人和孩子找到安全的地方，让他们免受袭击。

🔍 托福考试中，be secure from interruption（不受打扰）常会在对话中出现。

be stuck 卡住了

☞ A: I can't get this window open. It*'s* really *stuck*.

B: Why don't you try using this screwdriver and see if that works?

A：我打不开这扇窗户。它卡住了。

B：为什么不用这个螺丝刀试试，看能不能打开？

☞ get stuck

---

be superior to　地位高于；品质优于

☞ The experts are having a heated argument about whether photography *is superior to* other art forms. 专家们正在就摄影是否优于其他艺术形式而进行激烈的争论。

🔍 "地位低于；品质劣于"用 be inferior to 表示。

---

be supposed to　被期望；应该

☞ A: Sir, my adviser wants me to take the creative writing class that meets on Wednesday, instead of the Monday class because the instructor in the class *is supposed to* be great. But that would mean I'd have to spend the whole day on campus every Wednesday.

　 B: Well, but especially in creative writing the instructor can make a big difference in how much you get out of the class.

　 A：先生，我的指导老师想让我参加周三的创意写作课，而不选择周一的课程，因为大家认为这个课程的老师非常好。但是这意味着我每周三都要全天待在校园里了。

　 B：哦，不过尤其在创意写作课上，老师能够指导你从课外学到许多知识。

☞ I've ordered a radio and the company *is supposed to* ship it this week. 我已经订了收音机，公司应该这周就能把它运来。

☞ A: We *are supposed to* meet John here at the train station.

　 B: That's like looking for a needle in a hay stack.

　 A：我们应该在火车站这里和约翰见面。

　 B：那就像大海捞针一样。

☞ ought to

---

be sure of　确定

☞ A: So, have you finished reviewing all the material for the psychology exam?

　 B: Just about, but I still have details upon a few facts I'*m* not *sure of*.

　 A：你复习完心理学考试的所有内容了吗？

　 B：差不多了，但是我仍然对一些方面的细节不确定。

☞ Diana *was sure of* herself in the exam. 对于这次考试，戴安娜非常自信。

☞ be certain about

---

be surprised to/at　对…感到惊奇

☞ A: Hi Diana, mind if I sit down?

　 B: Not at all, Jerry. How have you been?

　 A: Good. But I'*m surprised to* see you on the city bus. Your car in the shop?

　 B: No. I've just been thinking a lot about the environment lately. So I decided the air will be a lot cleaner if we all use public transportation when we could.

A：嗨，戴安娜，介意我坐这里吗？

B：不介意，杰瑞。你最近怎么样？

A：很好。但是我很惊讶在公车上看到你。你的车送去修理了吗？

B：没有。我最近对环境问题想了很多。所以我决定如果我们尽可能地使用公共交通方式，空气就会清新很多。

be swamped with　忙于…

☞ A: Oh, Professor Jackson, I was wondering...but uh...well, if I had a chance yet to uh...look at my thesis proposal?

B: Well, I know you gave it to me over a week ago, but to be honest, I have **been swamped with** other things.

A：哦，杰克逊教授，我在想…但是…呃…我能不能看看我的论文开题报告？

B：嗯，我知道你上个星期就给我了，但是说实在的，我一直在忙其他事情。

be through（with）　完成，结束

☞ A: Please be sure to put all the lab equipment back on the shelves when you **are through with** your experiment.

B: Oh, don't worry; I'm always very careful about that.

A：完成试验后，请确保把实验室器材全都放回架子上。

B：哦，不用担心，我对这些事是很仔细的。

☞ A local business has donated these "Do Not Litter" signs to the club, so we'll need a couple of people to place them around the lake when we **are through**. 一个当地企业为俱乐部捐了几块写着"禁止乱扔垃圾"的牌子，所以等我们结束后，要找几个人把这些牌子放在湖边。

☞ finish, be finished with

be up to　取决于

☞ A: Should we call Marsha and tell her about the meeting?

B: I'm not sure. It**'s up to** you.

A：我们应该打电话给玛莎告诉她会议的事吗？

B：我不知道，你自己决定吧。

be/get used to　习惯于

☞ A: How's the new job going?

B: Well. I**'m getting used to** lots of new things. But I wish the supervisor would give me some feedback.

A：新工作怎么样啊？

B：嗯，我正在适应很多新事物。但是我希望主管可以给我些反馈。

☞ Johnson **is used to** the cold weather. 约翰逊适应了这寒冷的天气。

☞ be accustomed to

beaver fur　海狸皮

☞ A: This hat is great.

　　B: Yeah, it is made of **beaver fur**.

　　A: Oh, the price must be also great.

　　A：这帽子看起来很棒。

　　B：是啊，它是用海狸皮制成的。

　　A：哦，那价格一定也很高吧。

begin with　以…开始

☞ When I started my coin collection, I **began with** penny for several reasons. 当我最初收集硬币时，出于某些原因我从收集便士开始。

☞ We will **begin with** the first talking motion picture, *the Jazz Singer*, released in 1927. 我们从第一部有声电影《爵士歌手》开始，它发行于 1927 年。

☞ start with

behave yourself　行为规矩，遵守礼仪

☞ This book is about to teach you how to **behave yourself** at the party. 这本书是教你宴会礼仪的。

behavior communication　行为沟通

☞ The book about animal **behavior communication** is authored by David. 这本有关动物行为沟通的书是戴维编著的。

behave yourself

behind schedule　落后于预定计划；比预定的时间晚

☞ A: The subway is running **behind schedule**, and traffic is backed up for blocks. I don't know if we'll make the 7:15 show.

　　B: It's a beautiful night. Let's try to get there on foot. And if we don't make it, let's just have dinner near the theater.

　　A：地铁晚点了，而且好几个街区都在堵车。我不知道我们能否赶上 7 点 15 的表演。

　　B：今天夜景很美，我们走着去吧。如果没赶上，我们就在剧院附近吃晚餐好了。

☞ late

belong to　属于

☞ A: Excuse me, do you mind if I borrow that newspaper for a little bit?

　　B: I'm sorry, but it doesn't **belong to** me.

A：打扰一下，请问您是否介意我借阅一下那份报纸呢？

B：对不起，那不是我的。

☞ A: That sweater is so unusual, and yet it looks familiar. Did I just see you wearing it yesterday?

B: Well, not me. But—see, it **belongs to** my roommate Jill, and she is in your chemistry class.

A：那毛衣看起来很特别，而且很眼熟。我是不是昨天见你穿过？

B：哦，不是我。但是——其实它是我室友吉尔的，她和你一起上化学课。

benefit concert　慈善音乐会

☞ A: We need to let everyone know about the **benefit concert**, but we don't have much money for advertising.

B: How about using the school radio station? They broadcast free public service announcements.

A：我们需要让每个人都知道这场慈善音乐会，但是我们没有那么多钱做宣传。

B：用学校的广播站怎么样？那里可以免费播放公共服务通知。

benefit from/by　从…中受益

☞ A: Professor Brown, thank you for giving me so many suggestions about my paper.

B: I hope you could **benefit from** that.

A：布朗教授，非常感谢您为我的论文提了这么多建议。

B：希望能对你有所帮助。

🔍 be helpful 与该词组是近义词组，但是用法有所不同，要引起注意：The advice is helpful to me. = I could benefit from the advice. 在听力中，熟悉这类词组对把握对话和全文很重要。

bestow...on/upon...　把某物赠予某人

☞ A: It is said that the prize of this competition is wonderful.

B: It will be **bestowed upon** you if you are the winner.

A：据说这次比赛的奖品非常棒。

B：如果你是冠军的话，就会颁发给你的。

better watch one's step　谨慎行事

☞ A: This is the second time this month that my boss's asked me to work extra hours. I am glad to get a bigger paycheck, but I just don't want her to give me such a heavy schedule.

B: **Better watch your step**. A lot of people would like to trade places with you.

A：在这个月里，这是老板第二次让我加班了。我很高兴可以得到更多的报酬，但是我不想她将我的工作日程安排得这么满。

B：你最好小心行事。很多人想跟你换位子呢。

Unit 4

between you and me 只有你我知道，你我之间的秘密

☞ Just ***between you and me***, I think Jeff's sister swims better than he does. 我们俩私下说，我认为杰夫的妹妹游泳比他游得要好。

beyond one's control 超出某人的控制范围

☞ If the accident was because of heavy traffic or something, I'd be attributing the driver's behavior to an external factor, something ***beyond his control***. 如果事故的发生是因为交通拥挤或别的什么原因，我就会把司机的行为归结为外部因素，也就是超出了他的控制范围。

big deal 重要的事；大人物

☞ A: I'm sorry. Is that your coat over there? I just split coffee on it.
B: It's no ***big deal***. I was taking it to the cleaner's anyway.
A：真对不起，那边的外套是你的吗？我刚才把咖啡洒到上面了。
B：没什么大不了的，我正要把它送去洗呢。

☞ It's not a big deal.（没什么大不了的。）/ Don't make a fuss about it.（不用大惊小怪的。）

big bucks/megabucks 很多钱

☞ Those cheater made ***big bucks*** by telling lies to the kind-hearted. 那些骗子通过向好心人撒谎而骗取了大量钱财。

🔍 这个词组通常用在口语中。

bird migration 鸟类迁徙

☞ The changes of ***bird migration*** patterns reflect the adverse effects of greenhouse effect. 鸟类迁徙规律的变化反映了温室效应的负面影响。

birthday/Christmas greeting 生日/圣诞祝福

☞ A: I've heard ***Christmas greeting*** from Paul some days ago.
B: Oh, Merry Christmas.
A：我几天前收到了保罗的圣诞祝福。
B：噢，圣诞快乐。

🔍 Christmas（圣诞节）是基督教的传统节日，人们会通过寄送 greeting cards（贺卡）等方式送去祝福。

bitter flavor　苦味

☞ The bread sold in the new supermarket has a ***bitter flavor***. 这家新开的超市卖的面包有一股苦味。

blend in（with）　混合，混在一起

☞ The African grass mouse's furry stripe is like a chipmunk's, which helps it ***blend in with*** its environment. 非洲草原鼠毛皮上的条纹和花栗鼠的一样，这有助于它融入周围环境。

☞ mix with

block out　遮挡；封闭

☞ The lights make things look different, but they provide better visibility than regular lighting. The problem is that a lot of the colors are ***blocked out***. 这些灯使得东西看起来都不一样了，但是能见度会比普通灯要好。问题是许多颜色被遮挡看不出来了。

blonde hair　金黄色的头发

☞ A: Look at the girl with ***blonde hair***. She's really beautiful.
　 B: I thought you were interested in these books.
　 A：看那个金黄色头发的女孩，真漂亮。
　 B：我还以为你对这些书感兴趣呢。

blood sample　血样

blood sample

☞ A: What's the result?
　 B: The doctor said he could make a conclusion only after analyzing the ***blood sample***.
　 A：结果怎么样？
　 B：医生说他只能在分析完血样后才能下结论。

boundary line　分界线

☞ In the case of physical illness, the ***boundary lines*** between normality and pathology are often clearly delineated by medical science, making it easier to diagnose. 通常，在生理疾病的病例中，正常状态和病症之间的界线被医学清楚地划定，这样疾病诊断就更容易了。

brand of　…品牌

☞ A: I'm still not sure which ***brand of*** ice cream I should buy.
　 B: Oh, not that one, it's cheaper but other brands taste much better.
　 A：我还是不知道买哪个品牌的冰淇淋。
　 B：哦，不要买那个。它虽然便宜但是其他牌子的口感更好。

🔍注意两个词的连读。

break down 损坏；发生故障

☞ If the computer doesn't **break down** again, the data will be available to us soon. 如果电脑不再出问题，我们很快就能得到数据了。

☞ A: My car **broke down** and I've got to the doctor's appointment on the other side of town.

　 B: That's lucky you ran at me then. I can give you a ride on my way to work.

　 A：我的车坏了，而我与在城市另一边的医生约好了去看病。

　 B：你很幸运碰到了我，我上班途中可以载你一程。

☞ do not work

break out into 突然发出；迸发出

☞ These children **break out into** a cold sweat merely thinking about that terrible war. 这些孩子只要一想起那场可怕的战争就会出一身冷汗。

brief holiday greeting 简短的假日问候

☞ The first actual radio broadcast was made on Christmas Eve of 1906, arranging the program of two short musical selections of poem and **brief holiday greeting**. 第一次真正意义上的无线电广播是在 1906 年的圣诞前夜，安排的节目是两小段有音乐背景的诗歌节选和简短的节日祝福。

brief introduction 简短的介绍

☞ Could you please make a **brief introduction** on the current alternative fuels? 你能给我简单介绍一下当今的替代型燃料吗？

bring about 导致，引起，带来

☞ The development of science and technology has **brought about** many changes in our life. 科技发展给我们的生活带来了很多变化。

bring down 打倒；降低

☞ The scandal of corruption **brought down** the government, although it really did a lot for citizens. 虽然这个政府为市民做了很多事，但是那次贪污丑闻还是让政府垮了台。

bring forth 产生；提出；引起

☞ As we all know, careful production will **bring forth** better products which will result in good profit. 我们都知道，生产精细化会产出更好的产品，也将为我们带来好的收益。

bring home the bacon 赚钱谋生

☞ That old poor man had to **bring home the bacon**, or he couldn't afford his son's tuition. 那个男人又老又穷，还要赚钱谋生，否则他就付不起儿子的学费了。

bring sb. to trial　审判某人

☞ A: Is there anything new in the newspaper?

　　B: Yeah, a young man ill-treated his parents and will be ***brought to trial*** tomorrow.

　　A：报纸上有什么新闻吗？

　　B：有，一个小伙子虐待他的父母，明天就要被送去审判了。

broad claims　宽泛的观点

☞ A: What sort of grade did you get on your research paper? I know how hard you worked on it.

　　B: Yeah, well, I was hoping for something really good. But the professor said that i made too many ***broad claims*** that weren't supported enough.

　　A：你的论文得了多少分数？我知道你在上面花了很多功夫。

　　B：是的，嗯，我真的希望有个好结果，但是教授说我发表了太多宽泛的观点，而这些观点没有足够的论据来支持。

bubble economy　泡沫经济

☞ ***Bubble economy*** is doomed to collapse. It is just a matter of time. 泡沫经济注定是要崩溃的，只是个时间问题。

🔍 bubble economy 属于 financial speculation（金融投机），造成社会经济的虚假繁荣。

buck against　反抗，反对

☞ A: The girl we talked about during the class is really strong to ***buck against*** her misfortune fate.

　　B: Actually I don't know much about her.

　　A：我们课上谈论的那个女孩真坚强，能够与不幸的命运抗争。

　　B：事实上，我对她的事情知道得不是很多。

buck for　谋求，拼力争取

☞ A: Peter requires work for extra hours again this weekend?

　　B: Yeah, the only thing he thinks about is to ***buck for*** a raise.

　　A：彼得这周末又要求加班？

　　B：是啊，他所想的只有一件事，就是千方百计地谋求升职。

budget deficit　预算赤字，财政赤字

☞ As a result of ***budget deficit***, the government decided to raise tax and cut expenses. 由于财政赤字，政府决定提高税收并缩减开支。

🔍 相关的词组：

fiscal revenue 财政收入　　　　　　surplus 盈余

build nests 筑巢

☞ The lecture mainly talks the possible reason that birds began to ***build nests*** in trees. 这个讲座主要谈论了鸟开始在树上筑巢的可能原因。

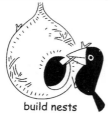

build nests

build on 建立于；依赖，依靠

☞ Figuratively speaking, both the cities of the Incas and the temples of the Mayas were ***built on*** corn. 比方说，印加人的城市以及玛雅人的庙宇都是依靠农作物(种植)建立起来的。

bulletin board 公告板，布告栏

bulletin board

☞ A: Hey Mark, have you been able to sell our old piano yet?

B: Ah, you were right, just posting notices on ***bulletin boards*** at a couple of supermarkets wasn't enough. I think I'll have to place an advertisement in the local newspaper.

A: 嗨，马克，你还没有卖掉我们的旧钢琴吗?

B: 啊，你倒提醒我了，只是在几个超市的公告板上贴通知还不够。我想应该在本地报纸上登则广告。

☞ A: Phil, could you give me a hand with this file cabinet? It belongs against the wall, next to the ***bulletin board***.

B: At your service.

A: 菲尔，你能帮我挪一下这个文件柜吗? 它应该靠着墙，挨着那个公告板。

B: 愿意为你效劳。

burn out 烧光，烧毁；(因燃料烧尽而)熄灭；(怒气、热情等)消失

☞ The factory was completely ***burnt out*** overnight. 这家工厂一夜间被烧为灰烬。

☞ burn down

burn up 烧起来；烧尽；发怒

☞ The research indicates that most of the water molecules from the comet would have ***burned up*** as they fell through the atmosphere. 研究表明，彗星上的大部分水分子在穿过大气层坠落时就已经燃烧殆尽了。

🔍注意两个词的连读。

business associate 生意伙伴

☞ A good ***business associate*** could bring you not only the profit but also valued friendship. 一个好的生意伙伴不仅可以给你带来收益，更能给予你珍贵的友谊。

☞ business partner

42

business management 商务管理

☞ The ***business management*** is very essential for a company. 商务管理对公司来说尤为重要。

busy schedule 忙碌的日程安排

☞ Lisa has a ***busy schedule***. 莉萨的日程安排很紧张。

busy signal 占线

☞ A: I've been calling David for the past half hour, but I keep getting a ***busy signal***.

　B: Well, if you don't get him soon we'll just have to go to the movies without him.

　A：这半小时内我一直给戴维打电话，但是一直占线。

　B：哦，如果你一会儿还联系不上他，我们只能自己去看电影了。

☞ busy line

by a small margin 小幅度地

☞ At the beginning of the financial crisis, people's consumption ability reduced ***by a small margin***. 金融危机刚开始时，人们的消费能力有了小幅度的下降。

☞ with a small margin

by any chance 可能，或许

☞ A: I can't seem to find my calculator. Did I lend it to you ***by any chance***?

　B: No, but you are welcome to mine if you need it, as long as I get it back by Thursday.

　A：我似乎找不到我的计算器了，我有可能借给你了吗?

　B：没有，但是如果你需要的话我可以借给你，只要在周四前还给我就行。

🔍 该词组通常用在问句中，表示委婉礼貌。

by chance 偶然，巧合

☞ A: How do you know Professor White isn't in his office?

　B: I met his assistant ***by chance*** just now.

　A：你怎么知道怀特教授不在办公室呢?

　B：我刚才碰巧遇见了他的助手。

by coincidence 巧合，碰巧

☞ The author tells how the symbol of Piggy Bank came about ***by coincidence***. 作者告诉我们小猪存钱罐的标志是如何巧合地想出来的。

by implication 含蓄地，暗示地

☞ Because he was afraid of revenge, that witness only admitted the fact ***by implication***. 那个目击者因为怕报复，只是含蓄地承认了那个事实。

by mail 通过邮件

☞ A: I need to get a copy of my birth certificate.

B: Sorry. But we can only accept requests *by mail* now.

A：我需要一份我出生证明的复印件。

B：对不起，现在我们只接受邮件形式的请求。

by the time 到…时候

☞ A: I was hoping we both would be in the discussion class.

B: Me too, Emmy. But *by the time* I got to registration, the course was closed.

A：我希望我们可以一起上讨论课。

B：我也这么想，埃米。但是我到报名处时，课程报名已经截止。

☞ A: How long can you keep the video tapes?

B: If they are not returned *by the time* the media center closes tonight, I'll have to pay a fine.

A：这些录像带你可以借多久？

B：如果在今晚多媒体中心关门前还不能还的话，我就要交罚款了。

> 🔍 托福考试中还常考到一个关于 by 的词组，by the way 表示"顺便说一下，顺便提一下"。

calculate the budget 计算预算

☞ *Calculating the budget* is a good way to check whether you have an overdraft. 计算预算是检查你是否透支的好方法。

☞ count the budget

calculate the number of calories 计算热量

☞ Many girls would like to *calculate the number of calories* in the food to decide whether to have or not. 许多女孩喜欢通过计算食物中的热量来决定是吃还是不吃。

calculus course 微积分课程

calculus course

☞ A: I'm really having trouble with this *calculus course*. If I can't start doing better soon, I'm going to have to drop it.

B: Why don't you get some help from the graduate assistance? That's what it is there for.

A：我学习微积分课程真的有困难。如果我再学不好的话，我就要放弃了。

B：你为什么不去学生辅导处寻求帮助呢？他们专门提供这方面的服务。

call for 需要；要求

☞ A: I can't find Elm Avenue anywhere on this map. I don't think there is such a street.

B: It's probably in the new part of town. We'll have to *call for* directions.

A：我在地图上找不到榆树大街，我认为根本就没有这条街。

B：可能是在小镇新建的地区，我们得找人问问方向。

☞ A: Someone just *called for* you.

B: Who, Helen?

A：刚才有人找你。

B：谁？海伦？

☞ be in need for

call for help 寻求帮助

☞ Lighting fire in the open is a common way to *call for help*. 在野外点火是一种常见的求救方法。

🔍 托福考试中 morning call（叫醒服务）也是经常考的词组，通常会出现在酒店的场景中。

call it a day 就此结束

☞ A: I'm really glad our club decided to raise money for the children's hospital, and most of the people we'd phoned seemed happy to contribute.

B: Yeah, I agree. Now we've gone through all the numbers on our list now, so I guess we can *call it a day*.

A：我真的很高兴我们俱乐部能为儿童医院筹款，而且我们致电的大多数人都很愿意捐款。

B：是啊，我同意。现在我们已经拨完了名单上的所有电话号码，我想我们今天可以收工了。

call off 取消

☞ A: Haven't you heard? The field trips have been *called off* because of the weather.

B: But Professor Lee told us just today to meet at four in front of the library.

A：你听说了吗？因为天气原因，野外实地考察旅行取消了。

B：但是李教授今天还告诉我们四点在图书馆前见面呢。

☞ A: Has tomorrow's meeting been confirmed?

B: Ahh, I was told it's been *called off*.

A：明天的会议确定了吗？

B：啊，我被告知会议取消了。

☞ cancel

call on/upon 拜访，访问；号召

☞ The company has good service that the salesmen will **call on** their clients every other month. 那家公司的服务很好，销售人员每隔一个月就会访问一次他们的客户。

☞ pag a visit to, drop in

call up 打电话

☞ A: How do I get one of those green buckets?

B: Oh, just **call up** the Sanitation Department. They'll deliver a bucket at no charge.

A：我怎么才能领到一个那样的绿桶呢？

B：哦，只要给卫生部门打个电话就行，他们会免费给你送一个的。

can't/couldn't help doing 禁不住；不得不

☞ After hearing the bad news, the mother **couldn't help** crying. 听到那个坏消息后，母亲禁不住哭了。

cancel out 抵偿，抵消

☞ The new headlights on cars **cancel out** the adverse aspects of sodium lighting and the colors appear natural again. 新式的车前灯抵消了钠光灯的弊端，而且灯光的颜色看起来也更自然了。

carbonic acid 碳酸

☞ Caves are normally created by **carbonic acid** that trickles down from above. 通常情况下，岩洞是由自上滴下的碳酸腐蚀形成的。

🔍 在托福考试中曾经出现了"硫酸"这个短语，即 sulfuric acid。

care for 喜欢；为…操心；照顾，照料

☞ A: You didn't **care for** the movie, did you?

B: You can say that again.

A：你不喜欢那部电影，是吗？

B：你说对了。

☞ A: Are you going to the conference in Chicago? I've already booked my hotel room.

B: Why **care for** hotel? My brother's got plenty of room in his place.

A：你去芝加哥开会吗？我已经订好酒店房间了。

B：为什么订酒店？我哥哥那里有很多地方可以住。

cash the check 兑现支票

☞ A: Could I borrow a twenty to tide me over till payday next Thursday?

B: You are in luck. I've just **cashed the check**.

A：你能借给我 20 美元帮我撑到下周四发工资的日子吗？

B：你真幸运呀！我刚刚兑了支票。

catch a flu　得了流行性感冒

☞ Every time I return to my hometown from Paris, I will *catch a flu* for dozens of days.
每次我从巴黎返回家乡，都会感冒一段时间。

catch up on　弥补；(事后)得到关于…的消息

☞ A: Hi, Anny, you're looking better. It's nice to have you back.

B: Thanks. I just hope I can *catch up on* all the work I've missed.

A：嗨，安妮。你看上去好多了。很高兴见到你回来。

B：谢谢，我只希望把我缺的课／落下的工作都补回来。

☞ A: I'm sorry I made you wait. The bus was stuck in traffic and took forever to get here.

B: No harm done. I was able to *catch up on* some reading.

A：抱歉让你久等了。公交车堵车了，用了好长时间才到这儿。

B：没关系的，我刚好可以多读几页书。

☞ make up for

change one's mind　改变主意

☞ A: Do you still want to go to graduate school after you get out of college?

B: I've *changed my mind* about that. I want to start working before I go back to school.

A：你大学毕业后还想上研究生吗？

B：我改变主意了。我想先工作再上学。

☞ A: I don't think I want to live in the dormitory next year. I need more privacy.

B: I know what you mean. But check out the cost of renting an apartment first. I wouldn't be surprised if you *changed your mind*.

A：我明年不想在宿舍住了。我需要有更多的私人空间。

B：我知道你的意思。但是先看一下租公寓的费用吧。如果你改变主意，我不会奇怪的。

change the channel　换频道

☞ The servant *changed the channel* immediately for the fat woman. 那名佣人马上为胖女人换了频道。

check in　登记；报到

☞ A: Have a good trip! I hope you won't have too long a walk from the car to *check in* at the hotel. That's a lot of luggage for you to carry by yourself.

B: Well, I'll get the driver to give me a hand.

A：旅途愉快！我希望你下车后去登记住宿不用走太远。你自己要拎很多行李。

B：哦，我会让司机帮忙。

check out 调查；结账离开，办妥手续离去；下班；符合要求，通过

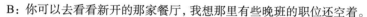
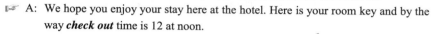
check out

☞ A: I really need to make some extra money. I've practically spent my entire budget for the semester.

B: You should **check out** the new cafeteria. I think there're a few openings left in the evening.

A：我真的需要多挣一些钱了。我已经把整个学期的预算都花完了。

B：你可以去看看新开的那家餐厅，我想那里有些晚班的职位还空着。

☞ A: We hope you enjoy your stay here at the hotel. Here is your room key and by the way **check out** time is 12 at noon.

B: Oh, thanks for reminding me. It's a lovely hotel and I'm not at all in a hurry to leave, but I wouldn't want to be charged for a second night.

A：希望您在酒店住得愉快。这是房间钥匙，顺便说一下，退房时间是中午12点。

B：噢，谢谢提醒。这酒店真不错，我也不急着走，不过我并不想花钱再住一晚。

check the scales 核对尺度

☞ People in our department use the standard weight to **check the scales** all over the country. 我们部门的人用标准重量衡量全国范围内的重量尺度。

check up on 校对，检查；验证

☞ An experiment will be made to **check up on** the reliability of this management system. 这个管理系统的可靠性将要通过一项实验来验证。

checking account 活期存款账户

☞ A: Can I open a **checking account** here?

B: I'm sorry. You'll have to step over to the manager's desk.

A：我可以在这里开个活期存款账户吗？

B：对不起。您得到经理办公桌那里。

🔍 相关词组：

saving account 储蓄账户　　　open an account 开户
interest rate 利率　　　　　　pay-in slip 存款单

Unit 5

chemical elements　化学元素

☞ The new X-ray microscopes can also be used to map the distribution of certain *chemical elements*. 这些新的 X 光显微镜也可以被用来绘制特定化学元素的分布图。

chemical pesticide　化学杀虫剂

☞ By enhancing the natural response in plants, researchers might reduce, some day even eliminate, the need for *chemical pesticide*, which can cause ecological damage. 通过促进植物的自然反应，研究者可能会减少，甚至会在未来的某一天停止使用化学杀虫剂，因为它会造成生态破坏。

chemical reaction　化学反应

☞ These unusual microorganisms' energy comes from *chemical reactions*, not sunlight. 这些不同寻常的微生物能量来自化学反应，而不是阳光。

🔍 "物理反应"在英语中是 physical reaction，"核反应"是 nuclear reaction。

chew over　反复思量，仔细考虑

☞ George *chewed over* the issue before making the final decision. 在做最后决定前，乔治反复思量这件事。

children development　孩子的发展

☞ The family education has a profound effect on *children development*. 家庭教育对孩子的发展有深远的影响。

chocolate syrup　巧克力糖浆

☞ A: Did you hear what George did last night? He was cooking dinner for the members of the drama club and he spilled spaghetti sauce all over the kitchen.

　B: Doesn't surprise me one bit. He did the same thing last semester, only with *chocolate syrup*.

　A：你听说乔治昨晚做的事了吗？他给戏剧俱乐部会员做晚餐时，把意大利面酱弄的满厨房都是。

　B：我一点都不觉得奇怪，上学期他也做过同样的事，只不过用的是巧克力糖浆。

chop down 砍下，砍伐，砍倒

☞ Everyone knows this story about Washington's **chopping down** the cherry tree when he was young and bravely confessing to his mischief later. 每个人都知道这个故事：华盛顿小时候砍倒了一棵樱桃树，后来他勇敢地承认了自己的错误。

🔍 两个单词连读时，p 的发音要弱化。

chunks of 大块的

☞ The impact caused the cores of the two planets to melt together and **chunks of** earth's crust to be thrown out into space. 这次撞击使得两个行星核融合到了一起，同时地表上大块的物质被抛到了太空中。

🔍 这个词组经常出现在学术文章中，所以考生平时要注意扩大自己的阅读范围，积累相关词汇。

city planning 城市规划

☞ Some officials in **city planning** organs were charged with taking bribe. 城市规划部门的一些官员被控受贿。

claim to 声称，主张

☞ Two groups were studied. One was a group of people who **claimed to** experience colors when they heard certain words. The other was a controlled group, people who experienced nothing out of the ordinary when hearing words. 有两组研究对象。一组声称在听到特殊词语时可以看到某些颜色。另外一组是对照组，在听到词语时什么也看不到。

class project 课题

☞ A: Excuse me, Prof. Davidson, but I was hoping to talk to you about my **class project** for economics.

B: I will have a class in a few minutes. Why don't you come and see me during office hours tomorrow?

A：打扰一下，戴维森教授，我想和您讨论一下我的经济学课题。

B：我几分钟后有课。要不你在明天的办公时间来找我？

classical music 古典音乐

☞ A: I think I'll put on some music now.

B: What do you have? I'm a **classical music** fan.

A：我想要放一些音乐。

B：你有什么音乐？我是古典音乐迷。

☞ A: How did you like the concert? I find it really moving.

B: I love **classical music**. But that conductor seemed a bit inexperienced.

A：你觉得音乐会怎么样？我觉得真的很有感染力。

B：我喜欢古典音乐。但是指挥似乎有点缺少经验。

clean up garbage

clean up garbage　清理垃圾

☞ The town's people used pigs to *clean up* the *garbage* that was thrown into the streets. 以前，这个小镇上的人用猪来清理扔在街道上的垃圾。

clear off　清除，收拾

☞ There isn't enough time to *clear* the table *off*. 没有足够的时间收拾桌子。

🔍 我们常说的"摆桌子吃饭"可说成 set / lay the table。

clear the way for　为…扫清道路 / 作铺垫

☞ It was that tragic fire that *cleared the way for* a new kind of city that used the new building techniques and new materials developed during the 1800's. 正是那场悲惨的大火为新的城市模式作下了铺垫，城市开始采用 19 世纪发明的新的建筑技巧和新材料。

clear up　（天气）变晴；整理，收拾，清除；解释，澄清

☞ A: If the weather doesn't get any better, we may have to scrap our plans for this afternoon's picnic.

　B: Don't give up yet. The forecast says the clouds should *clear up* by mid morning.

　A：如果天气没有转好，我们可能要放弃今天下午的野餐计划了。

　B：先别说放弃呀。天气预报说半上午的时候就会转晴。

☞ A: It's been pouring for three days now. I begin to wonder if it will ever stop.

　B: And tomorrow is going to be my day at the beach. But if it doesn't *clear up* by then, I'll just have to forget about that.

　A：已经下了三天大雨了。我在想它还会不会停。

　B：我原计划明天去海滩。但是如果到时候还不放晴的话，我就不得不放弃了。

clue to　提示，线索

☞ What's really interesting is the scientists are now able to recover DNA from these fossils and study the genetic material for important *clues to* evolution. 有趣的是，科学家们现在可以从这些化石中还原 DNA，并且研究遗传方面的材料以获取重要的进化线索。

college career　大学生活

☞ I've heard lots of first year students get into trouble with *college career* because they hang out every day in the student center till it closes. 我听说很多大一新生在生活上遇到麻烦，因为他们每天在学生中心消磨时光，一直待到关门。

collide with 　与…发生碰撞；与…发生冲突

☞ When Comets *collide with* the atmosphere, they break up. 当彗星和大气层发生碰撞时，它们就会分解掉。

colonial period 　殖民时期

☞ A: Hey Teresa! Thanks for agreeing to help me review all this history material.

　　B: No problem, Bob. So do you want to start with the stuff missed yesterday? They are part about urban problems in the *colonial period*?

　　A: Yeah, that'll be great.

　　A：嗨，特雷莎！谢谢你答应帮我复习所有这些历史材料。

　　B：不客气，鲍勃。那么你想从昨天落下的部分开始吗？一部分是关于殖民时期的城市问题。

　　A：是的，太好了。

color stripe 　彩条

☞ A: Do you like the bags with *color stripes* produced by the brand?

　　B: I've already had several ones.

　　A：你喜欢这个牌子的带条纹的包吗？

　　B：我已经有好几个了。

☞ color bar

combine with 　与…结合

☞ There are several specific human activities that when *combined with* a lack of rainfall encourage desertification. 人类的几项特定活动加之降雨量的不足共同导致了沙漠化。

come across 　偶遇

☞ I was looking through some of my roommate's science magazines and *came across* an article on phrenology. 我在翻阅室友的一些科学杂志时碰巧看到一篇有关颅相学的文章。

☞ meet with, encounter

come along 　跟着来，一起去

☞ A: Hey Neal, now that the midterms are over, a bunch of us are getting away for the weekend to go canoeing. Wanna *come along*?

　　B: Well, it'd be great to get away, but I've never done it before.

　　A：嗨，尼尔，现在期中考试结束了，我们一群人准备周末去划船，你想一起去吗？

　　B：嗯，一定很好玩，但是我从来没划过啊。

☞ A: I'm going over to see a car someone has for sale. It's just a year old, and it's supposed to be in excellent condition. Do you want to come with me to take a look at it? With all your experience as a mechanic, I'd appreciate your opinion.

B: That was twenty years ago. Cars have changed so much. I'm not sure how much help I might be, but sure I'll *come along* for the ride.

A：我要去看一辆待售的轿车。开了才一年，车况应该不错。你想和我一起去看一看吗？你有做技工的经验，我很想听听你的意见。

B：那都是 20 年前的事了。车更新得这么快，我不确定能给你多少帮助，但是我可以和你一起去试试车的。

---

come around　让步，改变立场；苏醒，恢复健康

☞ Gary's beginning to *come around* to my point of view. 加里开始转向我的观点。

---

come down with　染上(病)；付(钱)

☞ A: Hi, Dan, I just came by to see if you want to go to the gym with me this afternoon.

B: I'd love to but I don't think I'm up to it today. I'm *coming down with* a cold.

A：喂，丹，我来就是看你下午是否想和我一起去健身房。

B：我很想去，但恐怕今天不行。我感冒了。

🔍 考试中还常出现短语 come up with，但该短语不是 come down with 的反义短语，它的意思是"提出，想出"。

---

come into contact with sb.　接触某人

☞ You can *come into contact with* different people when you do part-time job. 在你做兼职工作的时候，你可以接触到各种不同的人。

---

come out　结果是；出现，出来；长出；出版

☞ A: How did your pictures at the Orientation *come out*? Did you get them back from the photo shop?

B: Actually the film is still in the camera. I haven't quite finished the roll.

A：你在新生见面会时照的相片效果怎样？你从照相馆取回来了吗？

B：事实上那个胶卷还在相机中，没用完呢。

☞ A: How clumsy of me, and all of your white table cloth.

B: Hey, it will *come out* with soap and water.

A：我太笨了！看我把你的白桌布弄的。

B：嗨，用肥皂和水洗一下就没事了。

☞ show up

🔍 表示"出版，发行"的词还有：release, launch。release 经常用于表示新专辑等的发行，launch 常用来指新产品的发布。

---

come out on top　占上风；最后成功

☞ A: I entered one of my new photographs in the newspaper's contest.

B: If it's anything like the others you've shown me, I'm sure you'll *come out on top*!

A：我把自己的一张新照片送去参加报纸的比赛了。

B：如果像你之前让我看过的那些，我肯定你会得第一的！

come over　　过来，顺便来访；改变立场或观点

☞ A: Listen, why don't you ***come over*** tomorrow and see the house for yourself? Ring my buzzer number.

B: Fine, see you then.

A：听着，你为什么明天不过来一趟，亲自看看房子呢？打我的手机就行。

B：好的，到时候见。

☞ A: Dr. Smith asked us to watch that special program on the Civil War on TV this weekend. Do you want to ***come over*** Saturday night?

B: Oh, I'm supposed to help my cousin move then. It's being rebroadcast on Sunday afternoon though. Is that OK for you?

A：这周末电视上会播放关于内战的特别节目，史密斯博士让我们到时候收看。你周六晚上想过来吗？

B：哦，我得去帮堂(或表)哥/弟/姐/妹搬家。周日下午还要重播，你那个时间方便吗？

☞ A: The basketball team is in the playoffs and I don't have a ticket. I guess I'll just watch it on TV. Do you want to ***come over***?

B: Actually I have a ticket, but I'm not feeling well. You can have it for what it costs me.

A：篮球队要参加决赛了，可是我没有票。我想我只能看电视了，你想过来一起看吗？

B：实际上我有票，但是我身体不舒服，我可以把票原价卖给你。

☞ drop in, pay a visit

come to terms　　达成协议，妥协

☞ I was glad that we had ***came to terms*** on this matter. 我很高兴我们在这件事情上达成了协议。

come up with　　想出，提出；赶上

☞ A: What have they decided to call the stadium?

B: No one has ***come up with*** a good name.

A：他们决定给这个体育场起什么名了吗？

B：还没想出来一个好名字呢。

☞ A: I've also arranged for you to give a speech during dinner tomorrow. At least five hundred of the students will be there. You will answer questions after you finish speaking.

B: That means I'd better ***come up with*** a speech pretty quickly.

A：我还安排了你在明天宴会时做一个演讲。至少有 500 名学生会出席。演讲结束后，你将回答他们提出的问题。

B：这就意味着我最好是很快想出一个演讲稿来。

☞ think up, put forward

come what may   不管怎样

☞ We'll pick you up tomorrow at eight *come what may*. 不管怎样，我们明天八点开车接你。

comment on/about   评论，对…发表意见

☞ One of his friend *commented on* Harry's haircut. 哈里的一位朋友对他的发型发表了意见。

☞ anyway, somehow

commercial success   商业成功

☞ Since sea captains often became part owners of their ships, they had a strong interest in the *commercial success* of their voyages. 因为船长通常是船只的拥有者之一，所以他们十分在意自己的航行在商业方面能否取得成功。

☞ make a comment on/about

committee meeting   委员会议

☞ A: Do you know if Sarah has reserved the room for the *committee meeting* yet?

B: No. But if she hasn't we should have her try to get it at the auditorium. We'll need the space.

A：你知道萨拉已经为委员会议预订好房间了吗？

B：不知道。不过如果她没订好的话，我们可以让她试试在礼堂找地方。我们需要空间。

☞ A: Professor, have you graded my term paper yet?

B: To tell you the truth, I've been tied up in *committee meetings* all week.

A：教授，您给我的学期论文评分了吗？

B：老实说，我整周都在忙委员会议，抽不开身。

☞ A: I think we should hold our *committee meeting* in one of the meeting rooms of the library. So far, there're 8 of us who plan to come.

B: Wow, if there were no more than four, I'd say that we have it over at my place; but with 8 of us, I guess I'd have to get along with your suggestion.

A：我想我们应该在图书馆的其中一个会议室里进行委员会议。迄今为止，我们有八个人要参加。

B：哇，如果是不超过四个人的话就可以在我那里举行。但是现在有八个人，我还是听你的吧。

🔍 另一个常考短语是 community committee，意思是"社区委员会"。

common sense   常识

☞ It may seem to run counter to *common sense* to say that introducing water into an area can cause it to become

55

more like a desert. 把水引入某地会使该地更像沙漠，这种说法似乎与常识相悖。

☞ public awareness

common use　广泛使用，普遍使用

☞ Before refrigerators come to **common use**, people in rural areas often have a ware to keep perishable fruits fresh. 在普遍使用冰箱前，农村地区的人们通常用器皿来使易腐烂的水果保鲜。

communicate with　与…沟通

☞ People who work at home and **communicate with** the office by the computer represent one of the trends Ms. Lambert has described. 在家上班并通过电脑与办公室人员沟通的人们代表了兰伯特女士描述的趋势之一。

comparative advantage　比较优势

☞ The principle of **comparative advantage** explains how trade is beneficial to all parties involved. 比较优势原则解释了所涉及的各方是如何从贸易中获益的。

comparative education　比较教育(学)

☞ The lecture for next time is mainly about the history and development of **comparative education**. 下次演讲的主要内容是比较教育学的历史和发展。

compare to　与…相比；把…比作

☞ **Compared to** French native paintings that are less realistic, native artists in United States painted images that were neat, positive, extremely accurate and almost photographic. 与法国本土不太现实的画作相比，美国本土艺术家的画作整洁、积极、极其精确，几乎和照相机拍得一样。

compare...with　将…与…比较/对照

☞ We know little about sea creatures **compared with** what we know about the animals on the land. 与对陆地动物的了解相比，我们对海洋生物知之甚少。

☞ be in comparison with

compensate for　弥补；补偿，赔偿

☞ A: Arm exercises? Is that because our arms are too fat or flabby?

　　B: Actually, that's not the main reason. They say that arm exercises are an ideal way to become physically fit.

　　A: But don't arm exercises raise your blood pressure?

　　B: That they do. But the article I read mentioned ways to **compensate for** that.

　　A：臂部锻炼？这样做是因为我们的胳膊太肥胖或者肌肉不结实吗？

　　B：事实上，那不是主要的原因。他们说臂部锻炼是让身体健康的理想方式。

　　A：但是臂部运动不是会增高血压吗？

　　B：的确会。但是我读过的一篇文章提到了弥补这一缺点的方法。

☞ make up with

complain about　抱怨，申诉

☞ Students who eat in the dinning-hall usually *complain about* the service quality. 在食堂吃饭的学生常常抱怨服务质量。

complain to　向···抱怨

☞ Students always *complain to* me about the food. 学生们总是向我抱怨食物问题。

complicated troubles　棘手的麻烦

☞ His mother allotted Sam 10 days to deal with all his *complicated troubles*. 山姆的妈妈给了他十天，让他处理自己的棘手问题。

computer data base　计算机数据库

☞ You also learn how to use the *computer data base* because the records are kept on it, and building up your computer skills is a good preparation for lots of jobs. 你也要学习如何使用数据库，因为数据都储存在里面。掌握计算机技巧对很多工作来说都是好的准备。

🔍 相关词汇：

keyboard 键盘　　　　　　　　hardware 硬盘
software 软件　　　　　　　　mouse 鼠标

computer literacy　计算机知识

☞ The job requires college degree or above and basic *computer literacy*. 这项工作要求大学本科及其以上学历，并且具备基础的计算机知识。

computer power button　计算机电源按钮

☞ Press any key or hit *computer power button* while it doesn't work. 如果电脑死机，请按任意键或按电源按钮。

concentrate on　专心于，全神贯注于

☞ A: Could you turn down your stereo a bit? I really can't *concentrate on* my book.
　 B: Why didn't you just say so?
　 A：你能把音响调小一点吗？我真的无法集中精力看书。
　 B：你怎么不早说呢？

☞ A: I can't *concentrate on* this final report any longer. Maybe I should take a nap before we continue.
　 B: They say the physical activity makes you more alert.
　 A：我无法专心做这份期末报告了。或许我应该小憩一会儿我们再继续。
　 B：有人说运动可以使人精神点。

☞ A: With so little time left to study for the history final. I think we should *concentrate on* going over our lecture notes.
　 B: That sounds good. At least we have an idea what Prof. Martin thinks is important.

A：历史期末考试的准备时间不多了。我认为我们应该集中复习讲座笔记。

B：好主意，至少笔记会告诉我们马丁教授的重点是什么。

☞ be absorbed in

confess to   承认，坦白

☞ Everyone knows this story about Washington's chopping down the cherry tree when he was young and bravely *confessing to* his mischief later. 每个人都知道这个故事：华盛顿小时候砍倒了一颗樱桃树，后来他勇敢地承认了自己的错误。

conflict of interests   利益冲突

☞ There is a growing *conflict of interest* between the two leading steel companies. 这两家龙头钢铁公司之间的利益冲突正在加深。

conflict with   与…冲突

☞ All the other work schedules *conflict with* my classes. 所有的其他工作日程安排都与我的课相冲突。

confuse...with   把…和…搞混，把…当成

☞ A: The dishes taste strange.

B: Well, it's easy to *confuse* sugar *with* salt.

A：这菜的味道吃起来很怪。

B：嗯，糖和盐很容易搞混。

🔍 通常听力考试中出现该词组时，confuse 的两个宾语是把握对话或全文意思的关键，所以在听到这个词的时候要多加注意。

Congressional Record   国会议事录

☞ The debates and votes are published in the *Congressional Record*. 议员的讨论和表决都会在国会议事录上公布。

congressional representative   国会代表

☞ We recently wrote to Herry James, one of the state *congressional representatives* from Texas. 我们最近给亨利·詹姆斯写信了，他是得克萨斯州的国会代表之一。

consensus on/about   关于…意见一致

☞ We'd better seek a *consensus on* this global issue. 我们最好在这一国际问题上达成一致。

consent to   同意，赞同

☞ We are fortunate that the famous professor *consented to* come share some of his experiences with us. 我们非常幸运，那位著名的教授同意前来和我们分享他的经验。

consider...done　当作…做完了

☞ A: Could you do me a favor? I really need to get this notebook to Kathy and I know she will be in your chemistry class this afternoon.

　B: Not a problem. *Consider* it *done*.

　A：你能帮我一个忙吗? 我急需把这个笔记本给凯茜。我知道她下午和你一起上化学课。

　B：没问题, 我来搞定。

consider to be　认为是

☞ Today, we'll cover what we *consider to be* the two great periods of Wright's career. 今天, 我们将谈到在我们看来赖特事业中的两个重要时期。

🔍 consider 后还可以直接加动名词, 如 consider resigning(考虑辞职)。

consist of　由…组成

☞ Because there was still no home radio receivers, Ben's audience *consisted of* only wireless operators on ships in New York harbor. 因为当时还没有家用收音机, 所以本的听众只是在纽约港船只上工作的无线操作员。

☞ be made up of

contemporary poet　当代诗人

☞ Gertrude Stein has been better known for her prose than for her poems. But I'd like to quote this line because of its musicality, and because I think it helps open up our awareness to the unconventional lyricism of *contemporary poets*. 一直以来, 格特鲁德·斯坦的散文比诗更要出名。但是由于其音乐感, 我想引用这行诗, 也因为我觉得它可以帮我们提升对当代诗人的非传统抒情诗的意识感觉。

🔍 现代诗人是 modern poets。

continental drift　大陆漂移(学说)

☞ The *continental drift* is the theory that the positions of earth continents have changed considerably overtime. 大陆漂移学说认为, 地球板块的位置随着时间推移发生了巨大改变。

contribute to　有助于, 促成

☞ I want to talk about some of the social elements that I believe *contributed to* the development of bebop music. 我想讲一下我认为促成比波普爵士乐发展的几个社会因素。

☞ make a contribution to

🔍 此短语中, to 是介词, 后面跟名词和动名词。

convert to/into　把···转化为

☞ When ultraviolet rays from the sun strike the vitamin D in our skin, the sunlight *converts* vitamin D *to* its active form, a substance called calciferol. 当阳光中的紫外线碰到我们皮肤中的维生素 D 时，就会把维生素 D 转化为其活跃形式，也就是一种叫"钙化醇"的物质。

NOTES

Unit 6

convey emotions to 向…传达情感

☞ Sometimes, we can only *convey* our *emotions* and ideas through the Internet and email *to* others. 有时，我们只能通过网络和电子邮件向别人表达情感。

coop up 禁闭，困住，把…关起来

☞ A: What are you doing *cooped up* here in the lounge on such a beautiful spring day? I can't understand why everyone isn't out there in the fresh air, getting some sunshine.

B: You won't be saying that if you have my allergies.

A：在这样一个阳光明媚的春天你把自己关在休息室干什么？我无法理解为什么没有一个人出去呼吸一下新鲜空气，晒晒太阳。

B：如果你也像我一样过敏的话就不会那么说了。

copying machine 复印机

☞ A: Are you just about done with the *copying machine*?

B: Pretty much. I just have to make sure the copy is clear.

A：你用完复印机了吗？

B：快了，我只要再看一下复印件是否清晰就可以了。

cosmic dust 宇宙尘埃

☞ Comets are made up mostly of *cosmic dust* and water. 彗星大部分是由宇宙尘埃和水组成的。

cost sb. an arm and a leg 耗资不菲

☞ A: Did you see the diamond ring Bill gave to Linda?

B: I sure did. It must have *cost him an arm and a leg*.

A：你看到比尔送给琳达的钻戒了吗？

B：当然看到了，他一定花了不少钱。

count on 期望，指望；依靠，依赖

☞ A: James, I don't know if you know this. But I'm prepared to run for class president and I'm wondering, if I can *count on* your vote?

B: Oh, maybe if you asked me sooner. But my roommate's running too and I've already promised him he had my support.

A：詹姆斯，我不知道你是否知道这件事。我准备竞选班长，我想问我能否算上你的一票？

B：哦，你早点说的话也许可以。但是，我的室友也参加竞选，我已经答应支持他了。

count...in 把…算在内

☞ A: I got an invitation to a financial planning seminar. And I don't want to go alone.

B: *Count* me *in*. I need all the help I can get managing my money.

A：我得到一份参加理财计划研讨会的请柬，但是我不想一个人去。

B：算我一个。我需要所有理财方面的帮助。

count...out 不把…算在内

☞ A: A bunch of us are going out for pizza.

B: *Count* me *out*, but have a good time.

A：我们一群人要出去吃比萨。

B：别算我了，你们吃得开心点。

cozy atmosphere 和睦的氛围

☞ People seem to think that the rounded logs give their homes a *cozy* warm *atmosphere*. 似乎人们都认为原木给他们的家营造出和睦温馨的氛围。

crash the rebellion 平息叛乱

☞ The only way for the country to survive in the war was to *crash the rebellion*. 这个国家在战争中幸存下来的唯一方式是平息叛乱。

creative thinking 创造性思维

☞ *Creative thinking* and innovation are particularly useful in decision and strategy. 创造性思维和创新在决策和战略方面尤其有用。

credit transfer 银行转账

☞ Many people doubt whether *credit transfer* is safe or not. 许多人怀疑银行转账是否安全。

🔍 现在流行信用卡结账，"信用卡"用英语说就是 credit card。

cultural diffusion 文化传播

☞ This definition tries to redefine classification of these traditional dwellings from the aspects such as immigration, *cultural diffusion* and dialect formation. 这种定义试图从移居、文化传播和方言形成等方面重新定义这些传统居住地的分类。

curl up 蜷缩，卷起，卷曲

curl up

☞ Although these bats sleep during the day, they do so *curled up* with their head exposed to the sun. 尽管这些蝙蝠在白天睡觉，但是它们却蜷缩着（身体），将脑袋暴露于阳光下。

current affairs 时事，新闻

☞ Readers are better informed about the *current affairs* through the new magazine. 通过这本新杂志，读者能更好地了解时事。

cursive script 草书

☞ The children had moved from writing in block capital letters to *cursive script*. 这些孩子已经从书写粗体大写字母转为写草书了。

🔍 相关词汇：
calligraphy 书法   penmanship 书法
handwriting 书法；笔迹

cut across 径直穿过，走捷径，抄近路

☞ These pupils *cut across* the park near their school. 这些小学生抄近路，径直穿过他们学校旁边的公园。

cut back 削减；修剪；急忙返回；倒叙

☞ A: I cannot believe my phone bill this month; it's way too high.

B: Yeah, that happened to me a lot last year, but this year I have just tried to *cut back* on my long distance calls.

A：我真不敢相信这个月的电话费会这么高。

B：嗯，去年我也经常发生这种情况，但是今年我努力削减了长途电话费。

☞ shorten, decrease, reduce

🔍 cut back 后常跟 on 搭配，表示"在某方面削减开支"。

cut down 砍倒；削减，减少

cut down

☞ In the past, we simply *cut down* infected trees to fight the disease. 在过去，我们只是把被感染的树砍掉来防御这种疾病。

cut down on 减少

☞ A: I'm having trouble fitting into my jeans. Looks like I'll have to get some new ones.

B: Oh, you wouldn't do that if you just *cut down on* what you eat.

A：我的牛仔裤都穿不上了。看来我不得不买几条新的了。

B：哦，如果你节食就不用买了。

☞ A: The doctor says I've to *cut down on* fattening foods. All the ones I like.

B: So that explains your mood.

A：医生说我得少吃油腻的食物。所有我喜欢吃的。

B：那就是你心情不好的原因吧。

cut down the budget　减少预算

☞ What do you think is the best way to *cut down* this kind of *budget* during the plan making process? 在制作这项计划过程中，你认为怎样才是减少这种预算的最佳方法？

cut in　插嘴；(汽车)超车抢档

☞ Please do not *cut in* when the professor declare the departing date. 在教授宣布出发日期的时候请不要插嘴。

cut it out　闭嘴

☞ I told you to *cut it out*. 我叫你闭嘴。

☞ shut up

dark pigments　黑色素

☞ The skin of the grass mouse contains lots of melanin, or *dark pigments*. 草鼠的皮肤中含有大量黑色素。

🔍 两个词连续时，k 的发音要尽可能弱化。

data process　数据程序

☞ A: Good morning, East Coast *Data Process*. May I help you?

B: Caroline? Oh, dear, I'm sorry. I thought I dialed Jack; your number must be just above his in my address book.

A：早上好，东海岸数据程序中心。有什么可以帮您的？

B：卡罗琳吗？哦，天啊，对不起。我以为拨的是杰克的号。在我的通讯录中，你的号码一定是正好在他的上面。

daylight hours　白天

☞ Most mice are nocturnal, but the African grass mouse is active during *daylight hours*. 大多数老鼠都在夜间活动，但是非洲草原鼠在白天非常活跃。

☞ daytime

debate over　关于…的争论

☞ The *debate over* social security will be shifted to the developing countries. 关于社会安全的争论马上就会转移到发展中国家上。

debate with 与…辩论

☞ He dared them to *debate with* him about it. 他向他们挑战，要他们和他辩论这个问题。

decent pay 可观的薪水

☞ A: Gee, Tom, I hear that you are working as a house painter this summer. It's got to be awfully hot working up there on a ladder in the blazing sun all day.

B: Well it's hard work, but I get to be outdoors and a *decent pay* is offered.

A：嘿，汤姆，听说你这个夏天在做房屋油漆工，烈日下整天在梯子上工作很难受吧。

B：嗯，工作是很辛苦，但是由于在室外工作，他们给的薪水很高。

☞ excellent salary

decide on 对…做出决定

☞ He couldn't *decide on* a topic for his paper. 他不能确定他论文的主题。

☞ make decisions on

dedicate one's energy to 将精力用于

☞ The professor *dedicated his energy to* the researching of this famous theory. 教授把精力都用在研究这个著名理论上了。

define...as 把…定义为

☞ A desert is *defined as* a place that receives a certain maximum amount of rainfall. 沙漠是根据最大降雨量来定义的地方。

delight at 因…感到快乐

☞ We can image the mothers' *delight at* the good news. 我们可以想想这些妈妈在听到这个好消息时的快乐表情。

deliver a judgment/verdict 做出判决

☞ The judge sometimes *delivers a judgment* after hearing the arguments or evidence given by plaintiff only. 法官有时候在单方面聆听原告的证据后就做出判决。

deliver a(n)speech/lecture/address 发表演讲/讲座/讲话

☞ The president *delivered a speech* on TV to the nation in the New Year. 总统在新年向全国发表电视演讲。

☞ give a speech / lecture

deny oneself sth./doing sth. 节制，戒绝，摒弃

☞ Ben decided to *deny himself* smoking and drinking. 本决定戒烟戒酒。

戒烟3!!

deny oneself

department chair   系主任

☞ I didn't write that letter to the **department chair** that day. 那天，我没有给系主任写信。

depend on   依靠，依赖，取决于

☞ Industries **depend on** our government agencies to monitor the accuracy of scales so that when they buy and sell their products there is one standard. 各行业依靠政府机构来监测尺度的精确度，以便他们在买卖产品时有相同标准。

☞ Algae are the base of the aquatic food chain, which means the other organisms **depend on** them for food. 藻类是水生食物链的基础，这就意味着其他生物体都以它们为生。

☞ count on, rely on, feed on, live on

deplete all natural resources   耗尽所有自然能源

☞ What will happen to the atmosphere as a result of burning out gasoline and **depleting natural resources** like fossil fuels? 当燃烧掉汽油、耗尽所有如化石燃料的自然能源时，大气会怎样？

deposit a layer of sediment   积蓄沉淀物

☞ Over the history of the area, every time the river flooded, it would **deposit a layer of sediment** all through with flood plain. 历史上，这个区域每经过一次洪水，就会在冲击平原上沉积一层沉淀物。

derive...from   从…获取，从…得到

☞ Like many other popular writers, Mark Twain **derived** much of the materials for his writing **from** the wealth and diversity of his own personal experiences. 就像许多其他著名作家一样，马克·吐温从他丰富的、多面的个人经历中得到了很多写作素材。

descend from   起源于；是…的后裔

☞ When the first Argentine ants came to California, their population must have been very small and all the later generations of Argentine ants there must have **descended from** the same few ancestors. 当第一批阿根廷蚂蚁来到加利福尼亚时，它们的数量一定非常少，而之后的所有阿根廷蚂蚁必定是由这些相同的祖先繁衍而来。

develop film   冲洗胶卷

☞ According to the conversation, it is inferred that it's a cheap process of **developing film** at home. 从对话中可以推断，在家冲洗胶卷很便宜。

develop film

digestive system 消化系统

☞ The article mainly talks about the feeding habits and *digestive systems* of starfish. 这篇文章主要讲述海星的进食习惯和消化系统。

🔍 呼吸系统：respiratory system

dirt cheap 非常便宜

☞ A: You've already furnished your apartment?

B: I've found some used furniture that was *dirt cheap*.

A：你布置完自己的公寓了吗？

B：我买了一些非常便宜的旧家具。

discussion class 讨论课

☞ A: I was hoping we both would be in the *discussion class*.

B: Me too, Emmy. But by the time I got to registration, the course was closed.

A：我希望我们可以一起上讨论课。

B：我也这么想，埃米。但是我到报名处时，课程报名已经截止了。

🔍 国外大学的上课形式多种多样，常见的有讲座（lecture）、导师个别指导（tutorial）和陈述（presentation）等。

disposable paper cup 一次性纸杯

☞ The scientist came up with *disposable paper cup* just as the nation was becoming concerned about their health risks associated with the tin cups. 正当国家开始担心锡铁杯带来的健康风险时，那位科学家发明了一次性纸杯。

distinctive characteristic 独特特征

☞ What does the speaker say as a *distinctive characteristic* of jazz musicians? 说话者指出的爵士音乐家的独特特征是什么？

distinctive feature 特色

☞ One *distinctive feature* of Moore's sculpture is his use of holes or opening to emphasize that he is indeed working in a 3-dimensional medium. 摩尔雕刻的一大特点就是他对洞孔或空穴的利用，以此来强调他实际上是采用三维空间的方法在雕刻。

distinguish...from 把…与…区分开

☞ Criteria must be worked out for *distinguishing* normal behavior *from* abnormal behavior in actual clinical cases. 必须制定标准来区分临床病例中的正常行为和异常行为。

☞ tell...from

distort history　歪曲历史

☞ Some newspapers are often responsible for *distorting history*. 一些报纸常常为曲解历史而负责。

distort the original meaning　曲解原意 / 本义

☞ The student *distorted the original meaning* of his teacher. 这名学生曲解了老师的本义。

distribution center　分销中心

☞ Many customers complained to *distribution center* about the quality of their products. 许多顾客向分销中心抱怨产品的质量。

dive in　（头朝下）跳水

dive in

☞ This is our last chance to take a break before finals. The scenery is beautiful, and if it gets too hot we can *dive in* whenever we feel like it. 这是我们期末考试前最后一次休息的机会。这里景色很美，而且如果天气太热的话，我们随时都可以跳水。

🔍 注意两词连读/'daɪvˌɪn/。

divide into　分成，分为

☞ Today I want to talk to you about the wasps and their nests. You recall the biologist *divided* species of wasps *into* two groups, solitary and social. 今天我想给你们讲的是黄蜂和它的巢。你们回想一下，生物学家将黄蜂的种类分为群居和独居两种。

do sb. a favor　帮忙

☞ A: Could you *do me a favor*? I really need to get this notebook to Kathy and I know she will be in your chemistry class this afternoon.

　B: Not a problem. Consider it done.

　A：你能帮我一个忙吗？我急需把这个笔记本给凯茜。我知道她下午和你一起上化学课。

　B：没问题，我来搞定。

☞ give sb. a hand

do with　对待，处理

☞ I don't know what to *do with* all the food that's left over. 我不知道怎样处理这些剩菜剩饭。

☞ What have you *done with* my umbrella? 你把我的伞弄到哪里去了？

dormitory area　宿舍区

☞ A: Excuse me, can you tell me the nearest telephone booth in the **dormitory area**?

B: Sorry. I'm a freshman.

A：劳驾，请问离宿舍区最近的电话亭在哪里？

B：对不起。我是新生。

dormitory officer　宿舍管理员

☞ Paul asked the **dormitory officer** for changing the room. 保罗请求宿舍管理员给他换宿舍。

dozens of　许多的

☞ I remember there were **dozens of** people waiting there for autographs. 我记得当时有许多人在那里等着要签名。

☞ **Dozens of** valuable paintings and frescoes were badly damaged today when rain water poured through a roof at the state museum. 今天，当雨水透过国家博物馆的房顶时，许多贵重的油画和壁画都被严重破坏了。

☞ lots of

🔍 注意连读 /ˈdʌznzˌəv/。

draft of paper　论文草稿

☞ The professor will expect a preliminary **draft of** each **paper** two weeks before the final due date. 教授期望在论文上交截止日期的前两周看到每份论文的初稿。

drag one's feet on　拖延，拖沓地进行

☞ A: I keep putting off getting my passport application.

B: Thank Goodness. I didn't **drag my feet on** that one.

A：我一直在推迟办理护照申请。

B：谢天谢地，我在这件事上没有拖拖拉拉。

drastic climatic variation　剧烈的气候变化

☞ Over the past decade, there has been a **drastic climatic variation** in the global. 在过去的十年间，全球经历了剧烈的气候变化。

dress up　打扮，装饰

dress up

☞ A: I'm thinking about wearing a suit to the party tonight. What do you think?

B: Well, I haven't heard anything about **dressing up**. I bet a sweater would be fine.

A：我在考虑今晚穿西装去参加宴会。你认为怎么样？

B：哦，我没听说需要什么特殊着装。我肯定穿毛衣就可以了。

drive apart 使···分离

☞ Brazil and Ascension Island were once much closer together, and continental drift *drove* them *apart*. 巴西和阿森松岛曾经离得很近，后来大陆漂移导致它们分开了。

drive home 开车回家

☞ A: There's a thunderstorm watch for this afternoon.

B: Ah nuts. And I was about to *drive home*.

A：今天下午有雷雨警报。

B：胡说。我马上要开车回家了。

drive sb. up the wall 把某人逼到绝境；使沮丧

☞ This computer is *driving me up the wall*. 这台电脑真令我抓狂。

drop by 顺便拜访

☞ A: Let's *drop by* the post office again, Fred, and see if there is any mail yet.

B: The post office again? It's only been an hour.

A：弗雷德，我们顺便再去一趟邮局，看是否有邮件。

B：还要去？你一个小时前刚去过啊。

☞ drop in

🔍 两词连读时，p 的发音要尽可能弱化。

NOTES

Unit 7

drop sb. off　让某人下车

☞ A: Where do you want me to *drop you off*.
B: Right here is fine.
A：你想在哪里下车?
B：这儿就行。

🔍 *在考试中还会考到另外一个短语：give sb. a lift 搭便车。*

drug trade　毒品交易

☞ The government official didn't really have the time to devote to investigation of the *drug trade*. 政府机关实际上没有足够的时间来进行毒品交易的调查。

due to　由于

☞ Some American researchers predicted that Antarctica would show early signs of global warning *due to* the green house effect. 一些美国的研究人员预测，南极洲将显示出由于温室效应而导致全球变暖的早期信号。

☞ Some leaves have withered and turned yellow, maybe *due to* Dutch elm disease. 一些树叶可能由于荷兰榆树病而枯萎变黄了。

☞ as a result of, because of, owing to

dust devil　沙尘暴

☞ It's reported that a *dust devil* swept across northwest of America. 据报道，一场沙尘暴席卷了美国西北部地区。

☞ dust storm

dust devil

eager for　渴望

☞ Audiences and dancers in the United States were *eager for* their own contemporary dance form, and so around 1900 dancers created one. 美国的观众和舞者都渴望拥有属于他们自己的现代舞形式，于是在 1900 年左右舞者们就创造了一种。

☞ keen for

eager to(do)　渴望做

☞ The man's parents are *eager to* see their son. 这个男人的父母渴望见到他们的儿子。

☞ keen to do

earn/gain/establish a reputation as 获得 / 建立…的名声

☞ Henry's teaching method had **gained** him **a reputation as a** good teacher. 亨利的教学方法使他获得了好老师的声誉。

eat away 侵蚀，消耗；痛快地吃

☞ It's the acid added to books that eventually **eats away** the paper. 正是加入书中的酸性物质最终腐蚀了纸。

🔍 注意连读 /'iːtəˌweɪ/。

ecological balance 生态平衡

☞ The government has taken measures to keep **ecological balance**. 政府已采取措施维持生态平衡。

ecological disaster 生态灾难

☞ Researchers might reduce the need for chemical substances, which can cause **ecological disaster**. 研究人员可能会减少对导致生态灾难的化学物质的需求。

🔍 另一常考短语是 ecological damage，意思是"生态破坏"。

economic conditions 经济条件

☞ This style became very popular, in part because of the **economic conditions** of the time. 这一风格变得很流行，部分是因为当时的经济情况。

🔍 注意 economic 和 condition 连读时会有吞音现象，第一个单词末尾 /k/ 音只到发音位置，而不发出声音。

economic crisis 经济危机

☞ Many artists who had been living in big cities were forced by the **economic crisis** to leave those big cities and move back to their small towns in rural America. 许多生活在大城市的艺术家为经济危机所迫离开了这些大城市，搬回到他们美国的小城镇里。

🔍 另一常考的短语是 financial crisis，意思是"金融危机"。

economic perspective 经济前景

☞ Three months ago, the May employment report revealed that the improving **economic perspective** will add more than 54,000 jobs soon. 三个月前，五月份就业报告显示，不断改善的经济前景将在不久增加 54000 个以上就业岗位。

effective measures 有效措施

☞ The government should take *effective measures* to stimulate the economic growth. 政府应该采取有效的措施来刺激经济增长。

effective remedy 有效治疗法；有效药物

☞ The new medicine developed by the research group can be an *effective remedy* for insomnia. 这个研究小组所开发的新药对治疗失眠有很好的疗效。

either of …中的任意一个

☞ A: I'm sort of upset with my brother. He hasn't answered *either of* my letters.

B: Well, just remember how excited your freshman year was. Give him a chance to get settled.

A：我有点担心我弟弟。他一封信都没给我回。

B：哦，想想你自己上大一时多么兴奋吧。给他个机会安顿好。

☞ If it's not to the President's liking, the bill can be vetoed or killed in *either of* the two ways. 如果议案不投总统所好，他可以采用两种方式中的任何一种进行否决。

🔍 either 在英音中读作 /ˈaɪðə(r)/，在美音中读作 /ˈiːðə(r)/。

electric bill 电费单

☞ A: You know, if you closed your windows all the way during the cold weather, your *electric bills* wouldn't be so high.

B: Sure, but my housemate will never agree to that.

A：知道吧，如果你冷天一直关着窗户，电费就不会这么多了。

B：的确，但是我室友永远不会同意这么做。

🔍 与"费用单据"相关的短语还有：

phone bill 电话费单   gas bill 煤气费单

heating bill 暖气费单   water bill 水费单

electrical impulses 电子脉冲

☞ Most of the fish here produce only weak *electrical impulses* that are useful for navigating, locating food and even for communicating. 这里大部分的鱼只能发出微弱的电子脉冲，这有助于它们游行，定位食物，甚至是相互交流。

☞ This fish navigates using tiny receptors in the skin that are sensitive to *electrical impulses*. 这种鱼利用皮肤上微小的感受器帮助游行，这种感受器对电子脉冲敏感。

☞ Fish use the ability to produce and detect *electrical impulses* to communicate. 鱼可以用这种特殊的能力发出并探测出电子脉冲，从而互相进行交流。

electrical signals 电子信号

electrical signals

☞ The knife fish produces an *electrical signal* and the receptors in its skin let it know when the signal is distorted by a tree root or some other obstacles so it can go around it. 刀鱼发出电子信号, 当信号被树根或其他一些障碍物挡住时, 它皮肤上的感受器就会感知并反馈, 从而使其能绕行。

electronics engineering 电子工程学

☞ John was an expert on *electronics engineering*. 约翰是电子工程学方面的专家。

elementary school 小学

☞ As you prepare to become *elementary school* teachers, you'll be hearing a lot of discussion about the relevance of teaching penmanship. 当你准备当小学老师时, 你会听到许多有关板书方面的讨论。

☞ Years ago when I was studying education in college, reading, writing and arithmetic were the basics of *elementary school* education. 许多年前, 我在大学里学习教育时, 阅读、写作和算术是小学教育的基础。

☞ In my states penmanship has been de-emphasized in a required curriculum, especially in the later years of *elementary school*. 在我所在的州, 书法不再被强调是必修课, 尤其在小学教育的后几年。

☞ primary school

🔍 中学是 middle school 或 high school。

elevation of …的海拔

☞ Not long ago, some of you may have read about the team of mountain climbing scientists who helped to recalculate the *elevation of* the highest mountain in the world, Mount Everest. 你们中的一些人可能已经通过阅读得知, 不久前, 登山科学队重新测量了世界最高峰珠穆朗玛峰的海拔。

☞ The *elevation of* Mount Everest was determined many years ago using traditional surveying methods. 很多年前, 珠穆朗玛峰海拔是通过传统的测量方法测定的。

elevation to 升职

☞ Many colleagues tried to block Peter's *elevation to* the manager. 许多同事试图阻止彼得晋升为经理。

☞ promotion to

employment agency 职业介绍所

☞ Many foreign students got part-time jobs through *employment agency*. 很多留学生通过职业介绍所来找兼职工作。

encounter difficulties/danger/trouble/opposition　遇到困难/危险/麻烦/反对

☞ The conversation mainly refers to the **difficulties** often **encountered** by psychologists. 对话主要涉及心理学家常常会遇到的一些困难。

☞ be confronted with difficulties / danger / trouble

encourage sb. to do sth.　鼓励某人做某事

☞ Although works are automatically copyrighted, artists are **encouraged to** register their work with United States Copyright Office. 尽管作品是自动生成版权的，但是艺术家仍被鼓励去美国版权署为他们的作品进行注册。

end up　结束

☞ Many pesticides that the farmers applied to their crops are eventually washed away by the rain and **end up** in ponds or other bodies of water where amphibians live. 农民在庄稼上用的许多杀虫剂最终都被雨水冲走，然后流到池塘或者其他两栖动物生活的水域里。

🔍 注意连读 /ˈendˌʌp/。end up 后可以接介词 with，还常接 doing 的形式表示"以…告终"。

endangered species　濒危物种

☞ Conservationists don't have enough funding to save every **endangered species** in the world, so they have to decide based on what would be lost if a species became extinct. 自然资源保护主义者没有足够的资金去救助这世界上每一个濒危的物种，所以他们会先考虑一个物种灭绝后，我们会失去什么，然后再做出决定。

☞ This is a wild life center, not a zoo. This place breeds **endangered species** and tries to prepare them for life in the wild. 这是一个野生动物中心，并不是动物园。这个地方繁殖着濒危物种，并试着培养它们野外生存的能力。

energy source　能源

☞ Prof. Collins is an authority on **energy sources**. 柯林斯教授是能源方面的专家。

energy source

engage in　从事，参加

☞ The major gourmet coffee merchants from other cities like Seattle, San Francisco, came to Boston where today they are **engaged in** a kind of coffee war with Boston's merchants. 现在，其他城市如西雅图、旧金山的主要精品咖啡商来到波士顿，与波士顿商人进行一场咖啡战。

enjoy the company of sb. / enjoy sb.'s company　喜欢某人的陪伴

☞ Susan *enjoys* her husband's *company* when traveling. 苏珊旅行时喜欢有丈夫的陪伴。

---

enormous expenditure　巨额开支

☞ The project will require *enormous expenditure*. 这项工程需要巨额开支。

🔍 常考的短语还有：
public expenditure 公共开支　　　　government expenditure 政府开支

---

entertain...with　用…娱乐

☞ Franklin wanted a paper that *entertained* the people *with* humors and critical news items. 富兰克林想办一份用幽默和批判性新闻来娱乐大众的报纸。

---

environmental issue　环境问题

☞ Let's talk about an *environmental issue* that has to do with how common household products have changed. 让我们来谈一个关于环境是如何使普通家居产品发生变化的问题。

🔍 issue 通常指"有争议的问题，悬而未决的问题"，例如：a global issue 全球性的问题，a complicated issue 麻烦的问题。

---

environmental science class　环境科学课

☞ I'm working on a report on energy sources for my *environmental science class*. 我正在做环境科学课程里的一个关于能源的报告。

---

erase data　删掉数据

☞ The computer crashed, and all our *data* were *erased*. 由于电脑死机，我们所有的数据都被删除了。

🔍 erase 后还常接 record，表示"删除记录"。

---

escape from　从…逃出来

☞ Julie is wishing she can *escape from* her hard labor. 朱莉希望自己能摆脱繁重的体力劳动。

☞ flee from

---

even if/though　即使，尽管

☞ *Even if* the bill passed in Congress, it still doesn't become a law until the President had a chance to review it too. 即使国会通过了该法案，也要等总统看过后，才能成为法律。

☞ A: Didn't Maria go shopping with you yesterday?

B: *Even if* she hadn't had a lot of studying, she would have preferred staying home to going shopping.

A：玛利亚昨天没跟你去购物吗？

B：即使她没有很多学习任务，她也宁愿在家待着而不去购物。

☞ *Even if* you're registered for classes during the summer, you must leave this dorm by June third. 即使你在暑假登记了要上课，也要在 6 月 3 日以前离开宿舍。

☞ This story evolved, *even though* no one knows for sure whether the incident ever occurred. 这个故事流传着，发展着，尽管没有人确切知道这件事是否真正发生过。

even now 甚至到现在；就在此刻；尽管这样，虽然情况如此

☞ A: What Carl did makes me angry *even now*.

B: Why not just forget about it?

A：卡尔所做的事让我现在还生气。

B：为什么不忘了这事呢？

☞ A: Growing up, we never had a TV. *Even now* I'm not used to watching it much.

B: Well, it's kind of like reading. Some things you find are great, but a little are real waste of time. You have to pick and choose.

A：我们的成长过程中从来没有电视。甚至到现在，我也不习惯看太多电视。

B：嗯，就像读书一样。有些你觉得很不错，但有些真的是在浪费时间。你不得不进行挑选。

exchange...for 以…交换

☞ A: I washed this sweater according to the directions on the label and look what happened to it.

B: It could be a manufactures' defect. We'll *exchange* it *for* a new one.

A：我按标签上的说明洗了这件毛衣，看看，现在它成什么样了！

B：这可能是生产厂家的问题，我们给您换一件。

☞ A: Excuse me, I bought the wrong math book a couple of weeks ago. Here is the receipt. Can I get my money back?

B: Oh, I'm sorry not after 10 days, but you can still *exchange* it *for* something else.

A：劳驾，我几星期前买错了一本数学书。这是收据，我能退款吗？

B：噢，对不起，购买后十天就不能退了，但是你可以换一本别的书。

exchange greetings 互相问候

☞ The two men *exchanged greetings* and began to talk about work. 两个人相互问候之后便开始谈论工作。

🔍 "贺卡"用英语说就是 greeting cards。

executive summary 执行摘要

☞ The *executive summary* contains useful information for the readers. 这篇执行摘要包含读者需要的有用信息。

🔍 执行摘要是整个商业计划书的精华部分，涵盖了计划的要点，是全文的概述部分。

exhaust a subject/topic 对一个主题研究透彻

☞ I'm afraid they can't *exhaust* this *subject* in such a short time. 我担心他们无法在这么短的时间内将这一主题研究透彻。

exhaust oneself 使某人筋疲力尽

☞ Joe *exhausted himself* carrying the heavy box upstairs. 乔把那只很沉的箱子搬上楼，累得筋疲力尽。

exhaust oneself

exist in 存在于

☞ In fact the word "weekend" didn't even *exist in* English until about the middle of last century. 事实上，"周末"这个词直到上世纪中期才在英语中出现。

☞ More salt *exists in* the atmosphere near the ocean, thereby attracting the increased moisture and producing rain. 海洋附近的空气中含盐量更多，从而增加了湿度，并形成降雨。

☞ It's interesting to note that insurance has *existed in* some form for a very long time. 有趣的是保险已经以某种形式存在了很长时间。

☞ be in existence

exotic plant 外来植物

☞ You will see many *exotic plants* and of course the world famous alligators. 你将看到许多外来植物，当然还有世界著名的短吻鳄。

🔍 注意两词连读时，c 要弱读。

expand productive forces 发展生产力

☞ It is a top priority to *expand productive forces* at present. 当前发展生产力是第一要务。

expect for 期望，期盼

☞ A: What do you *expect for* a starting salary?
B: Three thousand dollars.
A: 你期望起薪是多少?
B: 3000 美元。

experimental station　试验站

☞ The first actual radio broadcast was that someone working from an ***experimental station*** arranged the program of two short musical selections of poem and brief holiday greeting. 第一次真正意义上的无线电广播是试验站工作人员安排的节目，内容是两小段有音乐背景的诗歌节选以及简短的节日祝福。

explosive news　爆炸性新闻

☞ I got ***explosive news*** for you: the world popular band is about to hold concert in our college city. 我要告诉你一个爆炸性的消息，那支世界著名乐队就要在咱们大学城开演唱会了。

☞ shocking news

explosive situation　一触即发的形势

☞ The countries are all undergoing ***explosive situations*** and hard time. 这些国家都处在一触即发的形势下，处境困难。

☞ potentially dangerous situation, dire situation, critical situation

expose...to　显露，曝露；使遭受；使处于…作用（或影响）之下

expose to

☞ The animal ***exposes*** its eggs ***to*** strong sunlight. 这种动物将自己的卵暴露在强烈日照下。

☞ If our bodies are not ***exposed to*** ultraviolet rays from the sun we cannot convert vitamin D to its active form, and thus cannot make use of any of the calcium that we have consumed in our food. 如果我们的身体不能接触紫外线，我们就不能把维生素 D 转换成它的活跃形式，那么也就无法吸收从食物中所摄取的钙了。

☞ Although these bats sleep during the day, they do so curled up with their head ***exposed to*** the sun. 尽管这些蝙蝠在白天睡觉，但是它们却蜷缩着（身体），将脑袋暴露于阳光下。

🔍 名词形式 exposure 也会经常考到，注意后面也接介词 to。

extend the deadline　延长最后期限

☞ A: I've been working on this report all day. And I've still got 12 pages to write. At this rate, I'll never get it done by tomorrow.

B: Oh, that's right. You weren't in class today, so you probably haven't heard that ***the deadline*** has been ***extended*** a week.

A：我一天都在写这个报告。现在还有 12 页呢。照这个速度，我明天肯定完不成。

B：哦，对了，你今天没去上课，所以你可能还不知道，报告提交的截止日期已经延后了一周。

extinct species 已灭绝的物种

☞ The environmentalists pointed out that understanding of the new protection law was important to help people know more about how the *extinct species* gradually disappeared from the Earth. 环保主义者指出，很好理解这个新保护法有助于让人们知道更多关于那些濒临灭绝的物种是如何逐渐从地球消失的。

☞ endangered species

extra ticket 多余的票

☞ A: Say, Richard. If you like antique cars, we've got an *extra ticket* for the auto show on Saturday. Care to join us?

  B: Gee. How could I turn down an offer like that?

  A：喂，理查德。如果你喜欢老式汽车的话，我们现在有周六汽车展多余的票，有意一起去吗？

  B：呀，我怎能拒绝这样的邀请呢？

☞ A: Wanna come with me to the opera tonight? I've got *extra tickets* and I think it will take your mind off that math problem that you were swearing over for the last two hours.

  B: That'll be great but the opera is in what? Italian, right? I think I have a better chance of understanding a math problem.

  A：今晚想和我们一起去看戏剧吗？我有多余的票。我想它会使你放松，让你摆脱过去两个小时做数学题的烦恼。

  B：很好，但是戏剧是什么语言的啊？意大利语吗？我想和那个相比，搞定数学题的几率更大些。

extract the cellulose 提取纤维素

☞ The scientist tried dissolving mulberry leaves in nitric acid to *extract the cellulose*. 这位科学家试图把桑叶溶解在硝酸中以提取纤维素。

extracurricular activity 课外活动

☞ A: This campus offers a wide range of *extracurricular activities*, whether your interests are athletics.

  B: Thanks, I'm sure I'll get involved in it eventually. But since it is my first year that I'm taking extra courses, I'm really pushing as it is.

  A：不管你的兴趣是否在体育运动上，这个学校都会提供一系列的课外活动。

  B：谢谢，我相信最后我一定会参加的。但是因为第一年我会上很多额外课程，如果再参加课外活动的话时间就会很紧。

facial expression 面部表情

☞ Jane's *facial expression* didn't change on hearing the bad news. 在听到这个坏消息时，简的面部表情并没有改变。

fade away　渐渐消失；凋零；消瘦，憔悴

☞ Laughter *faded away*, leaving Linda with a sense of unease. 笑声过后，琳达感到浑身不自在。

fade out　渐弱；图像渐隐；褪色

☞ The street lights on campus are different. They gave off a hazy yellow glow that make some colors *fade out*. 校园的路灯不同，它们发出一种昏暗的黄色灯光，使一些颜色看起来变淡了。

faint hope/possibility/chance　希望/可能性/机会不大

☞ There will be a *faint chance* that you will pass the exam if you go on watching TV. 如果你继续看电视的话，你通过考试的机会就会很小了。

fair comment　公平的评价

☞ The teacher made a *fair comment* on my paper. 老师对我的论文作了公平的评价。

fair trial　公平审讯

☞ The person is waiting for a *fair trial* on his crime. 这个人正在等待对他的罪行作公平的审讯。

faith in　对…有信心

☞ The movement helped strengthen people's *faith in* their country, faith that had weakened as the result of the depression. 这场运动有助于增强人们对国家的信心，之前这种信心被经济萧条削弱了。

☞ belief in, confidence in

fall apart　破碎，破裂；崩溃

☞ It's a shame that those older wood pulp books are going to *fall apart* some day. Is there anything that can be done to preserve them? 那些用木浆做的书时间久了就会散开，真可惜。有没有什么方法可以保存它们呢？

fall back on　（在无其他办法时）求助于，转而依靠

☞ A: Were you able to understand that French novel without any help from the teacher?

　B: I did pretty well, but I had to *fall back on* my dictionary occasionally.

　A：你能在没有老师的帮助下读懂那部法语小说吗？

　B：我读得很顺，但是偶尔还是要求助于词典。

☞ turn to

fall behind　落后

☞ I wouldn't want you to *fall behind* in your course-work. 我不愿意你落下功课。

☞ lag behind

🔍 其反义短语catch up with 也比较常考，意思是"赶上"。

fall off 落下，跌落，下降；减少

☞The tree's leaves become dry, *fall off*, and eventually the tree dies. 树叶干枯、落下，最后树木死去。

fall out 脱落；争吵；结果是

☞Sidney's tooth *fell out*. 西德尼的牙掉了。

🔍注意连读 /ˈfɔːlˌaʊt/。

fall out

fall through 穿过…落下；落空，失败

☞The research indicates that most of the water molecules from the comet would have burned up as they *fell through* the atmosphere. 研究表明，彗星上的大部分水分子在通过大气层坠落时就已经燃烧殆尽了。

NOTES

Unit 8

---

family reunion 家庭聚会

☞ A: Where are you going next Monday?

B: California. We're having a *family reunion*. It's my grandmother's ninetieth birthday. So all the cousins and aunts and uncles are going. She planned the whole thing herself.

A：你下周一打算去哪里？

B：加利福尼亚。我们全家人聚会。那天是我(外)祖母的 90 岁生日。所有的堂(表)兄弟姐妹、姑妈和叔叔都来。全部事情都是(外)祖母自己一人操办的。

---

farewell party 告别晚会

☞ Students prepared a big *farewell party* for their Professor Green. 学生们为格林教授准备了一个盛大的欢送会。

🔍 表示"告别"的两个常用短语是：say goodbye to 和 bid farewell to。

---

feel like 感觉像是；想要(做)

☞ A: I really enjoy the play. The students did a great job with the scenery. It looks so authentic. I *felt like* I was back in the 19th century.

B: I wish you could say the same thing about the costumes.

A：我非常喜欢这场戏。学生们将场景布置得太棒了，看起来和真的一样。我感觉像回到了 19 世纪。

B：我真希望你也这样夸奖一下服装。

---

field study 实地考察；野外研究

☞ Now I hope you all follow my advice and wear comfortable shoes because as I said yesterday we are going to do a little *field study*. 现在我希望你们都能听我的建议，穿舒适一点的鞋子，因为昨天我说过我们还要做一些实地考察。

---

field trip 实地考察旅行；社会调查

☞ A: I am so angry. My biology professor would not even let me try to explain why I missed the *field trip*. He just gave me a zero.

B: That seemed not fair. I would feel that way too if I were you.

A：我太生气了。我的生物学教授都不让我解释我为什么没去实地考察旅行，就给了我零分。

B：这似乎不公平。如果我是你，我也会很生气。

☞ A: I think the whole class is going on the **_field trip_** next Friday.

B: I'm not so sure. Not everyone has paid the transportation fee.

A：我想下周五全班同学都会去做实地考察旅行。

B：我不太肯定。并不是每位同学都交了交通费。

🔍 两词连读时，d 的发音要弱化。

fierce rays of　⋯的强烈光线

☞ Human population near the equator have evolved dark skin over many generations because of exposure to the **_fiercest rays of_** the sun. 经历了数代进化，赤道附近的人类因暴露在最强的阳光下而形成了黑色的皮肤。

figure out　计算出；想出；理解，明白

☞ When the British were building cities in American colonies, they had to **_figure out_** how to make the cities run smoothly. 当英国人在美国殖民地上建立城市的时候，他们必须想清楚如何使城市平稳运转。

☞ A: I thought Paul might be able to help me **_figure out_** this computer program.

B: Paul is the last person I'd ask if I were you.

A：我想保罗可能会帮我编这个计算机程序。

B：如果我是你的话，保罗是我最后才考虑的人选。

fill in　填写；临时补缺

☞ The professor wants them to **_fill in_** a research questionnaire. 教授想让他们填写研究问卷。

☞ A: Roger was feverish yesterday. I'm not sure if he'll be up to attending today's meeting.

B: Then can someone **_fill in_** for him?

A：罗杰昨天发烧了。我不确定他能否参加今天的会议。

B：那有谁可以补上他的空缺吗?

🔍 注意该词的连读，过去式 filled in 也要连读。

fill out　填写

☞ **_Fill out_** this registration form and duplicate. Then keep one copy for your records. 填好这张登记表及其复印件。然后，你要自己保存一份复印件作为记录。

☞ A: I'd like to apply for the part-time job.

B: Fine, just **_fill out_** this form. Someone will be with you in a moment.

A：我要申请一份兼职工作。

B：可以，只要填一下这张表，很快就会有人跟您联系的。

84

fill with   充满，用…填满

☞ A bladder of oxygen is an inflatable sack *filled with* oxygen to simulate atmospheric pressure. 氧气囊是一种充满氧气的袋子，用来模拟大气压。

☞ be full of

final exam   期末考试

☞ A: Since there was no *final exam* scheduled, I thought I'd be able to leave for winter break a couple of days early.

B: But all presentations are taking a lot longer than Dr. Taylor expected, so he's going to hold class during exam week.

A：因为没有期末考试的日程安排，我想我可以早走几天过寒假了。

B：但是泰勒博士的所有讲座都比他预计的要长，所以他会在考试周内继续上课的。

☞ Now I'd like to talk to you about the *final exam*. The exam will be held next Thursday, the last day of the exam week. 现在我要和你们讲一下期末考试的相关事宜。考试会在下周四进行，也就是考试周的最后一天。

🔍 托福中还常考 midterm，是 midterm test（期中考试）的简写。

final grade   最终分数

☞ A: How did you do on the math quiz?

B: Well, I am lucky that it only counts for a small portion of our *final grade* for the course.

A：你的数学测试考得怎么样？

B：哦，我很幸运，这测验只占本课程最终分数的一小部分。

final paper   期末论文

☞ A: I can't remember the due date for our *final paper*.

B: I think it is the last day of class. But Professor Lee said not to wait until the last minute to hand it in.

A：我不记得交期末论文的最后期限了。

B：我想是最后一节课。但是李教授说不要等到最后一刻才交。

finalize one's plan   确定某人的计划

☞ A: Have you *finalized your plans* for spring break yet?

B: Well, I could visit some friends in Florida, or go to my roommate's home. It's a tough choice.

A：你定下来春季休假的计划了吗？

B：嗯，我可能去佛罗里达州看一些朋友，或者是去我室友的家乡。这真得很难选择。

☞ Loli hasn't *finalized her plans* for the summer. 洛利还没有确定她的夏季计划。

financial institution 金融机构，金融组织

☞ Many foreign *financial institutions* lowered their interest rates one after another.
众多国外金融机构纷纷降息。

financial plan 金融计划

☞ A: I don't think we have nearly enough information for
our *financial plan*. But it's due tomorrow. So I guess
there isn't a lot we can do about it.

B: Guess not. At this point, we will just have to make do
with what we have got.

A：我认为我们没有足够的信息来做金融计划。但是
明天就到期了，我想我们做不了什么了。

B：当然不是。此刻，我们要做的是利用我们已有的信息去做计划。

financial plan

🔍和"金融"相关的常考短语有：
financial crisis 金融危机   fiscal policy 财政政策
monetary policy 货币政策

financial regulation 金融监管

☞ The Prime Minister called for global *financial regulation* to maintain economic
stability. 总理呼吁全球实施金融监管以保持经济稳定。

find a way to 找到…的方法

☞ Scientists are trying to *find a way to* make fuel oil less polluting. 科学家正在试图找
到减少燃油污染的方法。

☞ find a method to

find out 找出，发现，查明

☞ A: Weren't you going to *find out* from the registrar if you have enough credits to
graduate next semester?

B: You're right. I'd better get over there. Their hours are limited, and they can get
pretty busy.

A：难道你没打算向注册员查明自己是否修够了下学期毕业的学分吗？

B：是呀。我最好去一趟。他们时间有限，而且相当忙。

☞ I know Doctor Wilson's out of town at a conference, but I was wondering since she
won't be back till next week, if you could check in your computer records and *find
out* how I did on her mid-term exam? 我知道威尔逊博士出城开会了。但是她要到
下周才回来，我在想你能否看一下你的电脑记录，看看我在她那门课的期中考试
考得怎么样？

find ways to　找到…的方法

☞ A creative architect can *find ways to* incorporate natural landscape into the overall design. 一名有创造力的建筑师可以找到方法将自然景观融合到整体设计中去。

🔍 该词组还可以变形为 find a way to。

finish the roll　用完一卷胶卷

☞ A: How did your pictures at the Orientation come out? Did you get them back from the photo shop?

B: Actually the film is still in the camera. I haven't quite *finished the roll*.

A：你在新生见面会时照的相片效果怎样？你从照相馆取回来了吗？

B：事实上那个胶卷还在相机中，没用完呢。

finish with　以…结束

☞ A: I never should have taken that biology course. I mean I barely *finish with* reading for one experiment and Professor Jordan slaps on another reading assignment.

B: Yeah, I know, that's what everybody said at first, but bear with her. The reading load's getting lighter, you see, and you won't be sorry.

A：我真不应该选那门生物课。我的意思是，我还没读完做一次试验要看的书，乔丹教授就又布置了新的阅读作业。

B：是，我知道。起初每个人都这么说，但是忍耐一下吧。你知道，阅读量正在减轻，你不会遗憾的。

☞ end up with

finishing touch　收尾；最后一笔，最后润色

☞ A: How's that project in your economics class coming along?

B: I just put the *finishing touches* on it this morning.

A：你经济学课上的那个项目进展得怎么样？

B：我今天早上刚做完收尾工作。

☞ A: Professor Jones, last night when I was putting the *finishing touches* on my paper, that electrical storm completely wiped out my computer files. Do you think I could have another day to retype it?

B: I'm sorry, Steven. I'm leaving for a conference tomorrow and I'll be away two weeks. I suppose you could send it to me there.

A：琼斯教授，昨晚我在对论文进行最后修改时，电暴使我电脑里的文件全被删除了。您能再给我一天时间把它再打一遍吗？

B：对不起，史蒂文。我明天要去开会，而且要离开两周。我想你可以把论文发送给我。

fix the heater 修理暖气

fix the heater

☞ A: It's so cold. Can you help me to *fix the heater* tomorrow?

B: Well, I'd like to, but I have promised James to go fishing with him.

A：天太冷了，你明天能帮我修暖气吗？

B：哦，没问题，但是我已经答应和詹姆斯一起去钓鱼了。

fix the problem 解决问题

☞ A: Do you have hot water in your dorm? Because we haven't had any for three days and I hate cold showers.

B: Oh, sounds miserable. Since the gym's usually open, why don't you just go over there to *fix the problem*?

A：你们宿舍有热水吗？我们已经三天没有热水了，我讨厌冷水淋浴。

B：哦，真可怜。健身房经常开着，你为什么不去那儿洗呢？

☞ solve the problem

fix/make an appointment with 与···预定一个约会

☞ A: I don't understand why I received such a low grade on my term paper.

B: You should *make an appointment with* the professor to discuss it.

A：我不明白我的学期论文为什么得这么低的分数。

B：你应该约教授谈一下这事。

☞ A: I'd like to *make an appointment with* the doctor for tomorrow.

B: Unfortunately he is completely booked.

A：我想明天约一下医生。

B：抱歉他的预约已满。

flavor of ···的风味

☞ A: I wonder what this new *flavor of* ice cream tastes like?

B: I tried it last week. If I were you, I would stick with an old favorite.

A：我想知道这种新口味的冰激凌吃起来怎么样？

B：我上周吃过了。如果我是你，还会吃以前喜欢的口味。

flexible schedule 灵活的日程表

☞ A: Oh, Mrs. Wilson, now the classes are starting again and I could probably keep working at the front desk if you are willing to give me a *flexible schedule* and let me come in and work between classes. I really would like to stay.

B: And we like that too, but trouble is, that means the front desk won't be covered and well, the hotel just can't operate that way.

A：哦，威尔逊女士，现在又重新开课了，如果您给我的日程表能宽松些，允许我边工作边上课的话，我就能继续在前台工作了，我真的愿意留下来。

B：我也愿意那样，但麻烦的是，前台不能空着，酒店也不可能按照那种方式营业。

☞ flexible time-table

flexible working hours 弹性工作时间

☞ The **_flexible working hours_** have been gradually accepted in business world. 弹性工作时间在商界渐渐得到认可。

☞ flexible working schedule

focus on 集中于

☞ Moving away from newspapers, let's now **_focus on_** magazines. 谈过报纸后，我们现在关注一下杂志。

☞ Today, we are going to continue our discussion on social insects, **_focusing on_** the Argentine ants, which as you might guess is a species of ants that are natives to Argentina. 今天，我们将继续有关群居昆虫的讨论，并着重关注一下阿根廷蚂蚁。就像你们猜测的那样，这是一种最初生活在阿根廷的蚂蚁种类。

☞ concentrate on

food allergy 食物过敏

☞ Due to **_food allergy_**, Bob rarely eats this kind of food. 由于食物过敏，鲍勃很少吃这种食物。

food chain 食物链

☞ In the 1970s, the peregrine falcons almost disappeared as a result of the contamination of the **_food chain_** by the DDT in pesticide. 在 20 世纪 70 年代，由于农药中的 DDT 污染了食物链，游隼几乎都消失了。

food chain

☞ Algae are the base of the aquatic of **_food chain_**, which means the other organisms depend on them for food. 藻类是水中食物链的最底层，也就是说其他生物都以它们为食。

food package 食品包装

☞ The government has placed a stricter restriction on **_food package_** and storage. 政府已对食品包装和储存施加了更严格的限制。

for a rainy day 未雨绸缪

☞ A: Gee, you have a lot of change in that jar. Are you a coin collector?
   B: No, I'm just saving them **_for a rainy day_**.
   A：哇，你的那个罐子里有那么多零钱。你是硬币收集爱好者吗？
   B：不是的，我只是把它们攒起来以备不时之需。

☞ Where did the term Piggy Bank come from? Today the simple piggy bank is seen everywhere as the symbol of saving and frugality, for putting away funds **_for a rainy day_**, or building a nest egg for life's sudden money needs, such as paying college expenses, buying a home, or financing retirement. "存钱罐"这个词是怎么来的？如今，这个简单的存钱罐被视为是省钱和节约的象征，用来把钱存起来以备不时之需，或者是为生活中突然需要用钱时建立储蓄金，比如支付大学学费、买房子或是养老。

for a while 一会儿

☞ These students will be away *for a while*. 这些学生将要离开一会儿。

☞ A: Mind if I borrow your economics notes *for a while*?
B: Not at all.
A：你介意我借你的经济学笔记用一会儿吗？
B：当然不。

☞ A bunch of us hang around *for a while* after class to talk with our professor and ask him questions. 我们一群人在课后逗留了一会儿，和教授交流了一下，并问了他一些问题。

for generations 几代人

☞ Women have been weaving the baskets *for generations*, handing down the skills from mother to daughter. 几代女性都在编篮子，由母亲传给女儿技术，一代一代传下去。

for instance 例如

☞ *For instance*, one painting shows Poke Hunters saving the life of John Smith, an English Colonist, who had been captured by her tribe. 例如，一幅画描述的是普克·亨特斯救了一个英国殖民者的命，这人名叫约翰·史密斯，是她部落的俘虏。

☞ for example

for nothing 免费

☞ To pay to see that movie would be foolish, when you can see it on television *for nothing*. 如果能在电视上免费看那部电影，花钱去看就太傻了。

☞ free charge

for one's sake / for the sake of 为了…的利益

☞ I'll be taking the courses just *for the sake of* learning. 我上这些课程只是为了学习。

for sale 待售

☞ A: I'm going over to see a car someone has *for sale*. It's just a year old, and it's supposed to be in excellent condition. Do you want to come with me to take a look at it? With all your experience as a mechanic, I'd appreciate your opinion.
B: That was twenty years ago. Cars have changed so much. I'm not sure how much help I might be, but sure I'll come along for the ride.
A：我要去看一辆待售的轿车。开了才一年，车况应该不错。你想和我一起去看看吗？你有做技工的经验，我很想听听你的意见。
B：那都是 20 年前的事了。车更新得这么快，我不确定能给你多少帮助，但是，我可以和你一起去试试车。

☞ A: Do we need to get the concert tickets in advance?

B: There may be some *for sale* at the door at a higher price.

A：我们需要提前买音乐会的票吗？

B：门口可能有高价的待售票。

🔍 注意词组 on sale 是"降价销售"的意思，不要混淆。

for some reason 不知什么原因

☞ There are two groups of different types of specialized cells in the bone. Sometimes after the first group of cells leaves a hole in the bone tissue, *for some reason*, the second group doesn't completely fill in the hole. It can actually lead to a disease in which the bone becomes weak and is easily broken. 骨骼中有两组不同类型的特殊细胞。有时候，在骨组织中，第一组细胞留下了孔洞，由于某种原因，第二组细胞不能完全填补上这个孔洞。这就会导致一种疾病，骨头变得脆弱，而且易断。

for sure 确实，肯定，毫无疑问地

☞ A: This rash on my arm is driving me crazy. What do you think it could be?

B: I really couldn't say *for sure*, but it looks like something you ought to have checked out.

A：我胳膊上的这个皮疹快把我折磨疯了。你认为它是什么？

B：我真的不能确定，不过看上去你应该检查一下。

☞ A: You are not much of a Rock music fan, are you?

B: It's far from being my favorite kind of music. That's *for sure*.

A：你不是摇滚乐迷，对不对？

B：可以肯定地说，摇滚乐远不会是我喜欢的音乐类型。

for the benefit of / for one's benefit 为了…的利益 / 好处

☞ The little boy tried not to go to any trouble *for the benefit of* his parents. 为了父母，小男孩尽量不惹事。

for the time being 当前，暂时

☞ A: I want to quit.

B: Why? Your company isn't moving to the west coast after all.

A: Well, only *for the time being*. But I've been looking into other employment opportunities here anyway. Just in case.

A：我想辞职了。

B：为什么？你们的公司毕竟还没有到山穷水尽的地步。

A：嗯，不过只是时间问题。不管怎样我已经开始在找其他就业机会了，为了以防万一。

for the world　无论如何

☞ I wouldn't miss the party provided by your families *for the world*. 无论如何我都不会错过你家人组织的晚宴。

force...out through　迫使…从…中出来

☞ The scientist noticed that the silkworms digested mulberry leaves into liquid cellulose, and then *force* the liquid *out through* tiny holes to form slender threads. 科学家注意到蚕把桑叶消化成液态的纤维素，然后迫使液体从小孔中流出形成细丝。

formulate a theory　系统地阐述一个理论

☞ Einstein *formulated* the *theory* of Relative in 1905. 爱因斯坦在 1905 年系统地阐述了相对论。

franchise store　专营店

☞ The company opened more than 50 *franchise stores* all over the country. 这家公司在全国开了 50 多家专营店。

☞ chain store

free verse　自由体诗

☞ Walt Whitman was among the poets to use *free verse*. 沃尔特·惠特曼是运用自由体诗的诗人之一。

🔍 托福考试中可能考到的短语还有：
blank verse 无韵诗　　　　　　　　　Sonnet 十四行诗

freeze over　（水池、湖等）结冰

freeze over

☞ The river *froze over* when the temperature was zero below. 这条河在零度以下时会结冰。

freeze up　（机器、引擎中的水）结冰；使（机器）无法工作

☞ I was really happy to be writing a detective story, but after the first few pages, I sort of *froze up* mentally. I just couldn't write any more. 我非常开心能写侦探故事，但是写了几页后，大脑就好像冻结了一样。我就再也写不下去了。

from a biology perspective　从生物学角度

☞ We have been looking at the fear *from a biology perspective*, and some one asked whether the tendency to be fearful is genetic. 我们一直从生物学视角来看恐惧，有人问是否恐惧也是遗传的。

from now on　从现在开始

☞ A: John, I'd like to talk to you about the way you come late every day. It disrupts the class.

B: I'm sorry professor, I didn't realize I was bothering anyone. I will watch *from now on*.

A：约翰，我想和你谈谈，你每天迟到扰乱了课堂秩序。

B：教授，我很抱歉。我没有意识到自己打扰到了大家。从现在开始我会注意。

fuel efficiency　燃料利用率

☞ A: What's the city gonna do? Install pollution filters of some sort on their buses?

B: They could, but those filters make the engines work harder and really cut down on *fuel efficiency*. Instead they found a way to make their engines more efficient.

A：城市的人们要做什么？在公交车上安装某种污染过滤器吗？

B：这样做可以，但是那些净化器会妨碍引擎工作，而且降低燃料利用率。相反，人们找到了让引擎更有效率工作的方法。

full refund　全额退款

☞ A: What if I bring home the pants and my daughter doesn't like it?

B: Well, you can bring it back to us for a *full refund* in seven days.

A：如果我把这裤子带回家后我女儿不喜欢怎么办？

B：嗯，您可以在七天内把它拿回来，我们会给您全额退款。

full scholarship　全额奖学金

☞ A: Mary looks surprised.

B: Didn't you hear? She won *full scholarship* for next year.

A：玛丽看起来很惊讶。

B：你没听说吗？她赢得了明年的全额奖学金。

🔍 其他"奖学金"还有：

assistantship 助教奖学金

research fellowship 研究生奖学金

major award / first scholarship 一等奖学金

minor award / second scholarship 二等奖学金

furious with sb. at sth.　因为某事对某人大发雷霆

☞ A: I feel horrible. Deborah was *furious with* me *at* my fault. Do you think I should apologize again?

B: If I were you I'd let her cool off a few days before I talked to her.

A：我感觉很不好，黛博拉对于我犯的错误大发雷霆，你觉得我应该再向她道一次歉吗？

B：如果我是你，我就先让她冷静几天再和她谈。

☞ be very angry with sb.

garbage can/bin 垃圾箱

garbage can

☞ A: When is the garbage picked up here?

B: On Wednesdays, but I always put the *garbage cans* out on Tuesday night, so I don't miss the trucks in the morning.

A：这里的垃圾什么时候被清理走？

B：每周三，但是我通常周二晚上就把垃圾箱放在外面，所以我早上不会错过垃圾车。

garbage collector 垃圾清理工

☞ The *garbage collectors* should pick up the garbage early in the morning on every Thursday, so that they could have enough time to transfer all to the garbage station. 垃圾清理工在每周四早晨很早的时候就要去收垃圾，这样他们才有足够的时间把所有垃圾运到垃圾站。

general response 普遍反响

☞ A: Joe, I thought your article on the school newspaper was right on target. You certainly convinced me anyway.

B: Thanks Mary. Unfortunately, based on the *general response*, you and I are definitely in the minority.

A：乔，我认为你在校报上的文章写得正中要害。你绝对说服了我。

B：谢谢你，玛丽。不幸的是，基于大众的反应，我跟你肯定是少数派。

generation gap 代沟

☞ The *generation gap* bothers most parents a lot. 代沟让大多数家长很烦恼。

🔍 "代沟"一词是从英文直译过来的，它的出现与社会的高速发展（rapid development）不无关系，两代人之间短短的几十年就会形成沟通的鸿沟，而手机（cell phone）、网络（internet）等现代产品为联络带来了便捷的同时，也为沟通（communication）制造了障碍。所以无论是父母还是子女，都应该经常面对面地（face-to-face）交谈，同时做一个好的倾听者（listener）。

genetic testing 基因测试

☞ Using *genetic testing*, researches found that all the Argentine ants in California were very similar genetically. 通过基因测试，研究人员发现加利福尼亚的所有阿根廷蚂蚁都有着非常相似的基因。

get a chance of 得到一个…的机会

☞ A: I think our baseball team's **got a** good **chance of** winning the championship this year.

B: What? Are you kidding? Have you seen them play recently?

A：我认为我们的棒球队今年获得冠军的机会很大。

B：什么？你开玩笑吗？你最近看他们打比赛了吗？

get/have a grasp on 理解，了解；抓住

☞ A: Jack, what are you doing here? Did you **get a grasp on** what your task is?

B: It seems that I misunderstood something.

A：杰克，你在这里干什么呢？你了解自己的任务了吗？

B：看起来我是理解错什么了。

get a job offer 得到工作机会

☞ A: I just **got** my first **job offer**.

B: I did too.

A：我刚刚得到第一个工作机会。

B：我也是。

☞ George **got three job offers**, but he turned them all down. 有三家公司向乔治发出了工作邀函，但是他都拒绝了。

get a lot out of 从…学到很多

☞ The training program was difficult, but she **got a lot out of** it. 培训课很难，但是她从中学到了很多。

get a refund 获得退款

☞ A: Sorry Sam, I just hate these kinds of movies. They always give me bad dreams.

B: I agree, let's go and see if you can **get a refund** at the front window.

A：对不起，萨姆，我只是讨厌这一类电影。我看了后总会做噩梦。

B：我同意，我们去看看售票窗口能不能退钱。

get a ride 搭便车

get a ride

☞ A: Could I **get a ride** with you to the concert tonight?

B: I can't go, but you might ask Bob. I think he's leaving around seven-thirty.

A：我今晚可以搭你的便车去音乐会吗？

B：我不去，但是你可以问问鲍勃。我想他应该是在 7 点半左右走。

☞ A: Can I **get a ride** into the office with you tomorrow?

B: Another day would be fine. But I got to be downtown for a meeting first thing in the morning.

A：我明天能搭你的便车去办公室吗?

B：改天吧，我明天一早要去市中心开会。

☞ thumb a ride / lift

get a scholarship to the university　获得大学奖学金

☞ Lucy *got a scholarship to the university* of her choice. 露西得到了她所选择的那所大学的奖学金。

get around to sth./doing sth.　找时间做某事

☞ A: Did you never *get around to* cashing that refund check from the bookstore?

B: Oh, gosh! You know what. I must have misplaced that in my desk somewhere. But thanks for reminding me. My funds are running low, so I'd better find it soon.

A：你还没来得及去兑现书店的退款支票吗?

B：哦，天呐。知道吗，我一定是把它随手放在书桌的什么地方了。但是谢谢你提醒我。我的钱不够花了，所以我最好赶快找到它。

☞ A: You look different today, but I can't quite put my finger on what it is.

B: I finally *got around to* trying that new hair saloon in the mall.

A：你今天看起来不太一样，但是我说不出来哪里不一样。

B：我终于找到时间去试大厦里新开的美发沙龙。

NOTES

Unit 9

get away with 逃避(处罚)，侥幸逃脱

☞ A: Did you know that Bob was leaving for home tonight? He isn't planning to take his final exams.

B: He can *get away with* that?

A：你知道吗？鲍勃今晚回家。他不打算参加期末考试了。

B：他能逃脱吗？

get caught 遇到，碰到

☞ A: Did you *get caught* driving in that downpour after work yesterday? Everyone had their lights on and I could hardly see where I was going.

B: That must have been a local storm.

A：你昨天下班开车时遇到倾盆大雨了吗？每辆车都打着车灯，我几乎都看不清向哪个方向走了。

B：那一定是局部暴雨。

get going 赶紧行动

☞ A: It looks like we won't have enough time to do all we wanted to.

B: Who says we won't? Let's *get going*.

A：我们好像没有时间做所有的事了。

B：谁说不够？我们赶紧行动吧。

☞ get moving

get in one's hair 惹恼某人

☞ A: What did you do to *get in* the boss's *hair*?

B: I've no idea. I just told him I wanted to get a raise.

A：你跟老板说什么了，把他气成这样？

B：我不知道，我只是跟他说我想涨工资。

☞ comb one's hair the wrong way

get into trouble 遇到麻烦

☞ I've heard lots of first year students *get into trouble* with college career because they hang out every day in the student center till it closes. 我听说很多大一新生在生活上遇到麻烦，因为他们每天在学生中心消磨时光，一直待到关门。

get off on the wrong foot 一开始就很不顺利；起步便错

☞ A: Have you tried talking the noise to your neighbor?

B: We haven't even really met them yet except to say a quick hello. I hate to **get off on the wrong foot**.

A：你和邻居说噪音的事了吗？

B：我们甚至都没正经见过面，只是匆忙打个招呼而已。我不想一开始就和邻居闹僵。

get off the ground 开始进行

☞ A: Say remember that proposal for an international art festival next spring? Do you think there's any chance it'll ever **get off the ground**?

B: I don't think it's a question of whether it'll happen. It's just a matter of where it'll be held.

A：还记得要在明年春天举行国际艺术节的提议吗？你觉得它能实施吗？

B：我认为不存在举行或不举行的问题，这只是在哪里举行的问题。

☞ get under way

get off work 下班

☞ A: I've been wanting to visit Pam at the infirmary, but I don't **get off work** until after visiting hours.

B: Don't they have hours on weekends?

A：我一直想去医院看望帕姆，但是探病时间时我还在上班。

B：周末没有探病时间吗？

☞ be off duty, be off from work

get on one's nerve 让某人很烦

☞ A: Why did you come to the meeting late? I left a message with your roommate about the time change.

B: She has a very short memory and it really **gets on my nerve** sometimes.

A：你为什么开会迟到？我让你的室友给你捎口信说时间改了。

B：她很健忘，有时真得让我很烦。

get/have one's hair cut / cut one's hair 剪头发

☞ A: Hi Joe! I just saw your roommate coming out of the library. She looks different. Did she **get her hair cut** or something?

B: Yeah, three days ago actually. And hardly any one has noticed.

A：喂，乔！我刚刚看见你的室友从图书馆出来。她看上去有些不一样。她剪头发了还是怎么回事？

B：是，三天前剪的。几乎没人注意到。

get one's hands full of sth. 忙于做某事

☞ A: Why did I ever agree to work on the school newspaper the same semester on taking 5 classes?

B: Yes, you've **got your hands full of** right.

A：一学期要上五门课，我那时为什么还同意在校报工作？

B：是啊，你已经很忙了。

☞ be busy doing

get paid　获得报酬

☞ A: I found a perfect book bag but I'm about 20 dollars short.

B: Don't look at me. I don't **get paid** for another week.

A：我发现一个非常棒的书包，但是我还差 20 美元左右。

B：别指望我。我又一周没领薪水了。

☞ A: Are you sure you don't mind getting the concert tickets? I wouldn't be able to pay you back until Friday when I **get paid**.

B: No problem. I'm glad I can help and we'll be able to go together.

A：你确定不介意帮我带音乐会的门票吗？我周五发工资时才能还你钱。

B：没问题。我很高兴能帮助你，并且我们可以一起去。

🔍 两词连读时，t 的发音要弱化。

get ready for　准备好做

☞ A: Congratulations! I heard your field hockey team was going to the mid-Atlantic championships!

B: Yeah! Now we're all working hard to **get ready for** our game tomorrow.

A：恭喜你们！我听说你们场地曲棍球队要冲击大西洋中部冠军。

B：是！我们现在都在努力为明天的比赛做准备。

☞ be ready for, prepare for

get started on　开始做

☞ A: We should **get started on** that project.

B: The sooner the better as far as I'm concerned.

A：我们应该开始做那个项目了。

B：就我而言，越早越好。

☞ go about

get stuck　被困住，陷入僵局

☞ A: So I hear you're really happy with your new car. I bet it's a lot better than the last one you **got stuck** with, the one you bought from Cathy?

B: You can say that again. I'm sure I've made a good choice this time.

A：我听说你很满意你的新车。我猜它一定比你上次那辆麻烦不断的车好吧？就是你从凯茜手里买的那辆。

B：你说的没错，我肯定这次的选择是对的。

get time off from work　从工作中抽时间

☞ A: Have you seen this postcard from John. He's in Florida.

B: Oh, so he was able to *get time off from work*.

A：你看到约翰寄的明信片了吗？他在佛罗里达。

B：哦，看来他能从工作中抽出时间偷偷闲。

get tired of（doing）sth./get tired doing sth.　厌烦某事/做某事

☞ A: Do you ever *get tired of* all the talk about fat and cholesterol?

B: Do I? You know sometimes I think it's just a fad.

A：你厌烦那些关于脂肪和胆固醇的谈论了吗？

B：厌烦？你知道的，有时候我只把这些谈论看作是一种时尚。

☞ A: Did Mary meet you at the airport yesterday?

B: Yes. But she sure *got tired* waiting for my flight to get in. We circled the airport for three hours.

A：玛丽昨天去机场接你了吗？

B：是的。但是她一定等我的飞机着陆等得不耐烦了。我们在机场上空盘旋了三个小时。

get to sleep　睡觉

☞ I tried enough to *get to sleep* but it's only eight o'clock. 我努力想睡觉，但是这才刚八点。

☞ Leon was about to *get to sleep* when the phone rang. 利昂正要去睡觉的时候，电话响了。

☞ go to sleep, go to bed

give in　投降，屈服；让步；呈交

☞ A: My boss keeps asking me to work overtime but I always said no because I don't wanna jeopardize my studies, but I'm starting to waver.

B: I wouldn't *give in* if I were you.

A：老板总是让我加班，但是我都拒绝了，因为我不想荒废学业。不过我现在又开始动摇了。

B：如果我是你的话就不会让步。

☞ yield to, surrender

give off　发出（光等）；放出，排出

☞ The street lights on campus are different. They *gave off* a hazy yellow glow that make some colors fade out. 校园的路灯不同，它们发出一种昏暗的黄色灯光，使一些颜色看起来变淡了。

关于 give 的词组也是托福考试中常考的，其他的还有：

give in 屈服；呈交

give out 分发；用完

give a way 赠送；分发；泄露

give sb. a break　给某人一个改过的机会，饶了某人

☞ A: I got out of a science class late again. I never make it here to work on time. I hope I won't get in trouble.

B: The boss is in a good mood. Maybe she'll **give you a break**, this time.

A：自然科学课下课又晚了。我从来就没有准时上过班。我希望自己不会有麻烦。

B：老板心情很好。或许这次她会给你一个机会。

give sb. a hand（with）　帮助某人

☞ A: These boxes are too heavy for me to move.

B: Here, I'll **give you a hand with** them.

A：这些箱子太沉了，我挪不动。

B：来，我帮你。

☞ help sb. in / with

give sb. a hand

give sb. a refund　退款

☞ A: Sorry, but we cannot **give you a refund**. It's out of the date.

B: Then could you change another one for me?

A：对不起，我们不能给您退款，已经过期了。

B：那你们能给我换一个吗？

相关词组：

tax refund 退税

refund annuity 退回年金

refund notice 退税通知

give sb. a ride to　送某人去，载某人去

☞ A: I'm having a few friends over for a lunch tomorrow. It'll be great if you can join us.

B: I doubt I'll be able to make it. My brother is leaving for Chicago tomorrow afternoon. And I promised to **give him a ride to** the airport.

A：明天我有几个朋友要过来吃午饭。如果你能和我们一起就太好了。

B：我怕我去不了。我哥哥/弟弟明天下午去芝加哥。我答应开车送他去机场。

☞ A: Do you think you could **give me a ride to** the library tonight?

B: I'd like to but I'm heading in the other direction. I'm meeting Jean tonight.

A：你今晚可以载我去图书馆吗？

B：我愿意，但是我要往另一个方向走。我今晚要去见琼。

☞ A: John, I really can't afford any more interruptions right now. I've got to finish this assignment.

B: I'm sorry, Cathy. Just one more thing, I forgot to ask you if you could *give me a ride to* school tomorrow.

A：约翰，现在真的不能再有任何事打断我了，我得完成这个作业。

B：对不起，凯茜。还有一件事，我忘了问你明天是否能载我去学校。

☞ drive sb. to, pick sb. up to

give sb. a ring 给某人打电话

☞ A: You know, Sally was supposed to meet us here an hour ago. Maybe we should *give her a ring*. After all, she is the one who organized the study session.

B: You're right. I'll do it.

A：知道吗，萨莉应该在一小时前就来跟我们会合的。或许我们该给她打个电话，毕竟，是她组织的这个学习讨论会。

B：你说的对，我去打。

☞ ring sb., call sb.

give sb. an ultimatum 给某人下最后通牒

☞ A: If George misses one more meeting, we are going to have to find one new committee secretary.

B: We'd better *give him an ultimatum*.

A：如果乔治再错过一次会议的话，我们就要找个新的委员会秘书了。

B：我们最好给他下最后通牒。

give sb. credit for 因…给某人肯定

☞ The professor *gave* the students *credit for* their term paper, though their works were not up to his expectation. 教授对学生们的学期论文给予了肯定，尽管他们的作业没有达到教授的预期。

give sth. a thought 考虑，想

☞ A: Have you decided what you are going to do over the summer break?

B: Well, I've *given it a thought*, and I'd like to get a job in something related to marketing. But I haven't come up with anything definite yet.

A：你决定暑假做什么了吗？

B：嗯，我想过，我想找份营销方面的工作，但是还没想出具体要做什么。

give up on 对…失望，放弃

☞ A: Where have you been? I was just about to *give up on* you.

B: Sorry, my bus was delayed. But I'm glad you were patient. It would have been hard for us to find another time to meet this week.

A：你去哪了？我刚刚都不对你抱任何希望了。

B：对不起，公交车来迟了。但是你能这么耐心地等我，我很高兴。我们这周很难再另找时间见面了。

☞ be disappointed in/with/at

---

glacial movement 冰川运动

☞ The causes of *glacial movement* are exceedingly complicated. 引起冰川运动的原因极其复杂。

glial cell 神经胶质细胞

☞ The professor devoted all his life to the study of *glial cell*. 那位教授一生致力于神经胶质细胞的研究。

go extinct 绝迹

☞ Kinds of species are *going extinct* if people keep on invading and destroying the nature. 如果人类继续入侵、破坏自然界，那么很多物种都将灭绝。

🔍 extinct 一词还可指"（火山等）停止活动或喷发的"，在托福中也常考到。

---

go jogging 去跑步

☞ A: Are you ready to *go jogging*?

B: Almost. I have to warm up first.

A：你准备好跑步了吗？

B：差不多了。我要先热身。

🔍 和"运动"相关的常考短语有：

go hiking 去徒步旅行　　　go for a walk 去散步

---

go to one's head 冲昏头脑

☞ A: Have you noticed how John's changed since he became student government president?

B: I think the whole thing's *gone to his head*, and he used to be so sociable and open.

A：你注意到约翰成为学生会主席后的变化了吗？

B：我想这一切都让他冲昏了头脑，他过去很爱交际，也很开朗的。

---

go to the gym 去健身房，去健身

☞ A: Where is Bob?

B: I'm not sure, but he wouldn't have *gone to the gym* without us, would he?

A：鲍勃呢？

B：我不知道，但是他不可能不等咱们就去健身房了吧？

go/be in one ear and out the other　听过即忘; 左耳朵进, 右耳朵出

☞ A: I must have told Mike five times not to forget the meeting. And he still missed it.

B: Well, you know Mike; everything's *in one ear and out the other*.

A: 我告诉迈克五次不要忘了开会, 可他还是没来。

B: 哦, 你知道迈克的, 他什么事都是左耳朵进, 右耳朵出。

go/walk/run across　穿过/越过/走过/跑过

☞ There's a border walk that *goes across* the marsh, so you can look down at the animals in the water from a safe distance. 有一条人行道穿过湿地, 你可以在一个安全的距离内看到水里的动物。

☞ A: I need to *go across* town, but the traffic is so heavy this time of day.

B: When you take the subway, you don't have to deal with traffic. I never drive any more.

A: 我要去城镇的另一边, 但是现在正是堵车的时候。

B: 你坐地铁就不会遇到交通问题了。我已经不再开车了。

gold reserve　黄金储备

☞ The quantity of the *gold reserve* is one of the aspects of measuring a nation's wealth. 黄金储备量是衡量一个国家财富的一个方面。

good/bad reputation　好/坏名声

☞ A: Professor Howl. Have you heard of him?

B: Eh, he does have a *good reputation* in the Political Science Department.

A: 你听说过霍尔教授吗?

B: 嗯, 他在政治科学系声誉很好。

got the time　几点了

☞ A: *Got the time*?

B: It's a little after ten.

A: 几点了?

B: 10 点过一点儿。

☞ What's the time?

gourmet coffee　极品咖啡; 精制咖啡

☞ Over the last few years, a trend has been developing to introduce premium specially blended coffees known as *gourmet coffees* into the America market. 在过去几年中, 一种特别的混合咖啡, 即众所周知的精制咖啡, 被引入美国市场, 这已经成为一种潮流。

gourmet coffee

government agency 政府办事处

☞ The organization is the ***government agency*** that supervises the property markets. 该组织是监管房地产市场的一个政府机构。

graduation announcements 毕业典礼请柬

☞ A: Have you ordered your ***graduation announcements***?

B: No, I had Joe do it for me.

A：你订毕业典礼请柬了吗？

B：没有，我让乔帮我去做了。

graduation ceremony 毕业典礼

☞ A: I don't know if I can make it to the ***graduation ceremony***. Is attendance required?

B: At one time it was, but not anymore.

A：我不知道能否参加毕业典礼，要求必须出席吗？

B：曾经要求过，但是现在不用了。

☞ We need to arrive early for the ***graduation ceremony***. 我们得早点到达，去参加毕业典礼。

grand canyon 大峡谷

☞ A: It's good to see you back. How was your trip to Arizona? Did you see the ***Grand Canyon***?

B: Yes, it was fantastic.

A：很高兴看见你回来。你去亚利桑那州的旅行怎么样啊？看大峡谷了吗？

B：看了，太棒了。

☞ A: The ***Grand Canyon*** is full of mysteries. Wouldn't you like to go to Arizona some day?

B: You bet I would.

A：大峡谷充满了神秘色彩。你不想某一天去亚利桑那看看吗？

B：当然会的。

🔍 Grand Canyon 位于美国亚利桑那州西北部的凯巴布高原上，以其形态奇特、色彩斑斓而著称。同时，因科罗拉多河穿流而过，又叫科罗拉多大峡谷，是联合国教科文组织选为受保护的天然遗产之一。

grant one's/a request 答应请求

☞ A: I wonder whether I could hand in my paper later. It's too hard for me to finish it in such a short time.

B: It seems to be little chance for the professor to ***grant your request***.

A：我在想能不能晚点交论文。在这么短的时间让我写完太难了。

B：想让教授答应你的请求恐怕不太可能。

grasp at 向…抓去，抓取

☞ The rescue group told the victim to ***grasp at*** the hanging rope and they would pull him up. 救援人员告诉遇难者抓住绳子，他们会把他拉上来。

🔍 谚语：Grasp all, lose all. 贪多必失。

gravitational force 重力

☞ Study shows that the young earth would not have had enough ***gravitational force*** to stop a body the size of a moon from traveling through the solar system and pull it into orbit. 研究表明，地球在早期没有足够引力让如月球大小的天体在太阳系中停止遨游，并将其拉入轨道。

Great Depression 大萧条

☞ As the workweek shortened during the ***Great Depression*** of the 1930s, the weekend expanded to two full days—Saturday and Sunday. 20 世纪 30 年代的大萧条时期，工作日缩短了，周末也随之延长到了两天，即周六和周日。

☞ During the ***Great Depression***, the economy suffered tremendously. 大萧条时期，经济遭遇重创。

☞ Around the time of the ***Great Depression***, the art movement known as the Regionalism had begun in the United States. 在大萧条时期，被称为"地方主义"的艺术运动在美国就已经出现了。

🔍 经济危机后常会伴随大萧条，经济危机在英语中是economic crisis。

greeting card 贺卡

☞ A: Monica finally got a job in Los Angeles.

B: How do you know?

A: I just received her ***greeting card*** saying "Merry Christmas" to me.

A：莫妮卡终于在洛杉矶找到了工作。

B：你怎么知道的？

A：我刚刚收到她的圣诞贺卡。

groan about 抱怨

☞ How come Michael's always **groaning about** something? 迈克尔为什么总是在抱怨?

☞ complain about

grow hemp 种植大麻

☞ Only being approved by the government can you **grow hemp**. 只有获得政府批准, 你才能种植大麻。

🔍 与毒品(drugs)有关的词:
heroin 海洛因   cocaine 可卡因
ecstasy 摇头丸

grow up 成长, 成熟; 逐渐形成, 发展

☞ A: You are such a good listener. What's your secret?

B: Well, when you **grow up** sharing a room with three older brothers, you get plenty of practice.

A: 你真是个好的倾听者。你的秘诀是什么?

B: 嗯, 当你成长过程中和三个哥哥共处一个房间, 你自然会得到很好的锻炼。

☞ A: It's no use. I'll never learn to swim as well as you do.

B: Don't give up so easily. Remember I practically **grew up** in the water.

A: 没用的。我再怎么学也不可能和你游得一样好。

B: 别这么轻易就放弃。记得吗, 我基本上是在水里长大的。

🔍 grown up 表示"长大了的", 在听力中出现时会连读, 要多加注意。

gym pass 健身卡

☞ Linda wanted to transfer her **gym pass**. 琳达想转让她的健身卡。

🔍 "体操鞋"用英语说就是 gym shoes。

habit forming 习惯的养成

☞ A: You know, I've heard that bridge is **habit forming**. You should be careful not to play so much that you don't get your studying done.

B: Don't worry about me.

A: 知道吗, 我听说玩桥牌会养成习惯。你要小心, 不要玩太多以免影响学习。

B: 不用担心我。

habitat destruction 栖息地的毁坏

☞ The rare species is on the verge of extinct due to natural **habitat destruction**. 由于自然栖息地遭到破坏, 这种珍稀物种濒临灭绝。

half off 打折

☞ A: This mirror is the perfect size for our bathroom, and it's *half off*.

B: We won't have time to hang it today. It'll still be here next week.

A：这个镜子放在我们的浴室大小正好，并且在打五折。

B：我们今天没时间了。这个镜子下周也不会被卖掉。

☞ at discount

hand in 上交

☞ A: I can't remember the due date for our final paper.

B: I think it is the last day of class, but Professor Lee said not to wait until the last minute to *hand* it *in*.

A：我不记得交期末论文的最后期限了。

B：我想是最后一节课。但是李教授说不要等到最后一刻才交。

☞ A: Oh. Hi, Dan. I was just at the library. I have to *hand in* my biology paper tomorrow.

B: Tomorrow? Oh, no, I thought it wasn't due till Monday.

A：哦，嗨，丹，我刚才在图书馆。我明天就要交生物论文了。

B：明天？哦，不，我还以为周一才交呢。

☞ submit to, give in

🔍 与 hand 有关的词组：

hand down 留传下来，传给 　　　 hand out 分发，散发

hand in hand 手拉手

hand out 分发，散发

☞ Based on your responses to a questionnaire that I'll *hand out* to you in a minute, we will match you with one or more sponsors. 一会儿我会发给大家一张调查表，基于该表上大家的反馈，我们会给你找到一名或者几名适合的赞助者。

☞ The calendars were *handed out* free to customers to thank them for their business. 日历是免费发给顾客的，以感谢他们的光临。

hand-me-down 送的东西；旧衣服

☞ A: What a gorgeous jacket! It must have cost a fortune.

B: Not at all. It's a *hand-me-down*.

A：这件夹克多好啊！一定花了不少钱吧。

B：根本没有。别人送的。

hands down 易如反掌

☞ Lee won the chess match *hands down*. 李赢得了棋赛，易如反掌。

hang out   闲逛；坚持，持续

☞ A: Where did you **hang out** last summer vacation?

B: I just **hung out** in this city.

A：你上个暑假都做什么了？

B：我就在这座城市中闲逛了。

happen to   恰好，偶然，碰巧；发生在…身上

happen to

☞ A: You didn't **happen to** bring a spare blanket, did you? Because this one is all wet now.

B: No. But I do have some folding tools in the car. Will they do?

A：你恰好没有带多余的毯子吗？这个毯子现在湿透了。

B：没有。但是我车上有些折叠工具，用得着吗？

☞ A: Oh, I'm so sorry. You must let me pay to have your jacket cleaned.

B: That's all right. It could **happen to** anyone. And I'm sure that orange juice doesn't stain.

A：哦，实在对不起。我一定要付钱为你洗这件夹克。

B：没关系。任何人都会碰到这种情况。而且我确信橙汁不会在上面留下痕迹。

☞ A: Would you **happen to** know somebody who'd like to buy my car?

B: Well, I don't know of anyone off hand. But I'll check with some of my friends.

A：你知不知道谁会想买我的车？

B：哦，目前我还不知道。但是我会问问朋友的。

hard line   强硬路线

☞ The new leader took a **hard line** to deal with diplomacy. 那位新的领导人在外交上采取强硬手段。

🔍 line 一词在托福考试的对话中还常考到"电话线"的意思，如：The line is busy now. 电话现在占线。

hardly anyone has noticed   几乎没有人注意到

☞ A: Hi Joe! I just saw your roommate coming out of the library. She looks different. Did she get her hair cut or something?

B: Yeah, three days ago actually. And **hardly anyone has noticed**.

A：喂，乔！我刚刚看见你的室友从图书馆出来。她看上去有些不一样。她剪头发了还是怎么回事？

B：是，三天前剪的。几乎没人注意到。

have a chance to 有机会做

☞ A: I hope you **had a chance to** pick up those financial aid papers.

   B: I thought I'd get Dave to do it later.

   A：我希望你能有机会来把财政援助文件拿走。

   B：我想我一会儿会让戴夫去拿。

☞ A: Bill Smith has volunteered to write a summary of the proposals we've agreed on.

   B: Will I **have a chance to** review it?

   A：比尔·史密斯自愿为我们同意的那个议案写份概要。

   B：我有机会看一下吗?

☞ A: Have you **had a chance to** wear your new shirt yet?

   B: That reminds me. I've been meaning to exchange it for a larger size.

   A：你有机会穿你的新衬衣吗?

   B：这倒提醒我了。我一直想去换件大一号的呢。

have a big/good/poor appetite 胃口好/不好

☞ A: Take two of these pills three times a day. And you shouldn't take them on an empty stomach.

   B: What if I don't **have a good appetite**?

   A：这药一天吃三次,一次两片,不能空腹吃。

   B：那如果我没有胃口该怎么办呢?

NOTES

Unit 10

have a habit of doing 有做…的习惯

☞ A: Where is Steven?

B: He *has a habit of* doing warm-up before running.

A：史蒂文去哪了？

B：他习惯在跑步前先热身。

☞ get used to doing, be accustomed to do

have a problem with 在…方面有问题

☞ A: I wish I could help you. I'm not really good with computers. Whenever I *have a problem with* my computer, I just turn the whole thing off and then start all over again.

B: Well, I try that already about a dozen times.

A：真希望我能帮你，但是我对电脑并不在行。通常我的电脑出问题时，我就把所有程序都关掉，然后重启。

B：嗯，我已经这样试了很多次了。

have a way with 擅长

☞ Bonnie really *has a way with* words. 邦妮真的很健谈。

☞ be good at

have a...trip 度过一个…的旅行

☞ A: *Have a* good *trip*! I hope you won't have too long a walk from the car to check in at the hotel. That's a lot of luggage for you to carry by yourself.

B: Well, I'll get the driver to give me a hand.

A：旅途愉快！我希望你下车后去登记住宿不用走太远。你自己要拎很多行李。

B：哦，我会让司机帮忙。

have abundant energy 精力旺盛

☞ The hero *has abundant energy*, so he could be back to his feet whenever he suffers setbacks. 那个男主角有着充沛的精力，无论他何时遭受了挫折，总能再站起来。

🔍 abundant 的用法还有 be abundant in(富于…)，在托福考试中也常见到。

have anything on   与…有关的任何事

☞ A: Excuse me, does this library **have anything on** the international arts festival coming this summer or should I go to the art library for that?

B: If you give a minute, I think we have a few sources for that kind of information.

A：打扰了，这家图书馆有关于今年夏天国际艺术节方面的资料吗？或者我是不是应该去艺术类图书馆找这些东西呢？

B：请等我一下，我想我们有这方面的一些资源。

have one's address   有某人的地址

☞ A: My cousin Lisa said she mailed me some books. But they never came.

B: Well, you just moved into a new dormitory. She probably sent them out before she **had** your new **address**.

A：我堂（或表）姐/妹莉萨说她给我寄了一些书。我却没收到。

B：哦，你刚搬入新宿舍。她可能不知道你的新地址就把书寄出了。

have problems with   对…有问题

☞ A: Do you have any idea why David wants to see me tomorrow? Is he **having problems with** his accounting project?

B: Yeah, he's been struggling with it from day on and I'm told you're an expert on that stuff.

A：你知道戴维为什么明天想见我吗？他的会计项目出了问题吗？

B：是的。他费力弄了一天也没结果，听说你是这方面的专家。

☞ have trouble with

have right to do   有权利做

☞ Artists keep the copyright even after selling the work of art. The purchaser may buy the physical work, but the right to make prints or copies is still the artists' and buyers does not automatically **have** any **right to** make and sell prints or copies of work.

艺术家即使卖掉艺术品之后，仍享有艺术品的版权。购买者可以买到实际的作品，但是制作印刷品或副本的权利仍归艺术家所有，购买者不会自动拥有制作和销售艺术品的印刷品或副本的权利。

☞ have access to, be entitled to

have room for   有…的空间

☞ A: Do you know anyone who is driving to the conference in Boston next weekend?

B: Pete is. I think he **has room for** another person.

A：你知道谁下周末开车去波士顿参加那个会议吗？

B：皮特。我想他的车应该还能再坐一个人。

☞ have space for

> 🔍 room 在这里为不可数名词，意为"空间"。

have the authority to do　有权利做

☞ A: Like usual, the lecture hall is a complete mess this afternoon. Newspapers, soda cans, used tissues, all of it, just thrown all over the floor. I can't understand how people can be so thoughtless.

　　B: Well, your professor should **have the authority to** get something done about it.

　　A：和往常一样，演讲厅今天下午还是一片狼藉。报纸、汽水罐、用过的纸巾等所有垃圾扔得满地都是。我不理解人们怎么可以这么草率。

　　B：嗯，你的教授应该有权利为此做点什么。

have time to do　有时间做

☞ I would hardly **have time to** come to the rehearsals. 我很难抽出时间来排练。

☞ A: I have an idea for a special issue of the school newspaper. Do you **have time to** discuss it?

　　B: My class is over at one. But I'm free after that.

　　A：针对校报的专刊发行，我想出了一个主意。你有时间讨论一下吗？

　　B：我的课一点结束。在那之后就没事了。

have to do with　与…有关

☞ A: What do your eyes **have to do with** the computer?

　　B: People who use computers tend to stare at the monitor and blink less often than they normally would. That leads to dry irritated eyes.

　　A：你的眼睛和电脑有什么关系？

　　B：常用电脑的人经常盯着显示器，比正常情况下眨眼的次数少，这样就会导致眼睛干涩。

☞ relate to

have/gain (...) access to　可以达到；可以使用

☞ A: You are going to the library again?

　　B: Yeah, we **have** free **access to** it. Then why not study there with so many reference books?

　　A：你又要去图书馆？

　　B：是啊，我们可以免费进去，那为什么不在那里学习呢？有那么多的参考书。

gain (...) access to

have/get a haircut　剪头发

get a haircut

☞ A: You look different today. Did you **get a haircut**?

　　B: That's funny. You are the third person to ask me that. But all I did was getting new frames for my eye glasses.

　　A：你今天看起来不太一样，是剪头发了吗？

　　B：真有趣，你是第三个这么问我的人了，其实我只是换了新眼镜框。

☞ A: What, you are going to the hairdressers again? Seems like you just *had a haircut*.

B: You kidding, it's been over a month.

A：怎么，你又去理发店了吗？你好像刚刚剪过头发。

B：开玩笑，都已经剪了一个月了。

head for 前往；驶向；走向

☞ A: I just called the travel agent. It's all set. On June the first, I'm *heading for* the mountains for an entire week.

B: Have you checked the academic calendar? Because my classes aren't over till seventh.

A：我刚刚给旅行社打了电话，所有事宜都定好了。6月1号，我将会去山里待整整一周。

B：你看过校历了吗？我的课得到7号才结束呢。

☞ be towards

head on 迎头地，迎面地；针对地

☞ A: People say the exercise is good for you, but I don't know. I mean dragging myself out of bed six-day and every day to go to the gym is risking *head on* my sleeping schedule.

B: Sure, but who says you need to go every day?

A：人们说锻炼有好处，但是我不知道。我的意思是说，每周六天都要强迫自己早起，而且每天都要去健身房，这与我的睡眠时间冲突。

B：的确，但是谁说你每天都要去？

head over to 向着…去

☞ A: Are you ready to *head over to* the library? Oh, do you have your student ID card with you this time?

B: It's right here...ah, I must have left it in my room. I'll be right back.

A：你准备好去图书馆了吗？哦，这次你带学生证了吗？

B：就在这……啊，我一定是忘在房间里了。我马上回来。

☞ make for, steer for

hear about 听说

☞ A: I *hear about* your appearing on the six o'clock news.

B: Oh, that. Some people were filming something on campus and I just happened to pass in front of the camera.

A：我听说你出现在了六点的新闻中。

B：哦，那个呀。有人在校园里录制节目，我正好从摄像机前经过。

☞ A: Did you *hear about* Jim?

B: I wouldn't give that rumor any credibility.

A：你听说关于吉姆的事了吗？

B：我可不相信谣言。

☞ A: Did you *hear about* the big snow storm in Iowa yesterday? Three feet and twelve hours.

B: Yeah, and I hear it's heading our way. We're supposed to get the same thing tonight.

A：你听说昨天爱荷华州的暴风雪了吗？连续下了 12 个小时，有三英尺厚。

B：是啊，而且我听说它正朝着我们这边来呢。今天晚上我们这儿可能会下同样大的雪。

🔍 hear about 指不仅听说了一件事或一个人，而且了解相关细节；而 hear of 指仅仅知道有这件事发生，或仅仅知道有这个人存在，但是具体细节并不了解。

---

hear of 听说

☞ A: Who is this twentieth century's Socrates?

B: Professor Brown. Have you *heard of* him?

A：谁是 20 世纪的苏格拉底？

B：布朗教授。你听说过他吗？

🔍 另一常考短语是 hear from，意思是"收到…的来信"。

---

heating system 供暖系统

☞ The building's *heating system* dries the air. 大厦的供暖系统使空气干燥。

---

heavy traffic 拥挤的交通

☞ If the accident was because of *heavy traffic* or something, I'd be attributing the driver's behavior to an external factor, something beyond his control. 如果事故的发生是因为诸如交通拥挤之类的原因，我就会把司机的行为归结为外部因素，也就是说超出了他的控制范围。

🔍 另一常考短语是 traffic jam，意思是"交通堵塞"。

---

help oneself to 自取所需(食物等)

☞ With the exception of Sunday evenings and vacation breaks, dining halls are open every day for breakfast, lunch and supper. Students simply present their meal tickets at the door and go through the line, *helping themselves to* as much food as they want. 除了周日晚上和假期，食堂每天都会开放，提供早餐、午餐和晚餐。学生可以在门口出示饭票并排队进入，随便吃他们想吃的食物。

help oneself to

115

help out 帮忙，帮助…解决困难

☞ A: The tents are for the many special events and displays. And this year there'll be quite a few new events. I am going to help serve food at the refreshment tent for a few hours Saturday afternoon.

B: Do many people volunteer to **help out**?

A: Oh, yes. I like helping, because I really enjoy seeing a lot of my friends at the food tent.

A：帐篷是用来举办许多特别活动和展览的，而且今年会有不少新的活动。周六下午我要去茶点帐篷几个小时，帮忙提供食物。

B：有很多人自愿提供帮助吗?

A：当然。我喜欢帮忙，因为我真的喜欢在食物帐篷中看到那么多朋友。

hesitate to do 犹豫做

☞ If you have any problems, please do not **hesitate to** call the students centre. 如果您有任何问题，请随时拨打学生中心的电话。

☞ be free to do

historical perspective 历史的视角

☞ The Great Depression seemed more serious when put into an **historical perspective**. 从历史的视角看，大萧条似乎更显严重。

historical significance 历史意义

☞ My parents have always liked taking my sister and me to different places in the United States, places with **historical significance**. 我父母很喜欢带我和妹妹去美国各种有历史意义的地方。

🔍 关于景点(scenery spot)：
natural landscape 自然景观   cultural landscape 人文景观
places of historical interest 名胜古迹

hold on(to) 抓牢，紧握；继续，坚持；停住，等一下；(打电话时)别挂断

☞ A: You took the European literature class last year. Are you interested in selling me any of the books?

B: I always **hold on to** them for future reference.

A：你去年修了欧洲文学的课程，可以卖给我几本书吗?

B：我通常会留着这些书以备将来参考。

☞ A: If I don't find my wallet pretty soon, I'm going to have to report it stolen.

B: **Hold on**. Before you call campus security office, have you checked your car or your jacket pocket, everywhere?

A：如果我一会儿还找不到钱包，就要报告被偷了。

B：等一下。在你给学校保安室打电话前，你检查了汽车、夹克兜，以及其他地方了吗？

☞ A: These summer days are getting to be more than I can take. It was even too hot to go to the pool yesterday.

B: *Hold on*. According to the weather report we should have some relief by the end of the week.

A：这几个夏日热得已经让我受不了了。昨天热得都不能去游泳池。

B：再坚持一下，天气预报说这个周末天气情况会有所缓解。

hold over 推迟，使延期

☞ A: Hey, Bond, do you know the party is *held over* till next week?

B: Oh, thanks for telling. I'm preparing for it.

A：嗨，邦德，你知道聚会推迟到下周了吗？

B：哦，谢谢你告诉我，我正为它做准备呢。

☞ put off, delay

hold the grudge 记仇

☞ A: I wish I hadn't hurt Mary's feelings like that. You know I never meant to.

B: The great thing about Mary is that she doesn't *hold the grudge*. By tomorrow she'll have forgotten all about it.

A：我真希望没有伤害到玛丽。你知道我是无心的。

B：玛丽的优点就是不记仇。到明天她就会当什么事也没发生过。

home radio receiver 家庭无线电接收器

☞ A: Is there something different in your room?

B: Oh, you are careful. I just sold the old *home radio receiver*.

A：你房间做什么变动了吧？

B：哦，你可真细心。我刚把那台旧的家庭无线电收音机给卖了。

🔍 家用电器：

microwave oven 微波炉	oven 烤箱
vacuum cleaner 吸尘器	digital camera 数码照相机
digital video camera 数码摄像机	

homework assignment 家庭作业

homework assignment

☞ A: I'm wondering whether I could borrow your *homework assignments* to have a look at.

B: I think you'd better do it by yourself.

A：我在想，能不能借你的家庭作业看一下。

B：我觉得你最好还是自己写。

horizontal movement 水平运动

☞ Remember, although there are both horizontal and vertical movements in air, the term "wind" applies only to *horizontal movement*. 记住，虽然在空气中既有水平运动又有垂直运动，但是风只有水平运动。

household utensil 家庭用具

☞ During the middle ages, mined metal was scarce and expensive, therefore was rarely used in the manufacture of *household utensils*. 在中世纪的时候，开采的金属很稀少而且昂贵，所以很少被用来制作家庭用具。

housing office 住宿部

☞ The *housing office* will help you find off campus housing. 住宿部会帮你在校外找房住。

🔍 大多数学校都会有专门的住宿部，能为学生找到合适的房子。通常是独立公寓，或者是和房东一起住，也可以和其他学生合租。

How about...? …怎么样?

☞ A: *How about* a little tennis? Say Saturday or Sunday?
   B: It sounds great. It seems like all I have been doing lately is sitting in front of this computer.
   A：一起打网球怎么样？周六或周日？
   B：听起来不错。我最近好像一直坐在这台电脑前。

☞ A: I wish we could talk some more Judy. *How about* going for a cup of coffee? I'm ready for a break.
   B: I'd love to, but I have to study for a history exam. In fact, I was just on my way to the study group, and I think I am already late. Maybe tomorrow?
   A：朱迪，我希望我们能多聊聊。去喝杯咖啡怎么样？我准备休息一下。
   B：我很想去，但是我还要准备历史考试。其实，我正要去参加学习小组，而且我想我已经迟到了。明天怎么样？

☞ A: I think this coat is in great color. And the price is certainly right.
   B: *How about* the weight, though? Remember we're supposed to have a really severe winter this year.
   A：我觉得这件大衣的颜色不错，而且价格也合理。
   B：够不够厚？今年我们可是要准备过一个寒冬哦。

🔍 这个词组是提建议的一种婉转的说法，以表示对对方的尊重，这样的用法还有 I wonder if... / Maybe... / Would you like...?

huge explosion 大爆炸，剧烈爆炸

☞ The *huge explosion* of the volcano caused a great black cloud of dust. 火山的剧烈爆发产生了一大片黑色尘云。

human race 人类

☞ What amazes me was that the ***human race*** survived before antibiotics. 令我惊奇的是，使用抗生素前人类居然活了下来。

☞ human being

hurry up 快点

☞ A: Hey, Dan, do you think you might ***hurry up*** just a bit? You've been standing in front of that sandwich counter forever. And you know, I got class in ten minutes. And so do you, by the way.

B: Sorry, oh, I just wish they didn't give me so many choices.

A：嗨，丹，你能快点吗？你已经在那三明治柜台前站好久了。而且你是知道的，我 10 分钟后还有课。顺便说一下，你也是。

B：对不起，哦，真希望他们没有这么多种类供我选择。

☞ come on, be quick

hydrothermal vent 深海热泉

☞ In some places of the ocean floor, there are ***hydrothermal vents***, which are small cracks on the sea floor. 海床的某些地方有热泉口，它们是海床上的小裂缝。

I bet... 我确定···

☞ A: I see you are having the fish for lunch.

B: That's right. Fish sticks and tomato soup, my favorites.

A: ***I bet*** they were frozen.

A：我知道你午饭要吃鱼。

B：是的，鱼排和番茄汤是我的最爱。

A：我敢说鱼是速冻的。

☞ I'm sure...

🔍 "You bet." 的含义为"的确，当然"。

I doubt... 我怀疑···

☞ A: I'm having a few friends over for a lunch tomorrow. It'll be great if you can join us.

B: ***I doubt*** I'll be able to make it. My brother is leaving for Chicago tomorrow afternoon. And I promised to give him a ride to the airport.

A：明天我有几个朋友要过来吃午饭。如果你能和我们一起就太好了。

B：我怕我去不了。我哥哥 / 弟弟明天下午去芝加哥。我答应开车送他去机场。

☞ A: I've got the leave for the airport right away. Bill's plane is due in an hour.

B: Judging by the weather outside, ***I doubt*** that the plane will land on schedule.

A：我马上要前往机场，比尔乘坐的飞机预计一小时后到达。

B：看外面的天气，我怀疑飞机可能会晚点。

☞ A: That's a long line. Do you think there'll be any tickets left?

   B: *I doubt* it. Guess we'll wind up going to the second show.

   A：队排得很长。你认为还会有票吗？

   B：估计没有了。我想我们只能去看第二场表演了。

☞ A: Do you think we should make reservations for dinner tonight?

   B: *I doubt* we'll need one. Lusia seems to be one of those places that is only crowded on weekends.

   A：你认为我们应该预订今天的晚餐吗？

   B：我想不用吧。路西亚餐厅似乎是只有周末才会爆满的地方。

I'd like to do... 我想做⋯

☞ In the few minutes that remain of today's class, *I'd like to* discuss next week's schedule with you. Because I'm presenting a paper at a conference in Detroit on Thursday, I won't be here for either Wednesday's or Friday's class. 今天的课剩下这几分钟里，我想和你们讨论一下下周的计划。因为我正在为周四在底特律召开的一次会议准备论文，周三和周五的课我不会来上。

identify (...)with 认同；认为⋯等同于

☞ The Depression had caused many Americans to begin to doubt their society. But regionalism artists painted scenes that glorified American values, scenes that many Americans could easily *identify with*. 大萧条让许多美国人开始怀疑他们的社会。但是地方主义艺术家所画的画却美化了美国的价值观，而且让很多美国人容易认同。

if only 要是⋯多好；要是，只要

☞ A: It's really cold outside. You should wear a scarf to keep your neck warm.

   B: That's a good idea. *If only* I had one with me.

   A：外面很冷。你应该围上围巾，脖子就暖和了。

   B：这主意不错。要是我有围巾就好了。

☞ A: This heat is unbearable. *If only* we'd gone to the beach instead.

   B: Why? With the museums and restaurants in Washington, I'd be happy here no matter what the weather.

   A：天热得让人受不了。要是我们去海边就好了。

   B：为什么？我喜欢华盛顿的博物馆和餐馆，无论天气如何，我在这里都很开心。

🔍 注意该词组用在虚拟语气中，用以表达自己的意愿或非真实条件。词组 only if 与这个词组很像，但意思是"除非⋯否则绝不⋯"，要注意区分。

igneous rock 火成岩

☞ *Igneous rock* is one of the three main rock types. 火成岩是三种主要岩石类型之一。

illegal earnings 非法收入

illegal earnings

☞ The corrupt official will not only be confiscated all those *illegal earnings* but also be fined. 那个贪官不仅会被没收所有的非法收入，还会被处以罚款。

illegal parking 违章停车

☞ A: Could you please just put me down at the gate of the cinema?

B: Sorry, but it is *illegal parking*.

A：您可不可以让我在电影院门口下车?

B：对不起，那是违章停车。

immerge oneself into 沉浸在…，专心做…

☞ The artist almost *immerged* herself *into* the paintings in the exhibition. 那位艺术家几乎完全沉浸于展览会上的绘画中了。

immune defense 免疫防御

☞ Some antibiotics are just slowing the bacteria down until our normal *immune defenses* can finish the job. 一些抗生素仅仅是在我们正常的免疫系统发挥功能前起到延缓细菌感染的作用。

impact on 对…的影响

☞ The accident really had a huge *impact on* us. 这次事故对我们的影响真的很大。

☞ influence on

implicit memory 内隐记忆

☞ The scientist issued an article titled *New Progress in Implicit Memory*. 这位科学家发表了一篇题为《内隐记忆研究新进展》的文章。

impose on 打扰；征(税)，加(负担、惩罚等)

☞ A: Elizabeth! She is a friend of mine. She'd be a big help right now. Why not you give her a call?

B: What! At this hour? It's already ten thirty. I don't wanna *impose on* her.

A：伊丽莎白! 她是我的一个朋友，她现在能帮我们的大忙。为什么不给她打个电话呢?

B：什么，现在吗? 已经十点半了，我不想打扰她了。

☞ We're supposed to write a short story that has some sort of limitation or, constraints *imposed on* it. 我们应该写一个有些许限制的短片故事。

☞ During the World War II the government *imposed* a new tax *on* public entertainment, what you might call performance tax. 在第二次世界大战期间，政府对公众娱乐征收了一项新税，我们可以称之为"演出税"。

improve one's grade　提高某人的成绩

☞ She thinks taking the course would *improve her grades*. 她认为上这门课会提高她的成绩。

improvement in　在…方面的改进

☞ Even with some major *improvement in* roadways, farmers still had to rely on rivers to move their crops to markets. 即使道路有了很大的改善，农民仍然需要依靠河运把农作物运到市场。

in (...) contest　在(…)竞赛中

☞ A: I'm sorry to hear that Helen failed *in* speech *contest*.
　 B: Well, she did her best.
　 A：听到海伦在演讲比赛中失利，我感到很遗憾。
　 B：嗯，她已经尽力了。

🔍 注意在英语中，contest, race, match 都是比赛的意思。contest 一般用在以下短语中：composition contest(作文比赛)，a speech (speaking) contest(演讲比赛)，a beauty contest(选美比赛)等；race 主要指"田径比赛或赛马、赛车、赛船"，如 a horse race(赛马)，a boat race(赛船)；match 则指双方对垒的比赛，如网球赛(a tennis match)，拳击赛(a boxing match)等。

in a furious way　采取激烈的方式

☞ A: I can't stand the noise. I'm going upstairs to argue with those crazy guys.
　 B: I don't think you could solve the problem *in a furious way*.
　 A：我实在受不了这噪音了，我要上楼去找那些疯子理论。
　 B：我认为采用这种激烈的方式是不能解决问题的。

in a furious way

🔍 反义词组：in a polite way (以礼貌的方式)

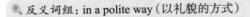

in a good mood 心情很好

☞ A: I got out of a science class late again. I never make it here to work on time. I hope I won't get in trouble.

B: The boss is **in a good mood**. Maybe she'll give you a break, this time.

A：自然科学课下课又晚了。我从来就没有准时上过班。我希望自己不会有麻烦。

B：老板心情很好。或许这次她会给你一个机会。

in a hurry 赶时间，匆忙地，急于

☞ A: We hope you enjoy your stay here at the hotel. Here is your room key and by the way check out time is 12 at noon.

B: Oh, thanks for reminding me. It's a lovely hotel and I'm not at all **in a hurry** to leave, but I wouldn't want to be charged for a second night.

A：希望您在酒店住得愉快。这是房间钥匙，顺便说一下，退房时间是中午12点。

B：哦，谢谢提醒。这酒店真不错，我也不急着走，不过我并不想花钱再住一晚。

☞ A: Excuse me. This roommate matching questionnaire is so long and I am kind of **in a hurry**. Do I have to answer all the questions?

B: Just the first side, the ones on the back are optional.

A：打扰了。这个室友组合调查问卷太长了，而且我有点赶时间。我必须回答所有问题吗？

B：只有正面是必须回答的，背面是自由选择的。

in a mess 混乱，一团糟

☞ A: I made my last exam **in a mess**.

B: Well, the past has passed.

A：我上次考试考得一团糟。

B：嗯，过去的都过去了。

🔍 注意区分 mess 与 mass 的发音，in the mass 指"总体上，整体而言"。

in a sense 从某种意义上说

☞ **In a sense** Selina might win the race if she hasn't got a bad cold. 从某种意义上说，如果赛琳娜没有得重感冒，她可能会赢得这场比赛。

🔍 在托福考试中，还经常考到一个关于 sense 的词组：make sense（讲得通，言之有理，有意义）。

in addition to 除…之外

☞ *In addition to* exercising regularly, eating a good breakfast is considered by many health experts to be a significant part of a successful way of reduction plan. 除了要有规律运动外，许多健康学专家还认为吃好早餐是成功减肥计划中非常重要的一个部分。

☞ *In addition to* being transported by train, ice was delivered by ships all along the east coast or further inland by boat. 除了用火车运输外，冰还被用大船运到东海岸，或用小船运到更远的内陆地区。

☞ besides

in advance 提前

☞ A: It's a really nice apartment. But the owners want two-month rent *in advance* and I just don't have it.

B: Do you think it would help if they know what a good tenant you are? You could get your landlord to write them a letter.

A: 这公寓真不错。但是房主要我提前交两个月房租，我现在没那么多钱。

B: 你觉得让房主了解你这个房客有多好会有帮助吗？你可以让你现在的房东给他们写封信。

☞ A: I think I'll take my mother to that French restaurant on Main Street for her birthday.

B: I hope it's not any time soon. They are usually booked up weeks *in advance*.

A: 我想带我妈妈去主街上的那家法国餐厅庆祝她的生日。

B: 我希望不是在近期去，那里的位子通常都是在几星期前预订的。

☞ A: I'm afraid this is the only room in the hotel we have free at this time. Sir, We weren't expecting you.

B: Oh, dear. I guess I'll take what I can get. Next time I'll be sure to call *in advance* and make a reservation.

A: 恐怕这是我们宾馆现在唯一一间空房了。我们没想到您会来，先生。

B: 哦，天啊，随便给我一间吧。下次我肯定会打电话提前预订的。

☞ A: My parents need a place to stay when they come to town next week. Do you have any suggestions?

B: I'd like to recommend the Clover Inn to visitors. But unlike the other places in town, they are usually filled months *in advance*.

A: 下周我父母要到镇上来，他们需要一个住宿的地方。你有什么建议吗？

B: 我愿意向游客们推荐三叶草旅馆。但是和镇上其他的旅馆不同，它们经常要在几个月前预订。

☞ ahead of time

in all aspects 全面地，各方面地

☞ A: Have you heard of our final exam?

B: Yeah, I think we should review what we've learnt *in all aspects*.

A：你听说我们的期末考试了吗？

B：是啊，我想我们得把所学过的东西全面复习一遍。

in all likelihood 十分可能，很可能

☞ *In all likelihood*, it was the ancient Greeks who first calculated the link of triangle's sides using square numbers. 很有可能是古希腊人首先使用平方数来计算三角形三条边之间的联系。

☞ as likely as not

in authority 有权

☞ A: I want to check my grades of my paper.

B: Sorry, only the professor *in authority* could take it to you.

A：我想看看我的论文分数。

B：对不起，只有负责分数的教授才能拿给你。

🔍 托福中还常考一个词组 in charge of，表示"负责"。

in brief 简单地说，简言之

☞ A: What do you think of my paper? Will it be OK if I hand in this to the professor?

B: Well, er, I think your point is vague, and the examples you gave are not strong enough to support the point, and ..., er, *in brief*, your work is bad.

A：你觉得我的论文写得怎么样？我把这个交给教授可以吗？

B：嗯，我觉得你的论点很模糊，而且所举的例子也不能有力地支持论点，而且…嗯，简单地说，你写得太差了。

in case (that) 假使；以防万一；也许，说不定

☞ A: Hi, thanks for your help. I guess I can handle the rest myself. But just *in case*, are you going to be around later?

B: I don't know, but you can always ask Judy. She's really good with these kinds of problems.

A：嗨，谢谢帮忙。我想剩下的我自己可以处理。但是为了以防万一，你一会儿还会过来吗？

B：我不知道，但是你可以随时问朱迪。她对这些问题很在行。

☞ A: I'm pretty confident the company where I worked the past two summers will hire me full time after graduation.

B: Well, just *in case that* it doesn't work out, Career's Service is having a work shop on campus next Thursday on applying for a job. They had one here last year, and I know a lot of people find it helpful.

A：我已经在一家公司实习了两个暑假，我很有信心毕业后他们会雇佣我。

B：嗯，为了以防万一，就业中心将于下周四在校园里举办一个招聘会。他们去年就办了一次，而且我听说很多人都觉得有帮助。

in coalition with　与…联合

☞ The two nations finally came to an agreement to be *in coalition with* each other to hedge against inflation. 这两个国家最终达成协议，联合抵御通货膨胀。

NOTES

Unit 11

---

in common 共用，共有，共同

☞ A: So, you and Julia are no longer roommates. I'm not surprised. You two never did things very compatible.

B: Yeah, well... It's not that we didn't get along... We just didn't have much *in common.*

A：你和朱莉娅不再是室友了。我一点也不惊讶，你们两个做事从来没一致过。

B：是啊，嗯…也不是我们相处不好…只是我们的共同点太少了。

☞ A: I can never tell if it's Lisa or Kate on the phone. Their voices are so similar.

B: That's about the only thing they have *in common* for sisters.

A：我永远分不出来电话里是莉萨还是凯特，她们的嗓音太像了。

B：这是她们姐妹俩唯一的共同点。

🔍 out of common 表示"非凡的，不寻常的，特殊的"。

---

in competition with 与…竞争，和…竞赛

☞ The biggest advantage of electric cars is that they don't pollute. However, they will be *in competition with* gas powered cars. 电力车最大的优点就是不会污染环境，但是它们将和天然气汽车一较高低。

in competition with

in conflict with 与…发生冲突

☞ When personal interests are *in conflict with* collective interests, personal interests must be subordinated to the collective ones. 当个人利益与集体利益冲突时，个人利益要服从集体利益。

---

in consequence 因此，结果

☞ The police was careless; *in consequence*, the thief fled away. 那个警察很粗心，结果小偷跑掉了。

☞ as a result

🔍 注意区分该词组与 in consequence of（由于），两个词组只差了一个词 of，但是含义和用法完全不一样。

in consequence of 由于，因为…的缘故

☞ ***In consequence of*** the police's neglect of his duty, the prisoner fled away. 由于那个警察的玩忽职守，犯人逃跑了。

☞ because of

in contact with 与…接触，与…联系

☞ A: Do you have any suggestions for coping with anxiety? You know how I hate exams.

B: Last year the university offered a stress management course at about this time. Have you been ***in contact with*** the student help services?

A: No. I haven't had time.

A：你有应对焦虑的建议吗？你知道的，我讨厌考试。

B：去年大概这个时候，学校开了一门应对压力的课程。你和学生帮助中心联系过了吗？

A：没有，我一直没时间。

☞ make contact with

🔍 反义词组：out of contact with（与…无联系）

in danger of extinction 处于灭绝的危险中

☞ In consequence of environmental pollution, many species including both plants and animals are ***in danger of extinction***. 由于环境污染，许多动植物物种都处于灭绝的危险中。

in detail 详细地

☞ Stowe, the writer of *Uncle Tom's Cabin*, usually succeeded, for her settings were often described actually and ***in detail***. 《汤姆叔叔的小屋》的作者斯托的成功之处主要在于，其作品的背景描写很真实、很细腻。

in due course 到适当的时候；及时地

☞ A: Excuse me. When shall I come again to make sure my application information?

B: We will inform you ***in due course***.

A：打扰一下，我什么时候要再来确认我的申请信息呢？

B：到时候我们会通知您的。

☞ A: What about the release dates for the new regulation?

B: The school authorities will announce ***in due course***.

A：新规章的发布日期是哪天？

B：校方会在适当的日期发布。

in exchange for 交换

☞ A: It's said that you could give the receipt *in exchange for* some coupons in the new supermarket.

B: Yeah, here are some that I've just got in it.

A：据说在那个新超市，你可以用收据换一些优惠券。

B：是啊，这些是我刚从那里换的。

in favor of 赞成，支持

☞ A: When shall we set off to go camping tomorrow?

B: My parents are not *in favor of* our idea.

A：我们明天什么时候出发去野营？

B：我父母不赞成我们的想法。

☞ support

🔍 托福考试中还经常在对话部分出现 do sb. a favor，表示"帮助某人"。

in good company 相处得好

☞ A: I'm going to meet Jackson at the airport.

B: Well, it seems that he is *in good company*.

A：我要去机场见杰克逊。

B：嗯，看起来他的人缘还挺好。

🔍 反义词组：in bad company（相处得不好）

in harmony with 与…协调，与…相一致

☞ That architect manipulated space extremely well. Some of his smallest houses look gigantic, and he had great respect for the materials he used and also a tremendous skill for placing his buildings *in harmony with* nature. 那个建筑师将空间利用到了极致，他所建的一些最小的房子看起来都很宽敞。他很尊重自己所使用的材料，并且拥有一种惊人的能力能够把建筑和自然融合成一体。

in imitation of 仿效，模仿

☞ This villa was built *in imitation of* a Roman style. 这个别墅效仿罗马风格而建。

in imitation of

in line 成一条直线，排成一行

☞ A: I had to stand *in line* at the bank for about half an hour. There were only two tellers open.

B: That's where you and I differ. I would've gone back another time.

A：我不得不在银行排半个小时的队，因为只有两个出纳窗口开着。

B：这就是你和我的不同。要是我，我会再找个时间去。

A: Waiting *in line* to copy just one page of an article wastes so much time.

B: Have you ever tried the photocopier on the third floor of the library? I don't think as many people know about it.

A：排了半天队就为了复印文章的其中一页，这也太浪费时间了。

B：你试过图书馆三楼的影印机了吗？我想可能很少有人知道那个。

in line with　与……一致，符合，按照

A: Would you like to have a break and a cup of coffee with me?

B: Your idea is *in line with* mine.

A：想休息会儿跟我喝杯咖啡吗？

B：你的想法和我的一样。

in motion　在开动中，在运转中

It's the solar radiation that causes the horizontal movement, and the atmosphere produces horizontal differences in air pressure. These differences set winds *in motion*. 正是太阳辐射引起了水平运动，而大气层的气压在水平方向出现不同，从而使得风运动。

in no time　立刻

A: How does your daughter like her new school?

B: Fine. She seems to have made new friends *in no time*.

A：你的女儿觉得新学校怎么样？

B：很好。她好像很快就交了新朋友。

☞ right away, right now, in a minute

in one's lifetime　在某人一生中

Gertrude Stein didn't publish any of her works *in her lifetime*. 格特鲁德·斯坦在有生之年没有发表她的任何作品。

A: I've never seen a larger collection of this author's books than the one here in this library. It's impressive how many she managed to write *in her lifetime*.

B: Yeah, actually a lot more than even this collection was Seger.

A：我从来没见过哪个地方收藏的该作家的作品比这个图书馆更多。她一生中写了多少部作品啊，真令人震惊。

B：是啊，但是这里收藏的赛格的作品比她的作品还要多。

🔍 英语中"寿命"一词常用"life expectancy"来表示。

in one's place　在某人的住处

A: Are you going to the conference in Chicago? I've already booked my hotel room.

B: Why care for hotel? My brother's got plenty of room *in his place*.

A：你去芝加哥开会吗？我已经订好酒店房间了。

B：为什么订酒店？我哥哥那里有很多地方可以住。

in order to　为了

☞ Enormous amounts of air enter and exit the cave *in order to* maintain balance of the pressure with the other side air. 大量空气进出洞口，这样就能够和另一边保持气压的平衡。

☞ so as to

in other words　换句话说

☞ We still have a huge amount of work to do before this weekend. *In other words*, you five can not go to the play. 我们在周末之前仍有大量工作要做，换句话说，你们五个不能去看戏。

in particular　特别，尤其

☞ Today I'd like to talk about the sculptor Henry Moore, *in particular* the ideas his work is based on, and also how he viewed the medium of sculpture. 今天我要介绍雕塑家亨利·莫尔，尤其是他作品依据的思想，还有他是如何看待雕刻方法的。

☞ especially

in perspective　正确地

☞ A: I don't want to talk to Anna. She is so unreasonable.

　B: But, Nick, you should put this *in perspective*.

　A：我不想跟安娜说话了，她太不讲理了。

　B：但是，尼克，你应该正确地看待这件事情。

in preparation for　正在为…准备

☞ A: I haven't seen Daniel for several days.

　B: He is *in preparation for* his final exam.

　A：我已经好几天没见到丹尼尔了。

　B：他正在准备期末考试。

☞ prepare for = be in preparation for

in relation to　与…有关系

☞ Most of the scholars thought the size of the universe have remained unchanged since the moment of its creation or perhaps forever, with all the stars remaining more or less in place *in relation to* each other. 大多数学者认为宇宙的大小自创造那刻起一直没变，甚至可能永远都不会改变，所有恒星之间的相对位置基本保持不变。

☞ be related to

in session　开会，开庭

☞ The court is going to be *in session*. 法庭就要开庭了。

in shape 处于良好的健康状况；健壮的体格，健美的体形

☞ A: Good news. I'm not going to need surgery after all. The doctor says I can start working out again soon. And maybe play soccer again in a few weeks.

B: That's terrific. It would be great if you could get back *in shape* in time for the state tournament.

A：好消息，我不用做手术了。医生说我很快就能恢复训练，而且可能几个星期后就可以再踢足球了。

B：太棒了，如果你能及时恢复身体，就可以参加国家锦标赛了。

in terms of 从…方面来说；按照，依据

☞ We talk about wind direction, *in terms of* where the wind's coming from, not where it's blow to. 我们谈论风的方向，是依据风吹来的方向而不是吹去的方向。

☞ If you compare the earth and the moon *in terms of* substance, you find the moon isn't much like the earth. 如果把月亮和地球的组成物质作比较，你就会发现月亮和地球一点也不像。

in the chain of 在…链条中

☞ If that toad became extinct, we'd lose an important link *in the chain of* revolution. 如果那种蟾蜍灭绝，我们会丧失进化链条中的重要一环。

in the course of 在…过程中，在…期间

☞ A: Hey, Dick, how was your presentation?

B: I'm not sure. I mean maybe I was too nervous *in the course of* it.

A：嗨，迪克，你的陈述怎么样？

B：我不知道，我在陈述的过程中可能太紧张了。

in the end 最后，终于

☞ A: All of your classmates seem so enthusiastic about running in the race.

B: But *in the end* only three of them actually took part.

A：你们班同学似乎对跑步比赛都很有激情。

B：但是，最后只有三个人参加了。

☞ finally

in the fresh air 在空气清新的地方，在户外

☞ A: What are you doing cooped up here in the lounge on such a beautiful spring day? I can't understand why everyone isn't out there *in the fresh air*, getting some sunshine.

B: You won't be saying that if you have my allergies.

A：在这样一个阳光明媚的春天你把自己关在休息室干什么？我无法理解为什么没有一个人出去呼吸一下新鲜空气，晒晒太阳。

B：如果你也像我一样过敏的话就不会那么说了。

in the margin 在空白处

☞ A: Jack, here is your paper. Professor told me to give it to you and he had already inserted his comments *in the margin*.

B: Thanks a lot.

A：杰克，这是你的论文。教授让我交给你，他已经在空白处做了批注。

B：非常感谢。

🔍 在经济学中，margin 一词是"最低利润，最低收益点"的意思。

in the red 赤字

☞ A: So far the clubs are about three hundred dollars *in the red*, and we still have four months to go before membership renewal.

B: Well, we may have to raise our dues.

A：到目前为止，俱乐部赤字约 300 美元。距会员资格更新还有四个月。

B：哦，我们可能得提高会员费。

🔍 反义词组：in the black（赢利）

in the way 以这种方式；妨碍，挡道

☞ I like to make some changes *in the way* we prepare our food. 我想在咱们做饭的方法上做出一些改变。

in theory 理论上

☞ A: I might argue with some of the details, but I basically agree with managing the economy.

B: Sure it sounds great *in theory*. My concern is in practice.

A：我可能不同意某些细节，但基本同意操纵经济。

B：理论上听起来的确不错，但我担心的是在实际中的情况。

individual action 个体行动

☞ Although sharing is a concept generally associated with promoting the greater good, it is also an *individual action*, a personal choice. 虽然"分享"这一概念总的来说和带来更多的好处联系在一起，但是它仍然是个体行为，是个人的选择。

🔍 反义词组：joint action（联合行动）

inherit from 从…继承，遗传自

☞ That generous man donated all the property *inherited from* his father to those victims. 那位慷慨的男士把从他父亲那里继承来的财产全都捐给了那些受害者。

ink stain 墨水印迹

ink stain

☞ A: Do you think it'll be able to get this **ink stain** out of my pants?

　B: It won't be a problem but I'll need to send them over to the main cleaning facility. That's an extra day's time.

　A：你觉得我裤子上的墨迹有可能洗掉吗？

　B：这没问题，但是我要把它们送到洗衣总店去，这还要额外花一天的时间。

insert a/the/one's card 插卡

☞ A: What's wrong with this machine? Why can't I start it?

　B: Did you **insert your card**?

　A：这机器怎么了？我怎么启动不了它呢？

　B：你插卡了吗？

insist on 坚持

☞ A: Gary **insists on** buying the food for the picnic.

　B: That's pretty generous. But shouldn't we at least offer to share the expense?

　A：加里坚持要为野餐买食物。

　B：他太大方了，但是我们应该提出分担一点费用吧？

☞ A: Why do you always **insist on** wearing blue?

　B: Because it suits me.

　A：你为什么总是穿蓝颜色的衣服呢？

　B：因为这个颜色适合我。

☞ stick to

inspect sth. for sth.　检查…中是否有

☞ The doctors are supposed to **inspect** the victims **for** epidemic carefully. 医生应该仔细检查难民是否有传染病。

🔍 注意区分 inspect for，表示"检查"。

inspect the damage　检查损坏，检查损失

☞ After **inspecting the damage**, the shipping company found that they couldn't afford that and may go bankrupt. 船运公司检查损失后，发现他们负担不了，而且还有可能破产。

🔍 该词组经常出现在与贸易有关的文章中，另外还可能考到的一个词是 compensation（赔偿）。

intelligence analysis 情报分析，智能分析

☞ Through *intelligence analysis*, FBI have uncovered a plot of explosion in public. 通过情报分析，美国联邦调查局破获了一起在公共场所实施爆炸的预谋案件。

intend to 打算做，计划做

☞ A: Now that you've finished writing your thesis, do you think you will have time to sit back and take it easy? Maybe take a little bit vacation?

B: Believe me, that's exactly what I *intend to* do.

A：既然你已经完成了论文写作，你认为自己有时间坐下来放松一下吗？或许休一段时间假？

B：真的，那正是我打算做的。

🔍 两词连读时，d 的发音要弱化。

intense cold 严寒

☞ A: Hey, Eric, I thought you went to the cinema.

B: Oh, I didn't because of the *intense cold*.

A：嗨，埃里克，我还以为你去看电影了呢。

B：哦，因为太冷了，我没去。

☞ severe cold, freezing

intense cold

intense sunlight 强烈的阳光

☞ A: I can't open my eyes because of the *intense sunlight*.

B: Why don't you wear your sunglasses?

A：这强烈的阳光照得我睁不开眼。

B：你为什么不戴上墨镜呢？

intense tropical sun 强烈的热带阳光

☞ Because it spends a lot of time in the *intense tropical sun*, the grass mouse has also evolved two separate safeguards against the sun's ultraviolet radiation. 由于长时间处在强烈的热带阳光下，这种草鼠还进化出了两种可以抵抗太阳紫外线辐射的保护功能。

interact with 与…相处 / 交流；与…互相影响

☞ I thought I'd interview the manager about how people in the office *interact with* each other and with outside clients. 我想我会去采访一下经理，关于办公室内的职员之间以及职员与客户之间是如何相处与交流的。

interest rate 利率

☞ The economic crisis is more and more serious, and most of the banks begin to lower their *interest rate*. 金融危机越来越严重，大多数银行都开始降低利率了。

interfere with 妨碍；干涉，干扰

☞ In the economic sense, laisser faire meant that while the government should be responsible for things like maintaining peace and protecting property rights, it should not *interfere with* private business. 从经济意义上讲，自由主义是指政府对于维护和平与保护产权负有责任，而不应该干涉私人事务。

☞ disturb, interrupt

interior decoration 室内装潢

☞ A: Hey, Paul, I remember that you have learnt *interior decoration*.

B: Why? Did you buy that house?

A：嗨，保罗，我记得你以前学过室内装潢。

B：为什么说这个？你买那个房子了？

interior design 室内设计

☞ A: What do you think of the *interior design* of this apartment?

B: You know I don't like light green.

A：你觉得这个公寓的室内设计怎么样？

B：你知道的，我不喜欢浅绿色。

> 🔍 其他"设计"：
> building design 建筑设计   costume design 服装设计
> hair design 发型设计   style design 造型设计

interior designer 室内设计师

☞ A: Take a look at the interior decoration and give me some suggestions.

B: Well, to be honest, I think you'd better employ a professional *interior designer*.

A：看看这室内装潢，然后给我提点建议。

B：嗯，说实在的，我觉得你最好还是雇个专业的室内设计师。

internal factor 内在因素

☞ According to this theory, there are two categories of reasons: *internal factors* and external factors. 根据这一理论，原因有两类：内在因素和外在因素。

internal mail 内部邮件

☞ Staffs communicate with each other by using *internal mail* system. 员工们通过使用内部邮件系统互相沟通。

internal metal skeleton 内部金属骨架

☞ What makes Chicago's Home Insurance Building important is that it had true skyscraper construction with an *internal metal skeleton* that carried the weight of the brick exterior. 芝加哥家庭保险大厦之所以重要是因为它有真正的摩天大楼结构，其内部是一个金属框架，支撑外部砖面的重量。

international trade　国际贸易

☞ Insurance could help encourage ***international trade***. 保险有利于刺激国际贸易。

internet plug-in　网络插件

☞ The computer browser can't find ***internet plug-in***. 这台电脑的浏览器找不到网络插件。

international trade

inventory report　存货报告单

☞ A: I tentatively scheduled the meeting on Thursday to go over your ***inventory report***, assuming you can meet that deadline.

　　B: Well, to be honest, even Friday might be pushing it a little.

　　A：我暂时把会议定在周四，到时候我会看你的存货报告单，如果你能在这个截止日期前完成的话。

　　B：嗯，说实在的，即使是周五，时间都有些紧张。

🔍 相关的词组还有：

inventory records 存货记录　　　inventory short and over 存货缺溢
inventory control 库存管理

involve in　涉及，卷入；使陷入

☞ A: Jonathan said he wanted to get ***involved in*** the student government this year.

　　B: But he hasn't gone to a single meeting, has he?

　　A：乔纳森说他想今年加入学生会。

　　B：但是他一次会议都没去参加过，对吗？

☞ drag into

isolate from　使与…隔离；使孤立

☞ The doctor suggested that the patients who have got epidemic should be ***isolated from*** others. 医生建议将传染病人与其他人隔离。

It doesn't seem to...　看起来不像…

☞ A: Could you take a look at my printer? ***It doesn't seem to*** be working.

　　B: I can't offer to set up this new one. Just give me a few minutes, OK?

　　A：你能看一下我的打印机吗？好像坏了。

　　B：这是新的，我不太会修，给我几分钟好吗？

It's hard to tell/say.　很难说。

☞ A: How do you think of this sweater?

　　B: ***It's hard to tell***. The style is in fashion, but it's a little expensive.

　　A：你觉得这件毛衣怎么样？

　　B：不好说，样子很流行，但是有点贵。

item on the agenda　议程条款，议程项目

☞ The stockholders will talk about the last ***item on the agenda*** in the tomorrow conference. 在明天的会议上，股东们将会讨论议程中的最后一项。

jigsaw puzzle　七巧板，智力拼图

☞ Even people who want to build a traditional log cabin on their own can buy a kits with precut logs that fit together like pieces of ***jigsaw puzzle***. 即使是那些想自己建造传统小木屋的人，也可以买到带有预先切好的原木的成套工具，那些原木可以很好地拼接在一起，就像七巧板一样。

jigsaw puzzle

job interview　工作面试

☞ A: I don't know what to think. Which outfit should I wear to my ***job interview***, the black dress or the navy blue suit?

B: Well, Jane, you've got to consider the image you want to present, and I say the suit is more professional looking.

A：我应该穿哪套衣服去参加工作面试，是黑色裙装还是深蓝色套装？

B：哦，简，你要考虑自己想展现的形象，我觉得，西服套装看上去更职业化一点。

🔍 在面试中，求职者可以说成 job applicant，而职位申请表是 job application form。

NOTES

Unit 12

job-search techniques　找工作的方法

☞ A: I heard that only 20% of summer jobs in this part of the country are advertised. The other 80% are filled some other way.

　 B: Really? Then maybe I need to change my *job-search techniques*.

　 A：我听说这个地区的夏季工作只有 20%刊登了广告，而另外的 80%则是用其他方式发布的。

　 B：真的吗？那么或许我该改变一下找工作的方式了。

🔍 关于找工作：

full-time job 全职工作　　　　　　　　　part-time job 兼职工作

recruitment information 招聘信息　　　　interview 面试

employer 雇佣者　　　　　　　　　　　　employee 被雇佣者

join sb. in doing　加入某人一起做

☞ Please *join me in* welcoming Mr. Daniel Robinson, one of the foremost pianists of our day. 请和我一起欢迎丹尼尔·罗宾逊先生吧，他是当代杰出的钢琴演奏家之一。

jot down　草草记下，匆匆记下

☞ A: Lucy, may I borrow your notebook to have a look?

　 B: Sorry, I just *jotted down* the main points without the details. Professor Black talked about the subject too fast.

　 A：露西，我能借你的笔记看一下吗？

　 B：对不起，我只是草草记下了主要的几点，细节都没有记。布莱克教授讲课太快了。

☞ write down quickly, take notes quickly

keep company with　与…交往，与…结伴

☞ A: It's strange. Steven now *keeps company with* Mike every day.

　 B: They are working on an experiment.

　 A：真奇怪，史蒂文现在天天和迈克在一起。

　 B：他们正在研究一个实验。

keep on doing 继续做；一直做

☞ The turtles *kept on* going back to the island where they hatched. 海龟不断回到它们孵蛋的那个岛屿。

keep one's head 保持镇静，不慌不忙

☞ When we are in danger, just *keep our head* and try to find a way to escape. 当我们处于危险的时候，要保持镇静，尽量找到方法逃跑。

☞ stay calm

🔍 反义词组：lose one's head (丧失理智)。keep one's head above water 是指"努力不让某人陷入财政危机"。

keep sth. handy 随时使用

☞ A: I don't want to buy the book Prof. Brown told us to read for the exam. Do you think you could lend me yours?

B: Well, I'm not using it right now. But I really need to *keep it handy*.

A：我不想去买布朗教授让我们准备考试要读的那本书，你能借给我你那本吗？

B：哦，我现在没在用，但是我需要随时查看。

🔍 另外一个与 handy 有关的短语是 come in handy，意为"迟早会有用 (派上用场)"。

keep (sth.) to oneself 保守秘密，不交际

☞ A: I'm amazed that you still haven't gotten to know your neighbors.

B: They tend to *keep to themselves*.

A：我很惊讶你还不认识你的邻居。

B：他们不太和外人来往。

keep up with 跟上

☞ A: Lisa is out of the office again, for another business meeting. She told me her flight was leaving late last night. I don't see how she does it.

B: Me either. I could never *keep up with* that kind of pace.

A：莉萨又没在办公室，她去参加另外一个商务会议了。她告诉我她的航班昨天深夜离开，我不知道她是如何做到的。

B：我也是，我从来都跟不上这种节奏。

key person 关键人物

☞ A: Have you heard that Leon was rewarded by our college?

B: Yeah, because he is the *key person* of that successful experiment.

A：你听说了吗？我们学院奖励利昂了。

B：是啊，因为他是那个成功实验的核心人物。

注意 key 这个词在音乐相关词汇中是"调"的意思，而在电脑相关词汇中，是"键"的意思。

key point 关键点

☞ A: Your paper need to be rewritten. I even can't see your **key point**.

B: OK, maybe I should do more research.

A：你的论文得重写，我甚至找不到你的关键点。

B：好吧，或许我得再多做些研究。

key word 关键词

☞ The **key words** should be listed in front of the article. 关键词应该写在文章的前面。

kind of 一点点

☞ A: Excuse me. This roommate matching questionnaire is so long and I am **kind of** in a hurry. Do I have to answer all the questions?

B: Just the first side, the ones on the back are optional.

A：打扰了。这个室友组合调查问卷太长了，而且我有点赶时间。我必须回答所有问题吗？

B：只有正面是必须回答的，背面是自由选择的。

☞ A: Uh, Joe, I'm really sorry about the misunderstanding. I know you thought I was waiting you and..., well, I apologize if I mislead you.

B: Actually I think it's **kind of** funny. Don't worry. We'll laugh about it later.

A：呃，乔，对于这次误会我真的感到很抱歉。我知道你原以为我在等你，而且…，嗯，如果我误导了你，我道歉。

B：事实上，我觉得这挺有趣。别担心，我们以后会把它当笑话的。

要与 a kind of, that kind of, some kinds of 等区分开，这些词组中 kind 是种类的意思。但这里的 kind of 表示程度，同时在听力中要注意连读。

kitchen utensil 厨房用具，炊具

kitchen utensil

☞ A: Jason, all the **kitchen utensils** are too old to cook.

B: I'll get some from the supermarket right now.

A：贾森，所有的厨房用具都太旧了，不能用。

B：我马上去超市买一些。

know of 听说，听说过；知道

☞ A: One of the members of the dormitory council is quitting. Do you **know of** anyone who would be interested in taking her place?

B: I'm not sure. But I'll certainly keep an eye out for you.

A：宿舍委员会的一个成员要辞职了。你听说谁想接她的班吗？

B：我不确定。不过我一定帮你盯着。

☞ A: Would you happen to know somebody who'd like to buy my car?

B: Well, I don't **know of** anyone off hand. But I'll check with some of my friends.

A：你知不知道谁可能会想买我的车？

B：哦，目前我还不知道。但是我会问问朋友的。

☞ A: Is it too late for me to withdraw from my music class?

B: Um, not that I **know of**.

A：现在取消我的音乐课是不是太晚了？

B：唔，我不知道。

label as　把…称为，把…说成是

☞ The lovely girl is **labeled as** a thief. 那个可爱的小女孩被说成是小偷。

landmark and historic sites　风景名胜

☞ The students of archeology department would like to go to **landmark and historic sites** during the holiday to do some research. 考古学系的学生想在假期的时候去一些风景名胜做研究。

language lab　语言实验室

☞ A: Shall I lock the **language lab** now before I go home?

B: Don't bother. I'll check it myself later.

A：我需要在回家前把语言实验室锁上吗？

B：不麻烦你了，一会儿我自己检查一下。

laryngeal cancer　喉癌

☞ The audience feel deeply grieved to hear the news that the famous artist died of **laryngeal cancer**. 观众们听到那位著名艺术家死于喉癌的消息时感到深深的悲痛。

late fee　滞纳金，过时附加费

☞ A temporary worker said Jack just had to pay a **late fee**. 一个临时工告诉杰克要交滞纳金。

🔍 相关短语：extra charge，意思是"额外费用"

lead a...life　过着…的生活

☞ At the end of every fairy tale, the prince and princess **lead a** happy **life** forever. 在每一个童话故事的结尾，王子和公主都永远过着幸福的生活。

☞ lead a life of ..., live a ... life

lead the way　带路，引路

☞ A: Tod, do you know how to get to the hotel?

B: Oh, my, I wish we had a guide to **lead the way**.

A：托德，你知道怎么去这个旅馆吗？

B：哦，天呐，真希望我们有个向导带路。

---

lead to 导致；通向

☞ Maybe the most ironic example of human behavior that can **lead to** desertification is irrigation. 也许在导致土地沙漠化的人类行为的例子中，最具讽刺意味的就是灌溉。

☞ For some students these part-time jobs could **lead to** full-time work after graduation as they may offer experience in their own fields, be that finance, marketing, or even management. 对于一些学生来说，这些兼职工作可以成为自己毕业后的正式工作，因为他们已经有了这些领域的相关经验，如金融、营销甚至是管理。

---

leading authority 权威人士

☞ One **leading authority** said that the mineral water was harmful to stomach. 一名权威人士说矿泉水对胃有害。

🔍 其他"权威"：

traditional authority 传统权威   legal authority 法律权威
medical authority 医学权威   access authority 访问权限
appropriate authority 有关当局   competent authority 主管当局

---

leave for 离开去(某地)；为…而离开

☞ A: The forecast calls for heavy snow again tonight. Aren't you glad we'll be getting away from this for a week?

B: I sure am. But let's call tomorrow morning before we **leave for** the airport to make sure our flight hasn't been delayed or canceled.

A：天气预报今晚又广播了大雪通知。我们将告别这糟糕的天气一个星期，你难道不高兴吗？

B：我当然高兴，但是我们明早去机场前，还是打个电话确认下飞机没有延时或取消吧。

☞ A: Since there was no final exam schedule, I thought I'd be able to **leave for** winter break a couple of days early.

B: But all presentations are taking a lot longer than Dr. Taylor expected, so he's going to hold class during exam week.

A：因为没有期末考试的日程安排，我想我可以早走几天过寒假了。

B：但是泰勒博士的所有讲座都比他预计的要长，所以他会在考试周内继续上课的。

🔍 注意 leave 后面可以直接加地点，leave somewhere 表示离开某地；leave for somewhere 表示要去某地。

leave over 剩下，留下，遗留

☞ A: You've made enough soup to feed an army.

B: This way we'll have plenty *left over* for lunch tomorrow.

A：你做的汤足够一支军队喝了。

B：这样我们就可以留着明天午饭时喝了。

lend sth. to 借…给

☞ A: I can't seem to find my calculator. Did I *lend to* you by any chance?

B: No, but you are welcome to mine if you need it, as long as I get it back by Thursday.

A：我似乎找不到我的计算器了，我有可能借给你了吗？

B：没有，但是如果你需要的话我可以借给你，只要在周四前还给我就行。

letter of recommendation/reference 推荐信

☞ I need to get a *letter of recommendation* from Prof. Jackson for graduate school. 我申请研究生院需要杰克逊教授的推荐信。

life image 生活映像

☞ This photo enlargement here is a *life image* of actual size space suit worn by astronaut on the last space shuttle mission. 这张放大的图片是上一次执行太空飞行任务的飞行员所穿太空服的实际大小的图像。

light up 放晴；点燃；照亮

☞ A: It's been hot and humid for three weeks straight. I wish it'd *light up*.

B: I love summer weather, but there is a limit.

A：接连三周天气都很潮湿炎热。我希望天可以变晴。

B：我喜欢夏天的天气，但也是有条件的。

light up

line up 排队，使排成一行

☞ A: Look at all those cars *lined up* for the ferry. There must be forty ahead of us.

B: Yeah. I think it's going to be a while.

A：看看那些排队等着渡船的车，我们前面得有 40 辆。

B：是啊，我想得等一会儿了。

linear algebra 线性代数

☞ A: Well, it looks like you are watching television. But we have a *linear algebra* mid-term tomorrow, so I thought you'd be studying for it and maybe I can study with you.

B: Oh, well, I was just taking a break. This linear algebra stuff gives me a headache if I work on it too long.

A：看起来你在看电视，但是我们明天有线性代数的期中考试，所以我觉得你应该学习了，而且我可以和你一起学。

B：嗯，好吧，我只是休息一下，如果我长时间看这些线性代数的问题，会感到头疼。

link to　与…联系，与…有关联

☞ One of the convenience of internet is that the network stations are *linked to* each other. 互联网的便利之一就是网站之间彼此有链接。

☞ connect to/with

literature class　文学课

☞ A: So we had better stop to read for a *literature class*. That novel the professor assigned us is so boring.

B: Really? I started it yesterday afternoon, and I couldn't put it down until I finished it.

A：我们最好停下来，去读文学课的文章，教授给我们布置的那部小说太无聊了。

B：是吗？我昨天下午开始读的，一直到读完才舍得放下它。

☞ A: You took the European *literature class* last year. Are you interested in selling me any of the books?

B: I always hold on to them for future reference.

A：你去年修了欧洲文学的课程，可以卖给我几本书吗？

B：我通常会留着这些书以备将来参考。

live on campus　住校

☞ A: I don't like *living on campus*. It's so boring.

B: You could move off next year.

A：我不喜欢住在学校，太无聊了。

B：你明年就可以搬出去了。

🔍 美国学校宿舍（dorm）的条件普遍都很好，有独立的卫浴（bathroom）、厨房（kitchen）、卧室（bedroom）等，但是价格比在外面合租要贵一些，所以很多学生更喜欢在校外租房。

liven up　（使）愉快；（使）有生气，（使）活跃起来

☞ A: You know Jean White, she teaches physics. She just told me about how she *livened up* her classes.

B: What did she do?

A: Well, basically, she takes something the students are interested in, like music, and tries to relate principal of science to that.

A：你知道琼·怀特吧，她是教物理的，她刚刚告诉我她是如何活跃课堂气氛的。

B：她是怎么做的？

A：嗯，基本上，她会介绍一些学生感兴趣的东西，就像音乐，然后试着把它们和科学原理联系起来。

☞ warm up

loan application　贷款申请

☞ A: Why are you going home to see your parents this weekend?

B: I need my dad's help to fill up this ***loan application***.

A：你这个周末为什么要回家看你的父母？

B：我需要我爸爸帮忙填写这个贷款申请。

local business executive　本地商务官员

☞ Facing the rising unemployment rate, those ***local business executives*** also suffered a lot. 面对不断上涨的失业率，本地的商务官员也很痛苦。

local dialect　方言

☞ Harriet Beecher Stowe was one of the first writers to use ***local dialect*** for her characters when they spoke. 哈丽雅特·比彻·斯托是第一批让小说里的人物用方言说话的作家之一。

🔍 语言（language）是总称，研究语言的学科称为语言学（linguistics），方言（dialect）是语言的变体，可以分为地域方言（territorial dialect）和社会方言（social dialect）。另外，手语是 sign language。

lock up　锁上，把…关起来

☞ Martin ***locked up*** the lab and went home. 马丁锁上实验室后回家了。

☞ coop up

lock up

lodge an application　提出申请

☞ Enterprises in this area could directly ***lodge an application*** to the local business executives. 这个地区的公司可以直接向当地商务官员提出申请。

☞ make an application

long distance calls　长途电话

☞ A: I cannot believe my phone bill this month; it's way too high.

B: Yeah, that happened to me a lot last year, but this year I have just tried to cut back on my ***long distance calls***.

A：我真不敢相信这个月的电话费会这么高。

B：嗯，去年我也经常发生这种情况，但是今年我努力削减了长途电话费。

146

☞ A: I want to pay you for that ***long distance call*** I made but I suppose you haven't got the phone bill yet.

B: Oh, but I have.

A：我想付给你上次我打长途电话的费用，但是我想你还没有电话缴费单吧。

B：哦，我拿到了。

look familiar　看起来眼熟

☞ A: That sweater is so unusual, and yet it ***looks familiar***. Did I just see you wearing it yesterday?

B: Well, not me. But—see, it belongs to my roommate Jill, and she is in your chemistry class.

A：那毛衣看起来很特别，而且很眼熟，我是不是昨天见你穿过?

B：哦，不是我。但是其实它是我室友吉尔的，她和你一起上化学课。

look forward to sth./doing　期盼

☞ A: Is your roommate ***looking forward to*** going home for the summer?

B: She is counting the days.

A：你的室友盼着暑假回家吗?

B：她正一天天地数日子呢。

☞ A: I'm really ***looking forward to*** this trip with our geology class. But I'm not certain I have the strength to carry a bag pack up and down the mountain, especially when it's full of tools.

B: They are taking two donkeys to carry the tools. We just have to carry our personal items, like clothing and sleeping bags.

A：我真的很期盼这次地理课的实地考察旅行，但是我不确定我是否有足够的力气背着满满一包工具上山下山。

B：他们用两头驴驮工具，我们只要拿着个人用品就行，比如衣服和睡袋。

look into　研究，调查；检查；窥视

☞ A: You could still apply for a student loan or sign up for a work-study program.

B: Yeah. I think I'll ***look into*** that.

A：你仍然可以申请学生贷款或者报名勤工俭学项目。

B：是的，我想我会考虑的。

☞ A: You know my car hasn't been the same since I bumped into that telephone toll.

B: You'd better to have that ***looked into*** before you drive to Florida.

A：自从我的车撞上了那个电话亭，就和以前不一样了。

B：你最好在开车去佛罗里达州之前，把车送去检查一下。

☞ investigate into

look over （从头至尾）详尽查阅；察看；（上下）打量

A: That was really nice of you to **look over** my application to graduate school. What did you think of my answer to that last question?

B: I think your statement is OK, but why do you mention only your course? It seems that you should also describe your work experience.

A：你能看我的研究生申请表真是太好了。你觉得我最后一个问题回答得怎么样？

B：我认为你的陈述还不错，但是你为什么只提到自己的课程？好像你也应该描述一下自己的工作经历。

🔍 注意 look 和 over 要连读。

loosen up 放松，松开

A: Don't you find Professor Johnson to be very intimidating? He seems so strict in class.

B: It might be early to tell. But I hear he usually **loosens up** by about middle terms.

A：你没发现约翰逊教授咄咄逼人吗？他在课堂上似乎太严肃了。

B：这结论下的有点早吧，我听说他通常到了学期中期就会放松的。

lose one's balance 失去平衡

A: Shirley, could you help me? I almost **lose my balance**.

B: Oh, why did you buy so much food?

A：雪莉，能帮我一下吗？我差点失去平衡。

B：哦，你怎么买这么多吃的呀？

lose one's head 不理智

A: I'm sorry Dick. I must **lost my head** to say such words to you.

B: Oh, come on, man, I even don't know what are you talking about.

A：对不起，迪克，我那时一定是失去理智了，才对你说那样的话。

B：哦，算了吧，伙计，我甚至都不知道你在讲什么。

🔍 反义词组：calm down（冷静）

lose one's temper 发怒，发脾气

A: Besty really **lost her temper** at that meeting. She's gonna have to learn to be a lot more diplomatic than that.

B: You are right, but you have to give a credit for taking a stand.

A：巴斯蒂在会议上真的失去控制了。她真得学着老练一些。

B：你是对的，但是她敢于表态，这一点也值得肯定。

lose one's temper

lose track of the time 忘记了时间

☞ A: Where have you been? We were supposed to meet at the library half an hour ago.

B: Yeah, I'm really sorry. I guess I just *lost track of the time*.

A：你去哪里了？我们应该半小时前在图书馆见面的。

B：是的，我真的很抱歉。我想我是忘记时间了。

☞ A: What happened? We were supposed to meet here at 5. I've been waiting for you almost 20 minutes.

B: Sorry. I was working all day for my history paper and I got to so wrapped up in the research that I completely *lost track of the time*.

A：怎么回事？我们应该五点在这见面的。我已经等你快 20 分钟了。

B：对不起。我一整天都在写历史论文，太专注于研究以至于把时间完全忘了。

☞ forget what time it is

🔍 track 的本意是"行踪，轨迹"，与 lose 搭配表示"脱离了…的轨迹"，因此有了引申的意思，如 lose track of sb.（与某人失去联系）、lose track of the money（数不清钱数）。

lost-and-found case 失物招领箱

☞ A: Excuse me. Could you tell me where the *lost-and-found case* is? I found a book in the dining hall.

B: It's downstairs, in front of the shop.

A：打扰一下，您能告诉我失物招领箱在哪里吗？我刚才在食堂捡了一本书。

B：在楼下，商店前面。

lost-and-found office 失物招领处

☞ A: David, I just picked up a wallet, but there isn't an ID card.

B: Why don't you send it to the *lost-and-found office*?

A：戴维，我刚刚捡到一个钱包，可是里面没有身份证。

B：你为什么不把它送到失物招领处呢？

lunar calendar 阴历

☞ Chinese traditional Spring Festival is from Chinese *lunar calendar*. 中国传统的春节是按中国阴历来计算的。

🔍 世界通用的公历，我们称为阳历，是 solar calendar。

lunar eclipse 月食

☞ It was reported that there would be a *lunar eclipse* tomorrow evening. 据报道，明天晚上会有月食。

🔍 相关天文现象：

solar eclipse 日食

partial solar eclipse 日偏食

meteor shower 流星雨

annular eclipse 日环食

transit 凌日

lunar month 阴历的一个月，太阴月

☞ The 15th day of the 1st *lunar month* is the Chinese Lantern Festival. 阴历一月的第15天是中国的元宵节。

🔍 "阳历"和"阴历"分别表达为：solar calendar 和 lunar calendar。

magnetic field 磁场

☞ To understand the cause of auroras, first picture the Earth enclosed by its magnetosphere, a huge region created by the Earth's *magnetic field*. 要想理解极光产生的原因，就要先看一下地球周围围绕的磁气圈，磁气圈是由地球磁场产生的一个巨大区域。

🔍 托福考试中与"磁"有关系的表达：

magnetic pole 磁极

magnetic line 磁力线

magnetic storm 磁暴

magnitude energy 震级能量；巨大能量

☞ The earthquake released the *magnitude energy* equivalent to a nuclear bomb's energy. 这场地震释放的震级能量相当于一颗原子弹爆炸的能量。

mail carrier 邮差

☞ A: I wish I didn't have to make a special trip to the post office to get my package.

B: Well, if you call them in the morning, they'll give your package to your *mail carrier* to bring out to you.

A：我真希望自己不用特意跑一趟邮局去取包裹。

B：嗯，如果你早晨给他们打电话，他们会让邮差把包裹送给你的。

mail carrier

main office 总公司(社、行、局、店等)办公处

☞ A: I need you to send this package to the *main office* so it'll arrive before Wednesday's meeting.

B: Is there anyone else who can do it? It's going to take me an afternoon to prepare this report.

A：我需要你把这个包裹送到总公司，这样它会在周三会议前到达。

B：还有别人能做这件事吗？准备这个报告还需要花我一下午的时间。

maintain balance 保持平衡

☞ People in that area had figured that there must be a cave nearby, because of the strong wind that blew from behind the huge rock that covered the entrance. Enormous amounts of air enter and exit the cave in order to *maintain balance* of the pressure with the other side air. 那个地区的人们认为附近一定有一个洞穴，因为堵住入口的大石头后面有强烈的风吹出来。大量空气进出洞穴，这样就能够和另一边保持气压的平衡。

maintain the integrity 保持…的完善；保持…的公正

☞ When people cheat, no one wins. Every student should try their best to *maintain the integrity* of the exams. 当有人作弊时，无所谓谁赢。每个学生都应该尽自己的最大努力来保持考试的公正性。

maintenance crew/man/staff 维修人员

☞ I'll be passing out a form for you to fill out concerning the condition of your room. You should report on the form any damage to your room which has occurred over the last year, such as holes in the room's walls, door or windows. That way, our summer *maintenance crew* will know where to make repairs before the next school year starts. 我会让你们填一张关于宿舍条件的表格，你们要在上面写下过去一年宿舍里面损坏的东西，比如墙上、门上或窗户上的洞。这样，我们的暑期维修人员就可以知道在明年开学前需要修理哪些地方了。

major in 主修，专攻

☞ A: I just heard about your acceptance into law college. Do you think you will be able to join your brother's firm when you graduate?

B: Not likely. He is a tax lawyer and I'm going to *major in* criminal law.

A：我刚刚听说你被法律学院录取了。你觉得毕业后你能加入你哥哥的公司吗？

B：不太可能，他是税务律师，而我将主修刑法。

Unit 13

make a buck 挣钱

☞ It is really a good way to **make a buck** and become famous by showing on the Internet for an ordinary people. 在网上展示自己，对于一个普通人来说是个赚钱和出名的好途径。

☞ Mark is always looking for ways to **make a** fast **buck**. His laziness and greed will soon make trouble for him. 马克总是在找可以大捞一笔的途径。他的懒惰和贪婪一定会让他惹上麻烦的。

make a call to 给···打电话

☞ A: I just realize my telephone isn't working and I'm just expecting for an important phone call in a few minutes.

B: Well, you can use my phone to **make a call to** the phone company, but it looks like there's not much that can be done about the one you're expecting.

A：我刚刚才发现我的电话坏了，我正在等一个重要电话，几分钟后就打进来。

B：哦，你可以用我的电话打给电话公司，但是这好像解决不了你眼前等电话的问题。

☞ call up, ring up, telephone

make a comment 发表评论

☞ The artist **made a comment** about the student's plagiarizing of the passage. 那个艺术家对于学生剽窃文章的事发表了评论。

🔍 make no comment 表示"不予评论，没有评论"。

make a difference/distinction 区分

☞ A: Oh, can you **make a distinction** between personal information and private information? How can you tell others about this?

B: I'm sorry. I must have copied a wrong page.

A：哦，你能分清个人信息和私人信息吗？你怎么能把这个告诉其他人呢？

B：对不起，我一定是复印错了。

🔍 注意 make a difference 还有"有影响，起重要作用"的意思，如 The sea air has made a difference to her health. 海上的空气改善了她的健康状况。

make a mess of　扰乱

make a mess of

☞ A: Larry certainly *made a mess of* that plain job.

B: Don't be too hard on him. He was only trying to help.

A：拉里把那个简单的工作弄得一团糟。

B：别对他太苛刻，他也只是想帮忙而已。

make a reservation　预约

☞ A: I'm afraid this is the only room in the hotel we have free at this time. Sir, we weren't expecting you.

B: Oh, dear. I guess I'll take what I can get. Next time I'll be sure to call in advance and *make a reservation*.

A：恐怕这是我们宾馆现在唯一一间空房了。我们没想到您会来，先生。

B：哦，天啊，随便给我一间吧。下次我肯定会打电话提前预订的。

☞ book, reserve

make a trade　做交易

☞ We should know clearly about the rules before *making a trade*. 做交易前，我们要了解清楚规则。

make a trip　旅行

☞ A: We are going to *make a trip* to Italy this summer. Would you like to join us?

B: I can't wait for it.

A：我们这个暑假要去意大利旅行，你想加入我们吗？

B：我都等不及了。

☞ take a trip

🔍 托福中还常考到 plan a trip，意为"计划一次旅行"。

make heads or tails of　弄清楚

☞ I couldn't *make heads or tails of* the memo myself. 我自己都弄不清楚这个备忘录。

make it　成功

☞ A: The subway is running behind schedule, and traffic is backed up for blocks. I don't know if we'll make the 7:15 show.

B: It's a beautiful night. Let's try to get there on foot. And if we don't *make it*, let's just have dinner near the theater.

A：地铁晚点了，而且好几个街区都在堵车。我不知道我们能否赶上 7 点 15 的表演。

B：今天夜景很美，我们走着去吧。如果没赶上，我们就在剧院附近吃晚餐吧。

☞ A: I'm having a few friends over for a lunch tomorrow. It'll be great if you can join us.

B: I doubt I'll be able to *make it*. My brother is leaving for Chicago tomorrow afternoon, and I promised to give him a ride to the airport.

A：明天我有几个朋友要过来吃午饭。如果你能和我们一起就太好了。

B：我怕我去不了。我哥哥 / 弟弟明天下午去芝加哥。我答应开车送他去机场。

> make it 在英美人的口语中出现频率很高，它可以用来表示"某人在某个方面取得成功"、"做成某事"、"赶得上火车、汽车等"、"约定时间"及"病情好转"等含义。

make sb. alert 使…清醒，使…精神

A: I can't concentrate on this final report any longer. Maybe I should take a nap before we continue.

B: You know they say the physical activity *makes you* more *alert*.

A：我无法专心做这份期末报告了。或许我应该小憩一会儿我们再继续。

B：有人说运动可以使人精神点。

make sb. drowsy 使某人昏昏欲睡

A: We need to drive to the city tonight. But the doctor said this medicine might *make me drowsy*.

B: In that case, I'd better drive.

A：我们今晚要到那个城市，但是医生说那个药可能会让我犯困。

B：那样的话，还是我来开车吧。

make sb. feel better 使某人感觉好一点

I wonder if using some kind of eye-drops will *make office workers feel better*. 我在想用滴眼液是否会使办公室人员感觉好一点。

A: I'm really disappointed about not getting that job.

B: An evening at the jazz club ought to *make you feel better*.

A：没有得到那份工作真令我失望。

B：晚上去爵士俱乐部吧，那会让你感觉好点儿。

make sense 有意义；讲得通，合情合理

Sodium bulbs might *make sense* for highway, if they really do improve visibility so much. 如果钠灯真的能大幅提高可见度，在公路上使用就很有意义了。

> make sense of 意为"理解，弄懂"。

make sth. clear 使…清晰

The dancers want to *make it clear* to their audience that they are not performing any dances used for secret ceremonies. 舞蹈家想让观众明白，他们表演的舞蹈并不用于任何秘密的仪式。

The Law *makes it clear* that when someone buys the work of art, they are not allowed to destroy or change that work of art. 法律清楚地规定，购买艺术品后，不能对该艺术品进行破坏或修改。

manage to 设法做到

☞ A: Your cousins just called; they're stranded at the beach.

B: So they didn't **manage to** get a lift after all.

A：你堂(或表)兄弟／姐妹刚刚来电话说他们被困在海滩上了。

B：这就是说他们根本没搭到便车。

☞ A: How did you ever **manage to** get through all 1000 pages of that new spy thriller?

B: It took a while. But once I had started it, I couldn't put it down.

A：你怎么读完那部新的、关于间谍的 1000 页恐怖小说的？

B：花了我一段时间。但是我一开始读，就对它爱不释手了。

managerial expertise 管理知识，管理经验

☞ At the beginning of the reformation and opening-up, Chinese only learned **managerial expertise** from the foreign companies. But now we've developed our own ways. 在改革开放初期，中国人只能从外国公司学习管理经验，但是现在我们已经可以发展自己的管理模式。

manifestation of …的显示，…的表现

☞ Stammer is a **manifestation of** being nervous. 结巴是紧张的表现。

manipulate sb. into （doing）sth. 操纵某人做某事

☞ The politician **manipulated** the officials **into** changing the result of election. 那个政客操纵政府人员，改变了竞选结果。

marine animal 海洋动物

☞ Different to the conventional viewpoints, the ocean is not the place where **marine animals** spend the majority of their lives. 和传统的观点不一样，海洋动物的大部分生活不是在海洋中度过的。

marketing research 市场调查

☞ The sales manager is going to do a **marketing research**. 销售经理打算做一次市场调查。

material benefit 物质利益

☞ The economic globalization really brought consumers more and more **material benefit**. 经济全球化确实为消费者带来了越来越多的物质利益。

🔍 其他"利益"：

mutual benefit 互惠互利

fringe benefit 福利，补贴

economic benefit 经济利益

accident benefit 意外保险金

material management 物资管理

☞ The government has taken effective measures to strengthen the railway *material management*. 政府已采取有效措施来加强铁路物资管理。

meal card 饭卡

☞ John borrowed his friend's *meal card* yesterday. 约翰昨天借了他朋友的饭卡。

mean to 打算做，故意做

☞ I didn't *mean to* cause you so much trouble. 我并不是故意要给你找那么多麻烦的。

☞ A: I wish I hadn't hurt Mary's feelings like that. You know I never *meant to*.

  B: The great thing about Mary is that she doesn't hold the grudge. By tomorrow she'll have forgotten all about it.

  A：我真希望没有伤害到玛丽。你知道我是无心的。

  B：玛丽的优点就是不记仇。到明天她就会当什么事也没发生过。

☞ intend to, be going to

medicine cabinet 药柜

☞ There should be a home *medicine cabinet* in the corner of the house. 在房间的角落里应该有一个药柜。

medicine cabinet

meet the deadline 赶在截止日期前

☞ A: I tentatively scheduled the meeting on Thursday to go over your inventory report, assuming you can *meet the deadline*.

  B: Well, to be honest, even Friday might be pushing a little.

  A：我暂时把会议定在周四，到时候我会看你的存货报告单，如果你能在这个截止日期前完成的话。

  B：嗯，说实在的，即使是周五，时间都有些紧张。

🔍反义词组：miss the deadline(错过了截止日期)

meet the standard 达到标准

☞ California is a huge market for the automobile companies. So they are working hard to *meet the standard* which indicates that the cars must put no pollutants whatsoever into the atmosphere. 加利福尼亚州对于汽车公司来说是一个庞大的市场。所以他们一直在努力使自己的汽车达标，即不能向大气排放任何污染物。

melting point 熔点

☞ Products with low *melting point* may not be stable in the summer or in hot climates. 低熔点的物品在夏季或高温条件下会不稳定。

mental faculty   智力

☞ Playing with the babies and buying suitable toys for them are good ways to develop their *mental faculty*. 与孩子一起玩以及给他们买合适的玩具是开发他们智力的好方法。

☞ intellectual faculty

mention sth.   提到某事物

☞ Before we start our lesson, I'd like to *mention* a few things your text doesn't go into. 讲课之前，我想提几点课本上没有涉及的内容。

☞ As you may recall, last time I mentioned that Robert E. Peary was the first person to reach the North Pole. What I neglected to *mention* was the controversy around peary's pioneering accomplishments. 你们可能还记得，上次我提到罗伯特·E·皮尔里是第一个到达北极的人。但是我忘记讲一点，关于皮尔里的先驱性成就存在着争议。

☞ A: That was really nice of you to look over my application to graduate school. What did you think of my answer to that last question? You know, where I have to state my career goals and how I've been working towards them the past few years.

B: I think your statement is OK. But why do you *mention* only your course? It seems that you should also describe your work experience.

A：你能看我的研究生申请表真是太好了。你觉得我最后一个问题回答得怎么样？关于我的职业目标是什么以及在过去几年中我是如何朝着那个方向努力的。

B：我认为你的陈述还不错，但是你为什么只提到自己的课程？好像你也应该描述一下自己的工作经历。

metal detector   金属探测器

☞ Scientists make use of *metal detectors* to detect the metal. 科学家们使用金属探测器来探测金属。

metal-frame construction   金属框架建筑

☞ Chicago's Reliance Building was another important building in the development of the skyscraper. It showed the architects' understanding of the possibilities of *metal-frame construction*. 芝加哥的雷恩莱斯大楼是摩天大楼发展中的另一个重要建筑，它体现了建筑师对于采用金属框架建筑的可能性的理解。

meteorological data   气象数据，气象资料

☞ The scientists invented a new device to gather the *meteorological data*. 科学家发明了一种新的装置来搜集气象数据。

meteorological instrument 气象仪器

☞ The heavy snow made the *meteorological instrument* not work, and it still needs an extra week to mend it. 大雪使得气象仪器无法工作，而且还需要一周的时间来修理。

metric ruler 米尺

☞ A: I sure wish I had a *metric ruler* with me. I need the measurements in millimeters, not in inches and I'm tired of converting.

B: Would it make things go faster if you borrowed mine?

A：我真希望有一把米尺，我需要以毫米为单位测量，而不是以英寸。我真是烦透了单位转换。

B：用我的尺子会不会快一点呢？

mild asthma 轻度哮喘

☞ If a camper in your group has even a *mild asthma*, you would be informed and given further instruction about what to do in case of an attack. 如果你们组里有野营队员患轻度哮喘，你会被告知，而且会获得详细的说明该怎么做，以防病情突发。

🔍 其他病情：

heart disease 心脏病	rheumatism 风湿
measles 麻疹	mumps 腮腺炎

mix...with 将…与…混合

mix with

☞ To start our experiment, we should use the special liquid *mixed with* water first. 要做实验，我们首先要用这种与水混合的特殊液体。

modern poetry 现代诗

☞ It's important to read the assigned poems aloud, so you can develop an appreciation of the sounds of the poetry: the rhymes, the rhythm, the repetition of words or sounds, and to get a sense of the interplay between the sounds of the words and their meaning. This is really critical as we move into *modern poetry*. 大声朗读所指定的诗是很重要的，这样可以培养你对诗歌音律的鉴赏力，比如：韵、节奏、词和音节的重复，同时对单词的读音与其意义间的相互作用有所感知。这对我们进入现代诗部分的学习非常重要。

monopolistic competition 垄断竞争

☞ The multinational company is operated under *monopolistic competition*. 这家跨国公司处垄断竞争操纵之下。

🔍 "贸易"相关短语：free trade 自由贸易，free market 自由市场

158

more likely 很有可能

☞ We'll be *more likely* to feel a need to explain the causes of the behavior. 我们觉得很有必要解释一下这些行为的原因。

motion picture 电影

☞ You see the relationship between different media is not always one of displacement, but can be one of reinforcement. However, this is not always the case. Take television and *motion pictures* for example, with the popularization of TV, the motion picture industry suffered greatly. 你们看到了，不同媒介间的关系并不总是互相取代的，也可以是互相促进的。但也并不总是这种情况。就拿电视和电影来举例吧，在电视越来越流行的情况下，电影业处境异常艰难。

motivation for doing sth. 做某事的动机

☞ I'm going to introduce two current points of view about the *motivation for* writing. 我要介绍一下关于写作动机的两个现代观点。

Mount Everest 珠穆朗玛峰

☞ Not long ago, some of you may have read about the team of mountain climbing scientists who helped to recalculate the elevation of the highest mountain in the world, *Mount Everest*. 你们中的一些人可能已经通过阅读得知，不久前，登山科学队重新测量了世界最高峰珠穆朗玛峰的海拔。

mount the steps 登上台阶

☞ A: Jerry, come on. We are going to reach the mountaintop.

B: Oh, I'm too tired to *mount these steps*.

A：杰里，加油，我们马上就到山顶了。

B：哦，我太累了，爬不动了。

mount the steps

mountain climbing 爬山运动

☞ A: Would you like to go *mountain climbing* with us?

B: That's the last thing in the world I'd ever want to do.

A：你愿意和我们一起去爬山吗？

B：我最不想做的事就是爬山。

move away 离去，搬家；改变原来的想法

☞ Andrew is glad he *moved away* from the airport. 安德鲁非常高兴自己搬离了机场。

move back 往后退；把…往后移；搬回原来住的地方

☞ A: Are these seats all right with you or would you like to *move back*?

B: I don't really like sitting so close.

A：这些位子行吗？还是你想到后面坐？

B：我真的不喜欢坐这么近。

move into 搬入

☞ A: I'm always late for my morning classes. It's because of all the traffic out near where I live.

B: Well, you wouldn't have that problem if you **move into** our campus.

A：我早晨上课总是迟到，因为我住的地方附近交通堵塞。

B：嗯，如果你搬入学校住，就不会有这种问题了。

☞ A: My cousin Lisa said she mailed me some books. But they never came.

B: Well, you just **moved into** a new dormitory. She probably sent them out before she had your new address.

A：我的堂(或表)姐/妹莉萨说她给我寄了一些书。我却没收到。

B：嗯，你刚搬入新宿舍。她可能不知道你的新地址就把书寄出了。

🔍 反义词组：move off（搬离某地）

move off 离去，出发

☞ Seeing that we had noticed her, the little girl **moved off** at once. 那个小女孩一看到我们注意到她就马上走掉了。

move to 移到，搬到

☞ A: Gee, it keeps raining like this. They'll probably cancel the play tonight.

B: Yeah, too bad they can't **move to** an indoor stage.

A：哎，像这样一直下雨，他们可能要取消今晚的演出了。

B：是啊，他们不能搬到室内的舞台上演，太糟糕了。

🔍 托福中还经常考到 move on to，意为"进一步做…"。

move up 上移；(使)升级，提升

☞ It's interesting that the actor's one eyebrow **move up** and not the other. 有趣的是那个演员的眉毛一边向上挑起，另一边却没有。

movie critic 影评人

☞ Some performers think that earning money is more important than being praised by the **movie critics**. 一些表演者认为挣钱比让影评人称赞更重要。

muscular cell 肌细胞

☞ A: Jenny, I don't quite understand the chapter of **Muscular Cell**.

B: Well. Let's go to the professor's office together.

A：珍妮，我不太明白"肌细胞"那一章。

B：嗯，我们一起去教授的办公室吧。

muscular dystrophy 肌肉萎缩症

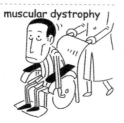

muscular dystrophy

☞ A: I'm sorry to say that you may get the *muscular dystrophy*. It may be inherited from your parents.

B: What? But my mother has never told me about that.

A：很抱歉，你可能是患了肌肉萎缩症，可能是从你父母那里遗传的。

B：什么？我妈妈从没跟我说过。

muscular tissue 肌肉组织

☞ The relaxation of *muscular tissue* is very necessary after the intense exercises. 剧烈运动后，让肌肉组织放松是非常必要的。

🔍 相关词组：

muscular system 肌肉系统　　　　circulatory system 循环系统
respiratory system 呼吸系统

mythical figure 神话般的人物

☞ History is full of people who were so admired that over the centuries they become almost *mythical figures*. 历史上有很多这样的人物，他们一直深受爱戴，几个世纪过后几乎成为神话般的人物。

narrow down 使缩小；使变窄

☞ A: You are on the right track. I just think you need to *narrow* the topic *down*.

B: Yeah. You are right. I always choose these broad areas when I'm doing a research paper.

A：你的思路是对的。我只是认为你需要缩小话题范围。

B：是，你说得对。我在写研究论文时总是容易选些宽泛的领域。

nasal asthma 鼻性哮喘

☞ A: Can you make a distinction between *nasal asthma* and asthma?

B: Your guess is as good as mine.

A：你能分清鼻性哮喘和哮喘吗？

B：我也分不清。

native plants 本土植物

☞ The research shows that some *native plants* can cure stomachache. 研究表明一些本土植物可以治疗胃痛。

natural habitat 自然栖息地

☞ The modernization of the buildings is achieved by invading the *natural habitat*. 建筑物的现代化是通过入侵自然栖息地实现的。

natural sight　自然景观

☞ Tourists were deeply impressed by the ***natural sight*** of the Great Canyon. 大峡谷的自然风光给游客们留下了深刻的印象。

🔍 和"旅游"相关的重要短语有：travel agency 旅行社，place of interests 名胜。

nearly perfect　近乎完美

☞ A: Congratulations! I heard about your new job.

　B: Thanks. ***Nearly perfect*** for me. It's really interesting. The hours are ideal and it's an easy walk from home.

　A：祝贺你！我听说了关于你新工作的事情。

　B：谢谢。这工作对我来说近乎完美。工作很有意思，工作时间也合理，并且离家很近。

negative consequence　负面结果

☞ When the reason of doing things is obvious, we usually don't question it. But when the reason is not so obvious and especially when the behavior could have ***negative consequences***, we are more likely to feel a need to explain the causes of the behavior. 当做事的理由很明显时，我们通常不会质疑。但是当原因不明显，特别是当行为会产生负面结果时，我们就更可能需要对该行为的原因作出解释。

☞ negative result

neither of　任何一个也不

☞ If these nutrients in the soil don't get replaced, the damaged soil stops producing ***neither of*** these two crops. 如果土壤中的营养物质没有得到更新，遭到破坏的土壤就不能种植这两种庄稼。

🔍 反义词组：both of（两者都）

nerve cell　神经细胞

☞ The medicine will do harm to ***nerve cells***. 这种药物对神经细胞有害。

neural transmitter　神经递质

☞ This special ***neural transmitter*** will help you relax, and you'll be on the way to get a good night's sleep. 这种特殊的神经递质会帮助你放松，并让你睡个好觉。

new around here　新来的

☞ A: Excuse me, could you tell me how to get to the post office?

　B: Your guess is as good as mine. I'm ***new around here***.

　A：打扰一下，您能告诉我怎么去邮局吗？

　B：我也不知道，我也刚来这儿。

☞ newcomer

new generation 新一代

☞ A: Why can't the procedure be worked in the computer?

B: You could try on Phil's. His is the *new generation*.

A：为什么这个程序在电脑上运行不了呢？

B：你可以在菲尔的电脑上试试，他的电脑是最新版的。

🔍在托福考试中，该词组还常用来指人或物种的新一代，考生要根据全文把握其含义。

NOTES

Unit 14

new type of fuel 新型燃料

☞ A: I have the flu. I was wondering if you could tell me what went on.

B: Actually we had an interesting class. Dr. Collin talked about a *new type of fuel*.

A: Oh, yeah?

B: Uh-hum. It's called dimethyl-ether of DME.

A：我感冒了，你能告诉我今天的课都讲什么了吗？

B：事实上我们上了一堂很有趣的课，科林博士讲了一种新型燃料。

A：哦，是吗？

B：嗯，燃料叫二甲醚。

news item 新闻条目

☞ Franklin wanted a paper that entertained the people with humors and critical *news items*. 富兰克林想办一份用幽默和批判性新闻来娱乐大众的报纸。

no kidding 不是开玩笑吧

☞ A: Professor Burns seems to think there is only one way to write paper and that's her way.

B: *No kidding*; she sure wasn't like that the last semester.

A：伯恩斯教授似乎认为写论文只有一种方式，那就是按她的方式写。

B：不是开玩笑吧。她上学期就不是这样的。

no longer 不再

☞ Dr. Parker is *no longer* teaching history. 帕克博士不再教历史了。

☞ A: So, you and Julia are *no longer* roommates. I'm not surprised. You two never did things very compatible.

B: Yeah, well... It's not that we didn't get along... We just didn't have much in common.

A：你和朱莉娅不再是室友了。我一点都不惊讶，你们两个做事从来没一致过。

B：是啊，嗯…也不是我们相处不好…只是我们的共同点太少了。

☞ not any longer

no wonder 不奇怪，难怪，怪不得

☞ A: You are looking a little overwhelmed.

B: *No wonder*. I got a million things to do and all of them have to be finished in the next twenty minutes.

A：你看起来有点疲惫。

B：这不奇怪，我有很多事情要做，而且所有的事情都要在接下来的 20 分钟内完成。

☞ A: Can you believe the way Larry was talking to his roommate? *No wonder* they don't get along.

B: Well, maybe Larry was just reacting to something his roommate said. There are two sides to every story you know.

A：你能相信拉里和他室友说话的方式吗？怪不得他们相处不好了。

B：嗯，或许这只是拉里对他室友所说的话的回应。你知道的，万事都有两方面。

☞ not surprising

nocturnal creature/animal　夜行生物

☞ Bats and owls classified as *nocturnal creature* only come out at night. 蝙蝠和猫头鹰属于夜行动物，它们只有晚上才出来活动。

nocturnal creature

nominate for　提名，推荐

☞ A: Did you have heard Carl being *nominated for* mayor?

B: Yes, it really floored me.

A：你听说卡尔被提名为市长了吗？

B：是的，这真让我吃惊不已。

☞ A: Guess what? I just *nominated* you *for* this year's class treasurer.

B: Oh, no, Sally, you didn't.

A：猜猜怎样？我刚刚推荐你为今年的班级财务委员。

B：哦，不，萨莉，你不会吧。

☞ recommend

North Pole　北极

☞ As you may recall, last time I mentioned that Robert E. Peary was the first person to reach the *North Pole*. What I neglected to mention was the controversy around Peary's pioneering accomplishment. 你们可能还记得，上次我提到罗伯特·E·皮尔里是第一个到达北极的人。但是我忘记讲一点，关于皮尔里的先驱性成就存在着争议。

🔍 与极地相关的词组：

polar aurora 极光

penguin 企鹅

polar night 极夜

polar bear 北极熊

polar day 极昼

not on your life 绝对不行

☞ A: There's a group of us going skiing this weekend. Are you interested?

B: *Not on your life*. Don't you remember that trip to Mountain Hope, when I went up to the cast for two months?

A：我们一群人周末要去滑雪，你感兴趣吗？

B：绝对不行。难道你忘了去希望山的那次旅行了吗，就是我去拍两个月戏的那次。

☞ absolutely not

not only... but (also)... 不但…而且…

☞ They missed *not only* the first train *but* the second one as well. 他们不仅错过了第一班火车，而且也错过了第二班。

☞ *Not only* can you look at some of the more unusual stamps issue *but* there's an interesting exhibit on how stamps are made. 你不仅可以看到一些更稀有的邮票，而且还会有一个关于邮票是如何制作的有趣展览。

🔍 以否定词或否定副词开头的句子要进行部分倒装，这些词有 not only, not until, no sooner... than, hardly, scarcely 等。在听力中出现时要多加注意，否则会影响对句子的理解。

notify sb. of sth. 通知某人某事

☞ We also need someone to *notify* the owners *of* the beach to leave their yard for the next couple of weeks. 我们还需要有人去通知海滩的所有者，在接下来的几个星期，把他们的庭院留给我们。

☞ inform sb. of sth.

🔍 该词组还可以变形为 notify sth. to sb.。

object to 反对

☞ Some parents *object to* the teaching of penmanship. 一些家长反对教授书法。

☞ be opposed to

occupy one's time 占用…的时间，打发时间

☞ A: You waited at the Tera's Cafe yesterday, didn't you? Was there much of a wait to be seated?

B: Was there? Wish I'd brought a book or something to *occupy my time*.

A：你昨天在泰瑞咖啡店排队等位了，是吗？要等很长时间才有座吗？

B：有座？我真希望我带了书或其他什么东西可以打发时间。

🔍 "打发时间"还可以有另一个表达 kill the time。

ocean plant 海洋植物

☞ There are a variety of *ocean plants* and animals. 海洋中动植物的种类繁多。

☞ marine plant

ocean plant

odd job 临时工作，零工，零活儿

☞ A: I haven't got a job yet. The ads on the newspaper are all about the *odd jobs*.

B: Take it easy. Rome can't be built in a day.

A：我还没找到工作呢，报纸上的广告都是招零工的。

B：放轻松点，罗马不是一天建成的。

🔍 注意区分该词组与 part-time job 的区别，odd job 是指杂工、零工，而 part-time job 是指利用业余时间做的兼职。

of course 当然，自然，无疑

☞ A: Excuse me, Professor Brown, but I'm still confused. Could you go over that last point one more time?

B: *Of course*, that's what I'm here for.

A：打扰了，布朗教授，我还是有些疑问。您能把最后一个知识点再讲一遍吗？

B：当然可以，这就是我在这里的原因。

☞ A: Jack, I'm so sorry. I don't know what I did with your dictionary. *Of course*, I'll buy you a new one.

B: Don't be silly. I've had that ragged old thing since junior high school and I hardly ever use it anyway.

A：杰克，真对不起，我不知道我都对你的字典做了什么。当然，我会再给你买本新的。

B：别傻了，那本破字典我从初中时就在用，现在几乎都不用了。

off and on 断断续续，不时地

☞ A: It rains *off and on* since yesterday.

B: Too bad. I thought to go picnic with you today.

A：从昨天就开始断断续续地下雨。

B：太糟糕了，我还想今天跟你去野餐呢。

off campus 校外

☞ If you've made plans to live *off campus*, you don't need to enter the lottery at all. 如果你已经打算在校外住了，就根本不必去抽号。

☞ A: Will you be living in the dormitory this year?

B: Maybe not. I've been thinking of renting an apartment *off campus* with some friends of mine.

A：你今年住宿舍吗？

B：可能不住。我一直考虑和一些朋友在校外租公寓。

☞ It's really tough getting around without a car when you live *off campus*. 住在校外要是没车的话真的很不方便。

☞ A: Have you guys decided whether you are going to get an apartment *off campus* next year or are you staying in the dorm?

B: We are still talking about the pros and cons.

A：你们决定明年到校外租公寓还是继续住校内宿舍了吗？

B：我们仍在权衡利弊。

☞ A: Hey, did you hear that they're going to raise the dorm fees again.

B: Really? Am I glad I decide to move *off campus*?

A：嗨，你听说宿舍费又要涨了吗？

B：真的吗？那我是不是应该为决定要搬出学校而感到高兴呢？

🔍 "校内"在英语中是 on campus，考生要多注意。

off hand 立刻，当即

☞ A: I don't remember the assignment *off hand*, but I've got it written down at home. How about if I call you tonight?

B: If you call before nine, just leave a message with my roommate.

A：我一时想不起作业了，但是我把它记下来放在家里了。今晚给你打电话怎么样？

B：如果你在九点前打，就给我室友留个口信吧。

off the mark 不相关，不切题，不准确

☞ A: Weren't you the person who said that not many students would sigh up for the talent show?

B: Yeah, I was really *off the mark* on that prediction.

A：难道你不是那个称不会有太多学生报名参加才艺表演的人吗？

B：是呀，我的预测真是错了。

☞ A: Didn't the committee say it would only take a month for them to complete the report? It took at least twice that long.

B: Yeah, there must be with way *off the mark*.

A：委员会不是说他们完成报告只需要一个月的时间吗？结果他们至少用了两个月。

B：是啊，一定是弄错了。

🔍 反义词组：to the point（切题，切中要害）

offer sth. to sb.　向某人提供某物

☞ A: It is said that the new French restaurant *offer* juice free to customers these three days.

B: Sorry. But I am going to see my parents later.

A：据说那家新开的法国餐厅这三天免费为顾客提供果汁。

B：对不起，我一会儿要去看我的父母。

☞ provide sth. to sb.

🔍 该词组还可以变形为 offer sb. sth.。

offer/give a discount　打折

☞ A: The supermall will *give a discount* during the holiday.

B: How about going there tomorrow?

A：那个商场在假日期间打折。

B：我们明天去怎么样?

official copy　正式副本

☞ A: You know that summer internship I applied for. They want an *official copy* of all my grades. But the records office charges 20 dollars for an official grade report. That's a lot, don't you think?

B: It really is. I only had to pay six for mine last year.

A：你知道我申请了那份暑假实习工作，他们想要一份我所有成绩的正式副本。但是档案处出具这样一份成绩单居然要收 20 美元。太贵了，你觉得呢?

B：确实是啊，去年我只花了六美元。

omit doing/to do　忘记做

☞ A: Don't *omit* locking the door when you go out.

B: It won't happen again.

A：你出去的时候别忘了锁门。

B：不会再发生那种事了。

on edge　紧张

☞ A: You seem *on edge* this morning.

B: I have to give a presentation in class this afternoon.

A：你今早看起来很紧张。

B：我今天下午要在课堂上做陈述。

☞ nervous

on edge

on good terms　相处得很好; 保持联系

☞ A: Do you know Sally's new address? She got some mail and I'd like to forward it to her.

B: Sorry, we weren't exactly *on good terms* when she left.

A：你知道萨莉的新地址吗？她有一些邮件，我得转寄给她。

B：对不起，事实上她走了之后我们就没再来往。

☞ get along well

---

on hold 暂停，搁置

☞ A: Thank goodness. Spring break starts next week. Are you doing anything special?

B: I have been planning to go to Florida with a friend of mine. But since she's backed out, everything's sort of *on hold*.

A：谢天谢地，春季假期下周就开始了。你有什么特别的事情要做吗？

B：我原打算和一位朋友去佛罗里达的。但是她不去了，所以一切就搁置了下来。

---

on one's way to 在某人去…的路上

☞ A: I hear you got lost *on your way to* the meeting at the hotel.

B: I don't know how I did it. I have been there a million times.

A：我听说你在去宾馆开会的途中迷路了。

B：不知道怎么搞的，我去过那儿无数次了。

---

on prescription 凭处方，根据药方

☞ The medication is only available *on prescription* from the doctor. 这些药只能凭医生开的处方来买。

---

on purpose 故意地

☞ If I imagined even for a minute, I would do a thing like that *on purpose*. 如果我再多想一分钟的话，就会故意做出那样的事。

☞ by intention

---

on schedule 按预定时间，及时，准时

☞ A: I've got to leave for the airport right away. Bill's plane is due in an hour.

B: Judging by the weather outside, I doubt that the plane will land *on schedule*.

A：我要马上去机场，比尔的飞机一小时后就到了。

B：看看外面的天气，我怀疑飞机能否按时着陆。

🔍 注意 schedule 的发音，英式发音是['ʃedjuːl]，美式发音是['ˌskedʒuːl]。

---

on the edge of 在…的边缘；濒于，快要，将近

☞ A: Who put the glass *on the edge of* the table? I almost broke it.

B: Oh, sorry, I drank some water just now.

A：谁把这个玻璃杯放在桌子边上的？我差点把它打破了。

B：哦，对不起，我刚才喝了点水。

---

on the front page of 在…的首页上

☞ Some early advertisements, now, still appeared *on the front page of* newspapers. 现在，一些早期的广告形式还会出现在报纸头版。

on the ground　依据，根据；当场，在现场

☞ Another scientist questioned this explanation *on the ground* that it would be very unlikely that conditions would allow generations of turtles over hundreds of millions of years to keep going back to the same nesting ground every single year. 另一位科学家质疑这一解释，依据是几亿年来环境不可能允许一代又一代的海龟每年都回到同一筑巢地。

🔍 on the ground 意为"根据，依据"时，可与 of 搭配，后面接名词，也可与 that 搭配，后面接从句。

on the mood of　处于…情绪之中，想要

☞ A: Hi Susan, if you are not doing anything for dinner tonight, a bunch of us are going to that new Italian restaurant in town.

B: Well, I am *on the mood of* some spaghetti and I have heard the food there is not bad.

A：喂，苏珊，如果你今晚没有准备晚饭的话，我们一群人打算去镇上新开的那家意大利餐馆吃饭。

B：哦，我也想吃意大利面了，听说那儿的食物不错。

on the rise　正在上升

☞ A: I read that the enrollment in the School of Business is *on the rise*!

B: Well, that's been a trend for several years now.

A：我看到报道说报名商学院的人数正在上升！

B：嗯，这几年都是这种趋势。

🔍 在关于物价上涨和涨工资的对话中，也会出现这个词组。

on the verge of　接近于，濒于

☞ A: Did you read today's newspaper? I heard there is something about a new wonder drug.

B: I did read an article about medical researchers being *on the verge of* a major breakthrough.

A：你读了今天的报纸了吗？我听说现在有一种神奇的新药。

B：我读到了一篇关于研究者在医学方面即将有重大突破的文章。

on top of　在…的上面；掌握，完全控制着；除…之外；紧接着…

☞ A: That bread I bought yesterday isn't in the kitchen. Someone must have eaten it.

B: Look *on top of* the refrigerator.

A：我昨天买的面包不在厨房里，一定是有人吃掉了。

B：看看冰箱上面吧。

☞ A: I'll read you the main points of the report over the phone.

B: Great. That'll help me stay *on top of* the project till I'm able to come back to work.

A：我将在电话里给你讲报告的要点。

B：好的。这会帮我在重新工作前一直掌握这个项目的信息。

☞ A: I can't find my notes from history class anywhere. They are not on my desk.

B: You may want to check behind it. Sometimes it happens to me, especially when there are a lot of papers still piled *on top of* it.

A：我到处都找不到我的历史课笔记。它们不在我的桌子上。

B：你在桌子后面找找。有时我也会遇到这种状况，尤其是当桌子上还堆满了很多试卷的时候。

on trial 在实验中；在审讯中

☞ A: Who is he?

B: Oh, he was put *on trial* for corruption.

A：他是谁?

B：哦，他因为贪污而被审讯。

🔍 该词组通常与 put 搭配, put on trial 是"审讯"的意思。

one's motivation 某人的动力

☞ A: It seems that you need more stress to motivate.

B: Oh, *my motivation* has been depleted by too much stress.

A：看来你需要些压力来激励一下。

B：我的动力都已经被压力消磨光了。

only if 只有当，除非

☞ A: What a great television program! That was really stimulating. Don't you think?

B: Well, *only if* you like politics.

A：多棒的电视节目呀! 真的很激励人。难道你不认为吗?

B：哦，只有爱政治的人才会这么认为。

☞ I usually watch TV *only if* I have nothing better to do. 只有当没有更好的事情做时，我才会看电视。

🔍 短语 if only 的意思是"要是…多好", 注意区别。

operate the machine 操作机器

☞ A: Have you finished your work?

B: Well ... er ... I don't know how to *operate the machine*.

A：你做完工作了吗?

B：嗯…呃…我不知道怎么操作这台机器。

opportunity cost　机会成本

☞ The problem results from the lower *opportunity cost*. 该问题是由机会成本的降低引起的。

🔍 "机会成本"是一个经济学概念，即作了一种选择而放弃其他选择所失去的可能产生的最大价值。

optical instrument　光学仪器

☞ Today we will learn how to use microscope which is an *optical instrument* to observe the cell. 今天，我们学习如何使用显微镜这种光学仪器来观察细胞。

organic chemistry　有机化学

☞ A: Don't you think Mike will succeed in the *organic chemistry* course?
B: Well. It depends on how much time he spent on study.
A：难道你认为迈克考不过有机化学课吗？
B：嗯，这取决于他花了多少时间进行学习。

organic material　有机材料

☞ One way to keep the lead in the soil and out of the vegetables is to add lime and *organic material* rich in bacteria to the soil. 使铅留在土壤中而不进入蔬菜中的一个方法是向土壤中加入石灰和富含细菌的有机材料。

original handwriting　原始笔迹，真迹

☞ The *original handwriting*, stamp and signature provided great quantities of documents to study the civilization of that period. 原始笔迹、印迹和签名为研究那段时期的文明提供了大量文献。

original landscape　原始景观

☞ By building, people are already damaging the *original landscape*. 由于建造房屋，人们已经破坏了原始景观。

original topic　原先的主题

☞ A: We'd better go back to our *original topic*.
B: What's that?
A：我们最好回到原先的主题上。
B：那是什么？

original viewpoint　独到的观点/见解

☞ In this paper the author proposed his *original viewpoint* aiming for establishing a recycling system. 在他的论文中，作者就建立回收系统提出了他独到的见解。

out of the question　毫无可能

☞ A: If I can borrow your Spanish notes this weekend, I'll be in a lot better shape for the quiz on Monday.

B: I'm afraid it is *out of the question*. Don't forget I have the same quiz.

A：如果这周末我能借你的西班牙语笔记看看，周一的测验我会考得好点。

B：这恐怕不可能，别忘了我周一也要参加同样的测验。

☞ A: Could I hand in my paper a few days later?

B: I'm afraid that's *out of the question*.

A：我可以晚几天交论文吗？

B：我想这不可能。

🔍 out of 有"越出…范围"的含义，和一些名词搭配组成固定词组，如：out of practice 荒疏的，不常练习的；out of sight 在视野之外，看不到；out of work 失业；out of touch 不联系；不接触。

out-door club　户外活动俱乐部

☞ A: I'm pretty excited. The *out-door club* is going hiking on Mount Herry Forest this weekend.

B: Yes. Finally, I've been looking forward to it all year.

A：我太激动了，这周末户外活动俱乐部要去亨利弗雷斯特山徒步旅行。

B：是啊。终于可以去了，我都盼了整整一年了。

out-door club

🔍 cycle tour, bicycle club 也是常出现在托福听力中的俱乐部名称。

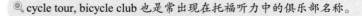

outer atmosphere　大气层

☞ A: Apparently, space satellites recently detected thousands of small comets colliding with earth's *outer atmosphere*, almost 40,000 per day.

B: OK, so that's what created the water?

A：很显然，空间卫星最近探测到有数以千计的小彗星与地球大气层相撞，每天达到将近四万个。

B：哦，这就是产生水的方式吗？

outline of a speech　演讲提纲

☞ Today I want to explain how to make a clear *outline of a speech*. 今天，我要讲一下如何做一个清楚的演讲提纲。

outline one's idea　概括想法

☞ A: Excuse me, Professor Smith. I want to say something about my paper.

B: Well, you may just *outline your idea*. I'm in a hurry to the meeting now, and maybe we could talk about the details this afternoon in my office.

A：打扰了，史密斯教授，我想说一下我的论文。

B：嗯，你可以概括一下你的想法。我现在急着去开会，或许今天下午，我们可以在办公室谈一下细节。

🔍托福中还常考到 outline your plan，意为"概括出你的计划"。

outstanding student　杰出/优秀的学生

☞ A: It is said that the university will award the *outstanding students*.

B: Yeah, and I got the second scholarship last semester.

A：听说这个大学会奖励优秀学生。

B：是啊，我上个学期获得了二等奖学金。

overcome the problem　克服这个问题

☞ These days, the students *overcame the problem* of weak light. 这些天来，学生们克服了灯光微弱的问题。

owe sb. a favor　欠某人的情

☞ A: Thanks Tom. I *owe you a favor*.

B: Oh, come on. Just drive you home.

A：谢谢你，汤姆，我欠你一个人情。

B：哦，得了吧，只是开车送你回家而已。

🔍do one's a favor，意为"帮助某人"，也常在托福的对话中考到。

owe...to...　感激；把…归功于

☞ I *owe* a lot *to* Professor Mercheno. He wrote a letter of recommendation for me and he bought me a set of practice tapes. 我非常感激摩切诺教授。他为我写了推荐信并给我买了一套练习磁带。

☞ thanks to, be credited to

ozone molecule　臭氧分子

☞ By breaking down and analyzing this light, the scientists hope to learn about the chemical composition of these planets' oxygen and *ozone molecules*. 通过打散这种光和分析它，科学家希望了解这些行星上氧气分子和臭氧分子的化学成分。

pain reliever/killer　止痛药/镇定剂

☞ A: Oh my god, you still don't look good. Didn't you take the *pain reliever* I gave you?

B: Yeah, an hour ago. Guess I've got a headache that just won't quit.

A：哦，天啊，你看起来还是不太好，你吃我给你的止痛药了吗？

B：嗯，一个小时前吃了。但我想我这次的头痛是不易退去的那种。

☞ By examining the students' blood after they listened to a variety of classic music collections, the researchers found that some students showed a large increase in endorphin, a natural *pain reliever*; this supports what music therapists have known for years: Music can help rejuvenate or soothe patients. 学生们在听过各种经典音乐之后，研究人员通过检查他们的血液发现，有些学生血液中的内啡肽大幅上升，这是一种天然的止痛剂。这就证实了多年来音乐疗法专家所倡导的：音乐可以让患者振奋或起到安抚作用。

☞ pain killer

🔍 stress reliever 减轻压力的东西
常见的止痛药有：
aspirin 阿司匹林   ibuprofen 布洛芬
panadol 扑热息痛   pethidine 哌替啶（又名杜冷丁）

---

paper topic   论文主题

☞ Mary found it very difficult to figure out the *paper topic*. 玛丽觉得想出论文主题很难。

---

parking lot   停车场

parking lot

☞ Interested cyclists should meet at eight a.m. in the *parking lot* at the corner of Hamilton Street and College Avenue in New Branderswork. 感兴趣的自行车爱好者应于早八点在位于新布兰德斯沃克的汉密尔顿路与学院大街拐角处的停车场集合。

☞ parking ground, parking place

🔍 parking lot 通常指"存放车辆的多层建筑物"；另外，park-and-ride place 指"换乘停车场"，是为驻车换乘提供存放车辆的场地。

---

parking meter   （投币式）停车计费器

☞ A: Excuse me, but do you happen to have some change for the *parking meter*?
     B: No. But if you go into the restaurant you'll probably be able to change a dollar bill.
     A：打扰一下，你有没有零钱换给我，投给停车计费器。
     B：没有。但是如果你去那家餐厅，可能会换开一美元钞票。

☞ She put too little money in the *parking meter*. 她向停车计费器中投的钱太少了。

🔍 相关词汇：
running time meter 计时器   an egg-timer 煮蛋计时器
pedometer 计步器

parking place 停车处

☞ I find it difficult to pick out my car from others in the *parking place*. 我觉得在停车场里从很多车当中找出自己的车很难。

☞ parking lot

parking sticker 停车许可证

☞ A: The sign says this is reserved parking only and your student *parking sticker* has expired, too.

B: I was just running in to turn in a paper, officer. I haven't been here for more than five minutes.

A: 这个标牌上说这是预留停车位, 而且你的学生停车许可证已经到期了。

B: 长官, 我只是进去交论文, 我到这儿还没有五分钟。

☞ The female student has lost her *parking sticker*. 那名女学生把停车许可证弄丢了。

☞ parking permit

part-time job 兼职工作

☞ A: I've been just told that my *part-time job* is going to end next month.

B: It's probably for the best. Your skills are sure in demand now. And that job wasn't exactly what he called interesting.

A: 我刚刚被通知, 我的兼职工作要在下个月结束了。

B: 这可能再好不过了。你的技能现在很抢手。况且那份工作也没有他说的那么有趣。

☞ A: I'd like to apply for the *part-time job*.

B: Fine, just fill out this form. Someone will be with you in a moment.

A: 我想申请这份兼职工作。

B: 好的, 先填下这个表格吧, 等会儿就会有人来对你进行面试。

☞ A: Sally really is amazing, isn't she? She has that *part-time job* and she studies harder than most of us.

B: I know, yet she still finds time to volunteer at the hospital.

A: 萨莉真的令人惊奇, 不是吗? 她做着兼职工作, 同时她比我们中任何一个都学习刻苦。

B: 我知道, 不只这样, 她还找时间在医院做义工呢。

☞ part-time position, part-time employment

> 🔍 托福中常谈到打工问题, 一般涉及的工作有: teaching assistant, lab assistant, research assistant, baby sitter, house-sitting。找工作要看报纸上的 help-wanted section, 申请工作要先 fill out the form, 并且要遵照 application procedure。

pass around 分发, 传送

☞ The next sample that I'll *pass around* is a microcline mineral, also called amazon stone. 接下来我要传给大家看的样品是微斜长石, 又称为"亚马逊石"。

pass on to　把…传给

☞ A: Mary, I lent you a couple of videos last week. I'd like to **pass** them **on to** another student today.

B: I have one in my bag, but could I keep the other one until tomorrow? I haven't quite finished it yet.

A：玛丽, 我上周借了两盒录像带给你。我今天想把它们给另一个学生看看。

B：我包里现在装着一盒, 但是我可不可以明天再给您另一盒? 我还没看完那盒呢。

☞ A: Do you have your film festival schedule with you? I'd like to find out what's playing this weekend.

B: I **past** it **on to** my roommate, but there should be more in the bookstore. I can pick one up for you next time there.

A：你带着电影节时间表了吗? 我想看看这周末放什么。

B：我把它给我的室友了, 但是书店应该还有很多。下次我去的时候可以给你带一份。

🔍 pass 的相关词组还有: pass by 经过, pass down 传给后代。

N O T E S

Unit 15

pause to do　停下来去做

☞ Nobody has *paused to* talk to the old man that evening. 那天晚上没有人停下来和那位老人说话。

☞ How often do you pause to appreciate what you have in life. 你多久才会停下来欣赏一下你生命中已拥有的东西。

☞ stop to do

pay attention to　注意，关注

☞ Society will not *pay attention to* the new laws. 社会将不会关注这项新法律。

☞ Do you think we should *pay attention to* these opinions given by the actors and the celebrities? 你认为我们应该对演员和社会名流所发表的见解给予关注吗？

☞ take note of, keep one's eyes on

pay for　付钱

☞ The man would like to *pay for* the woman's lunch. 男士愿意为这位女士的午餐付账。

☞ If you can see the movie on television, why *pay for* it? 如果你能在电视上看到那部电影，为什么还要花钱去看呢？

☞ A: Would it be better to buy a monthly meal ticket or *pay for* each meal separately?
　B: What difference does it make? The price per meal is the same either way.
　A：我们吃饭是买月票好呢，还是每顿饭分别付钱呢？
　B：有什么区别吗？两种方式的价钱是一样的。

☞ pony up

🔍 在托福听力中，"付电话费"为 pay the phone bill。

pay for admission　花钱入场

☞ The organizers built large arenas and earned money by requiring spectators to *pay for admission*. 组织者建造大型竞技场，通过向观众收取入场费来赚钱。

🔍 这里介绍几个和 admission 相关的表达方法：gain admission 得到…的录取，the admission of guilt 认罪，open admission 免试入学制，admission ticket 准考证，入场券。

pay phone 付费式电话

pay phone

A: Excuse me, could you tell me where the nearest ***pay phone*** is?

B: Well, the nearest one is in the library. But that closed an hour ago. I think the next closest one is probably in the student center.

A：打扰一下，请问最近的付费电话在哪里？

B：哦，最近的一个在图书馆，但是一小时前关门了。我想其次最近的可能是在学生中心。

🔍常考的短语还有 a long distance call，意思是"长途电话"。

payroll department 薪资部门

The lecture mainly talks about the basic functions of the ***payroll department***.
讲座主要讨论了薪资部门的主要职责。

🔍人力资源部用英语说是 Human Resource Department。

permission slip 请假条

When carrying on outdoor survey all members must have a ***permission slip***. If you have lost or forgotten yours, print and fill out the form, and return to the committee. 所有做户外调查的成员都必须有一个许可证。如果丢了或者是忘带了，请打印并填写这个表格，然后交给委员会。

☞ note for leave, request for leave

perpetual circulation 循环流通

A: I'm sorry, but I can't let you check out these books.

B: What do you mean?

A: Wow, the computer shows you got an overdue book, *Art Work*, and your ***perpetual circulation*** is revoked until you return it.

A：对不起，我不能让你借这些书。

B：什么意思？

A：哦，计算机上显示你有一本过期的书，书名是《美术作品》。在你还这本书前你的循环借书的权利被取消了。

personal characteristics 个人特质

Washington's ***personal characteristics*** make him a great leader. 华盛顿的个人特质使他成为一位伟大的领袖。

personal opinion 个人主张

What anthropologists find interesting is that T-shirts are used to express ***personal opinions***. T恤可以被用来表达个人主张，人类学家觉得这很有趣。

personal statement 个人陈述

☞ Students were asked to make **_personal statements_** on the first day of the school. 开学的第一天，学生们被要求做个人陈述。

personality trait 个性特征

☞ Self-image can be indicated by a tone of voice that is confident, pretentious, shy, aggressive, outgoing, or exuberant, to name only a few **_personality traits_**. 自我形象可以通过说话的语调得以显示，比如自信、自命不凡、害羞、盛气凌人、外向或活跃，这里只提到了几种个性特征。

☞ personal characteristics

pesticide residue 农药残留

☞ The factors that could be contributing to the world-wide decline in the number of amphibians include acid rain and the spread of the **_pesticide residue_**. 导致世界范围内两栖类动物数量减少的因素包括酸雨和农药残留物的扩散。

🔍 说某种食物或其他东西无农药残留用 "... shows no evidence of pesticide residue"。

pesticides-free 无农药的

☞ Well, a lot of food is pure and **_pesticides-free_**. They also have Vitamin supplements and soy and Toufu and that kind of thing. 嗯，许多食物都是纯天然无农药的。它们还含有维生素成分以及大豆、豆腐和类似物质。

pet peeve 让人气恼的事情，个人习惯上的一些小忌讳

☞ A: I can't stand know-it-alls.
   B: Tell me about it. They are one of my **_pet peeves_**.
   A：我不能忍受那些自以为无所不知的人。
   B：和我说说啊，我也很讨厌这样的人。

🔍 两个单词连续时，t 的发音要弱化。

phone bill 电话费单

☞ A: I want to pay you for that long distance call I made but I suppose you haven't got the **_phone bill_** yet.
   B: Oh, but I have.
   A：我想付给你上次我打长途电话的费用，但是我想你还没有电话缴费单吧？
   B：哦，我拿到了。

🔍 托福听力中出现的其他"单据"：
electric bill 电费单   mechanic's bill 修车费

physical activity 体育活动，身体运动

☞ A: I can't concentrate on this final report any longer. Maybe I should take a nap before we continue.

B: They say the *physical activity* makes you more alert.

A：我无法专心做这份期末报告了。或许我应该小憩一会儿我们再继续。

B：有人说运动可以使人精神点。

☞ physical exercise

physical characteristic 物理特征

☞ I'm not sure exactly what the connection is between a person's abilities and the *physical characteristics* of the head. But although there's no scientific basis for phrenology, it is true that the head is the center of control for the rest of the body.
我并不能十分肯定一个人的能力和其头部物理特征之间的关系。但是尽管颅相学没有科学依据，可以肯定的是头部是掌控身体其他部位的中心。

☞ There is a new school of thought called Cladistics where scientists determine relationships among the animals according to common *physical characteristics*.
有一种叫遗传分类学的学派，这些科学家根据共同的物理特征来确定动物之间的关系。

🔍 化学性质：chemical property

pick out 选出，挑出，拣出；辨认出，辨别出

pick out

☞ It took us a long time to *pick out* new costumes for the party. 我们花了很长时间挑选晚会穿的礼服。

☞ choose, select

pick up 拾起，捡起；（开车）接人；学会；偶然得到

☞ A: Would you like to go with me to the airport to *pick up* Frank?

B: I'd like to, but I have class till 2:00. And I know Frank's decided to take the early flight.

A：你愿意和我一起去机场接弗兰克吗？

B：我想，但是我要到两点才下课，而且我知道弗兰克决定坐早班飞机。

☞ A: Do you think I could borrow your car to go grocery shopping? The supermarkets outside the city are so much cheaper than the one by the school. But they're so far away. I'd be happy to *pick up* anything you need.

B: Well, I don't like to let anyone else drive my car. Tell you what, why don't we go together? That way I can learn the way.

A：我能借你的车去杂货店买东西吗？城外的超市比学校旁边的要便宜得多，但是太远了。我愿意帮你带任何东西。

B：嗯，我不想让别人开我的车。为什么我们不一起去呢？这样我也可以熟悉路线。

☞ A: So, did you ***pick up*** that orange juice for me like you said you would?

B: I meant to. But I'm short of cash. I'll be going back later though, after I stop by the bank if you can wait that long.

A：那么，你说要帮我带橙汁，带了吗？

B：我想带，但是现金不够了。如果你能等的话，我会在银行取些钱，再回去买。

pin...down   使说清楚；使某人就范；固定，使不能动

☞ A: It sounds like Karen isn't happy at all with her new roommate. Did she say why?

B: Believe me, I tried to find out. But I simply couldn't ***pin*** her ***down***.

A：听起来卡伦好像和她的新室友相处得一点都不开心啊。她说了是什么原因吗？

B：相信我，我是想搞明白怎么回事，但是却不能让她说清楚。

☞ bring sb. to heels, bring sb. to terms

> 🔍 pin sth. down 是"明确说明某事"，pin sth. on sb. 是"将某事推到某人身上"。

place reliance on   信赖，依靠

☞ Do not ***place*** too much ***reliance on*** her words. 不要太相信她的话。

☞ rely on, depend on

plan a trip to   计划去…的旅行

☞ A: Did you hear that my parents are ***planning a trip to*** Vancouver?

B: What for?

A：你听说我父母计划去温哥华旅行了吗？

B：为什么？

planet formation   行星构成

☞ Star's dust shows signs of possible ***planet formation***. 恒星的尘埃显示了行星的可能构成方式。

planet's orbit   行星轨道

☞ A: What is the shape of a ***planet's orbit***?

B: An ellipse.

A：行星的轨道是什么形状？

B：椭圆形。

planetary motions 行星运动

☞ The lecture mainly contains an introduction to the problem of *planetary motions*. 这个讲座主要包括了对行星运动问题的介绍。

plant fiber 植物纤维

☞ Each wasp nest has a special combination of *plant fibers* and so the wasps that live there have a unique smell. 每一个黄蜂窝都是由植物纤维经过特殊组合而成的，所以栖息在里面的黄蜂会有股独特的气味。

☞ The female wasp produces the paper by chewing up *plant fibers* or old wood. They spread the papers in thin layers to make cells, in which the queen lays her eggs. 雌性黄蜂通过咀嚼植物纤维或是朽木来制造蜂窝壁。它们把蜂窝壁铺成薄层，做成蜂房，供蜂王在此产卵。

🔍 托福中常见与"fiber"相关的短语如下：
glass fiber 玻璃纤维　　　　　　synthetic fiber 人造纤维

plastic bead 塑料珠子

☞ These *plastic beads* aren't for jewelry. They can be used for many scientific purposes, from conducting cancer research to calibrating microscopes. 这些塑料珠子不是做首饰用的，它们可以用于多种科研目的，从癌症研究到显微镜测量等。

plastic trash bags 塑料垃圾袋

☞ We'll put the litter in these *plastic trash bags*. 我们会把垃圾放在这些塑料垃圾袋里。

plastic trash bags

🔍 相关词汇：trash cans 垃圾桶

play in cooperation with 与…合作一起玩

☞ A: Don't you play with a partner?
　　B: Yeah. Four people play, two against the other two.
　　A: So you try to *play in cooperation with* your partner.
　　A：你难道不和搭档一起玩吗？
　　B：是啊，四个人玩，二对二。
　　A：所以你要试着和搭档合作才可以。

play one's heart out 全心投入

☞ A: Losing the championship must have been a big disappointment to the players on our volleyball team.
　　B: Yeah, but they really *played their hearts out*. They are still champions in my book.
　　A：锦标赛失利，我们排球队的队员一定很失望。
　　B：是，但是他们真的尽力了。在我看来他们依然是冠军。

plenty of 许多

☞ If we leave home at eight, we should get there in *plenty of* time. 如果我们八点离开家，那么我们应该有充足的时间到达那里。

☞ lots of

plough through 费力地阅读

☞ A: That's a pretty thick book. Are you sure Fram will want to *plough through* that?

B: Are you kidding? She'll be through it in two days.

A：这本书真厚啊，你确定弗兰姆想读吗？

B：你开玩笑吗？她两天就会读完。

☞ wade through

point out 指出

☞ The first thing I'd like to *point out* is that the workbook contains a very large amount of material, far more than you could ever handle in a single semester. 我要指出的第一点是这本练习册里包含了大量习题，远非你在一个学期内就能做得完的。

☞ In my opinion, Frank Lloyd Wright was the greatest American architect of the 20th century. People who know his designs well *pointed out* that his roofs often leaked, his ceilings were too low, and his houses were uncomfortable. In my presentation, however, I'll be focusing on the virtues of his designs. 在我看来，弗兰克·劳埃德·赖特是 20 世纪美国最伟大的建筑师。熟悉他设计的人指出他设计的房顶漏雨，天花板太矮，房子不舒服。尽管这样，在我的介绍里，我仍会着重于他设计的优点。

☞ indicate

political management 政治手段

☞ Last time we outlined how the Civil War finally got started. I want to talk today about the *political management* of the war on both sides, the north under Abraham Lincoln, and the south under Jefferson Davis. 上次我们大概讲了内战最后是如何爆发的。今天我要说一下双方在此次战争上使用的政治手段，北方的领导是亚伯拉罕·林肯，南方的是杰弗逊·戴维斯。

political science 政治学

☞ A: Have you heard of Professor Howl?

B: Mh, he does have a good reputation in the *Political Science* Department.

A：你听说过霍尔教授吗？

B：嗯，他在政治科学系声誉很好。

☞ A: My *political science* class ran overtime.

B: That's been happening quite a bit lately, hasn't it?

A：我上的政治学课拖堂了。

B：最近这经常发生，不是吗？

population distribution 人口分布

☞ The *population distribution* is closely related with the development of social economy at any time. 在任何时候，人口分布都和社会经济发展有着密切的联系。

🔍 表达"分布不均匀"用 uneven 来形容，如 uneven distribution of the air 空气的不均匀分布。

pore over 仔细钻研，仔细阅读

pore over

☞ We always spent all day long in the library *poring over* those texts books and other useful materials. 我们经常在图书馆苦战一天阅读教科书和其他一些有用的资料。

portray the cruelty of hunting 描述打猎的残忍

☞ The pictures exhibited in the house *portray the cruelty of hunting*. 这个房间里展出的画描述了打猎的残忍。

positive side 积极的方面

☞ There is a *positive side* of the way to start your college career. 以这种方式开始你的大学生活有其积极的一面。

postpone doing 推迟做

☞ She'd like to *postpone* working on the proposal. 她想推迟开展提议书上的工作。

☞ delay doing, put off doing

precious stone 宝石

☞ It is really a small amount to pay for such a *precious stone*. 要买这枚珍贵的宝石，这点钱真的是太少了。

☞ gemstone

precise elevation 精确的海拔高度

☞ Now these receivers have been reduced to about the size and weight of a hand-held telephone, so climbers were able to take the receiver to the top of the Everest, and from there, to access the satellite system signals that would allow them to determine the *precise elevation*. 如今，接收器的重量和大小都被减到与手提电话一般，所以攀登者可以把接收器带到珠穆朗玛峰顶，从那里，他们就可以接收到卫星系统信号，从而测定珠穆朗玛峰的精确海拔高度。

precise measurement　精确测量

☞ These scientists wanted to make a more **precise measurement**, using a new method that takes advantage of recent advances in technology; it's called the Global Positioning System. 这些科学家想利用最新科技成果做一次更为精确的测量，这种方法叫做"全球定位系统"。

predict weather　预测天气

☞ The traditional forecasting models do a much better job to **predict** general **weather** conditions over large regions. 传统的预报方法在预测大范围天气状况时要更准确一些。

prepare for　为…做准备

☞ The professor told the students that they would have enough time to **prepare for** the final exam. 教授告诉学生他们有充足的时间来准备期末考试。

☞ make provision for

🔍 在托福听力中，prepare for 后面常加 test 和 exam 之类的词汇做宾语。

press conference　记者招待会

☞ A **press conference** will be held in the main hall in the library for the art exhibition. 为了此届艺术展览，图书馆的大厅里将会召开一次记者招待会。

☞ news conference

pretty heavy workload　非常繁重的工作量

☞ I have a **pretty heavy workload** this semester. I already spend my evenings doing, but I don't really know when I can finish them. 这个学期我的工作量很重。我已经晚上都在工作了，但是真的不知道什么时候才能完成。

prevent...from　阻止，阻挡

prevent... from

☞ The fire was **prevented from** spreading because of Sandra's quick action. 由于桑德拉迅速采取了行动，才使得火势没有蔓延。

🔍 注意 prevent 后面要加 doing，prevent sb./sth. from doing。

primary school　小学

☞ A：Do you know each other?

　B：Of course, we are best friends since **primary school**.

　A：你们认识彼此吗？

　B：当然，从小学开始我们就是最好的朋友。

private company 私人公司

☞ Within a short time, the first east-to-west roads were built. They were called "turnpikes". *Private companies* built these roads, and collected fees from all vehicles that traveled on them. 在很短的时间内，第一条横贯东西的道路建成了，人们称之为"收费高速公路"。这些路是由私人公司修建的，他们对路上行驶的所有车辆收费。

🔍相关词语：

state-owned enterprise 国有企业　　　　registered capital 注册资金
legal person 法人

private residence 私人住宅

☞ The house, a *private residence* in western Pennsylvania, completed in 1936. 这座位于宾夕法尼亚州西部的房子是一处私人住宅，于 1936 年建成。　·

proceed to 往下进行；向…进发

☞ A: My chemistry project is in trouble because my partner and I had totally different ideas about how to *proceed to* the next step.

B: You should try to meet each other half way.

A：我的化学项目遇到麻烦了，因为我的搭档和我对如何继续进行下一步存在严重分歧。

B：你们应该试着折中一下。

☞ Let's *proceed to* the main exhibit hall and look at some of the actual vehicles that played a prominent role in speeding up mail delivery. 让我们前往主展厅，看看在加速信件邮递中起到重要作用的一些车辆。

proceed with 开始或继续做

☞ How do you *proceed with* your thesis proposal? 你的论文开题报告进行得怎么样了？

☞ start to do, begin to do

productive meeting 富有成效的会议

☞ A: How about the meeting last weekend?

B: It was not a *productive meeting*.

A：上周末的那个会议怎么样？

B：没有什么成效。

productive writer 多产的作家

☞ The young man was known as the most *productive writer* in the country. 这位年轻人以该国家最多产作家而闻名。

professional football player　职业足球选手

☞ A: Did you want to be a university football coach?

　　B: First, I wanted to be a *professional football player* in no more than three years.

　　A：你想成为大学足球队教练吗？

　　B：首先，我想在三年之内成为一个职业足球选手。

professional knowledge　专业知识

☞ I have obtained *professional knowledge* about management this semester. 这学期我学习了一些有关管理的专业知识。

☞ specialized knowledge

proficient at　对…精通

☞ The scrolls were written in a language that is really rare today. Only a few people are *proficient at* it. 那些经卷所使用的语言现在很少见到，只有一小部分人对该语言精通。

☞ be good at

promise to do　承诺做，保证做

☞ My father made me *promise to* study hard. 我父亲让我保证努力学习。

☞ A: Is it all right if I ask you a personal question?

　　B: You can ask. I don't *promise to* answer.

　　A：我可以问你个私人问题吗？

　　B：可以，但是我不保证会回答。

☞ A: I know I *promised to* drive you to the airport next Tuesday. But I am afraid that something has come up. And they've called a special meeting at work.

　　B: No big deal. Karen said she was available as a backup.

　　A：我知道我答应下周二开车送你去机场。但是我恐怕临时有事去不了了。他们要召开一个特殊工作会议。

　　B：没关系的。卡伦说她随时可做候补。

🔍 该词组用于被动语态时，形式为 be promised to sb.，意为"把…许配给某人"。

proposal for sth./doing sth.　…的提议

☞ A: Say remember that *proposal for* an international art festival next spring? Do you think there's any chance it'll ever get off the ground?

　　B: I don't think it's a question of whether it'll happen. It's just a matter of where it'll be held.

　　A：还记得要在明年春天举行国际艺术节的提议吗？你觉得它能实施吗？

　　B：我认为不存在举行或不举行的问题，这只是在哪里举行的问题。

proposal to do 做…的提议

☞ Many candidates have raised the *proposal to* investigate into the weird accident. 很多议员提议调查那场怪异的事故。

propose a resolution 提出决议

☞ The shareholders will not *propose a resolution* to appoint Johnson as a director at the enterprise. 股东们将不会提出任命约翰逊为这家企业执行官的决议。

propose a toast to 向…敬酒

propose a toast to

☞ Allow me to *propose a toast to* our honor guest Mr. Wright on behalf of our group. 请允许我代表我们团队向贵宾赖特先生敬酒。

propose an amendment 提出修正案

☞ The government officer *proposed an amendment* to the ban on children drinking. 那名政府官员对儿童禁酒令提出修正案。

propose marriage 求婚

☞ The bunch of people are discussing the interesting ways of *proposing marriage*. 那群人正在讨论求婚的有趣方法。

pros and cons 利弊, 正反两方面的意见

☞ A: Have you guys decided whether you are going to get an apartment off campus next year or are you staying in the dorm?

B: We are still talking about the *pros and cons*.

A：你们决定明年到校外租公寓还是继续住校内宿舍了吗?

B：我们仍在权衡利弊。

protective tariff 保护性关税

☞ The government decided to impose a *protective tariff* on the import cars. 政府决定对进口汽车征收保护性关税。

public sphere 公共领域

☞ The group defined the *public sphere* as a virtual or imaginary community which does not necessarily exist in any country. 这个组织把公共领域定义为一个虚拟或想象的社区, 该社区不一定存在于任何一个国家。

public transportation 公共交通

☞ A: I'm surprised to see you on the city bus. Your car in the shop?

B: No. I've just been thinking a lot about the environment lately. So I decided the air will be a lot cleaner if we all use *public transportation* when we could.

A：在公交车上碰到你，让我很惊讶啊。你的车送去修了吗？

B：没，我最近考虑了很多环境问题。如果我们都能乘坐公共交通工具的话，空气就会清新很多。

🔍 美国的公共交通工具主要包括 train, bus 和 subway。

public visit　公众参观

☞ The national museum will open to *public visit* next year. 国家博物馆将于明年对公众开放参观。

Unit 16

pull...into orbit 把···拉入轨道

☞ Study shows that the young earth would not have had enough gravitational force to stop a body the size of a moon from traveling through the solar system and *pull it into orbit*. 研究表明，地球在早期没有足够引力让如月球大小的天体在太阳系中停止遨游，并将其拉入轨道。

pump up through 从···中抽取

☞ The kind of water is *pumped up through* the bored hole and sprayed over the land to irrigate the crops. 这种水通过钻孔抽上来，喷洒到地面灌溉庄稼。

put air in 给···充气

☞ A: I think I need a new tire. I had to *put air in* it twice this week.

B: That happened to me once. It was just a nail, and they were able to repair it.

A：我想我需要换个新轮胎，我这周打两次气了。

B：我曾经也遇到过这种情况，这只是个钉子的问题，可以修好的。

put air in

put back 把···放回原处；延误，拖延，推迟

☞ A: Please be sure to *put* all the lab equipment *back* on the shelves when you are through with your experiment.

B: Oh, don't worry; I'm always very careful about that.

A：当你做完实验后，请确保把所有的实验器材都放回到架子上。

B：哦，别担心，我做这种事一直都很仔细。

☞ postpone

put down 放下

☞ A: I hope you like the novel I lent you. I wasn't sure whether it was the kind of book you would be interested in.

B: You know, I had the same doubt at first. But once I started I simply couldn't *put* it *down*.

A：我希望你喜欢我借给你的小说。我不确定你是否感兴趣。

B：知道吗，我刚开始也有这个疑虑。但是我一开始读，就对它爱不释手了。

☞ A: I started reading that book you loaned me, but I'm having a tough time keeping up with the main characters. It's hard to remember them all.

B: Yeah, I know. The first part isn't easy. All I can say is to stick with it. Once you get halfway through you won't want to **put** it **down**.

A：我开始读你借给我的那本书了，但是很难分清里面的主要人物。要记住所有人物很难。

B：是的，我知道，开始的部分确实不容易。我能说的就是坚持下去，一旦你读到一半，就不想放下了。

☞ drop down

🔍 该词组在托福考试中通常会出现在谈论书籍的对话中。另外要注意 put oneself down 表示"看轻自己"，而 put the phone down 意为"挂断电话"。

put on air 摆架子，装腔作势

☞ Our boss is always **putting on air**. 我们老板总是摆架子。

put off 推迟；关掉，熄灭

☞ A: What a day! We haven't had weather like this for ages.

B: I know. What you say if we **put off** studying for a little while and take the advantage of it?

A：天气真好！我们好久都没有过这样的天气了。

B：我知道。不如我们等会再学习，先享受一下这好天气？

☞ delay, postpone

put our heads together 共同想办法

☞ A: I am having such a hard time with the history assignment. It's taking for ever. How about you?

B: I'm struggling too. Why don't we **put our heads together**?

A：我做历史作业的时候真的很痛苦，总是做不完，你做得怎么样？

B：我也很吃力，我们为什么不一起想办法呢？

quarterly review 季度报告

☞ The **quarterly review** released yesterday presented an overview of recent developments in financial markets. 昨日发布的季度报告总体介绍了金融市场的近期发展。

quit school 退学，辍学

☞ The students from India once thought of **quitting school**. 来自印度的那几名学生曾经想过退学。

☞ drop out

quit smoking/drinking 戒烟/酒

☞ A: The doctor told me to quit drinking.

B: Shouldn't you *quit smoking*, too?

A：医生告诉我要戒酒。

B：没告诉你也要戒烟吗?

🔍 退出某项比赛或某项游戏也可以用 quit，如 quit the game。

quitting time 下课时间

☞ A: I'm glad it's almost *quitting time*.

B: Me, too. I have been watching the clock all afternoon.

A：我很高兴马上要下课了。

B：我也是。我整个下午都在看表。

quote this line 引用这行诗

☞ Gertrude stein has been better known for her prose than her poems. But I'd like to *quote this line* because of its musicality, and because I think it helps open up our awareness to the unconventional lyricism of contemporary poets. 一直以来，格特鲁德·斯坦的散文比诗更要出名。但是由于其音乐感，我想引用这行诗，因为我觉得它可以帮我们提升对当代诗人的非传统抒情诗的意识感觉。

radiation therapy 放射疗法

☞ The new *radiation therapy* can kill cancer cells and keep them from growing and multiplying. 这种新型放射疗法可以杀死癌细胞并且抑制它们生长和繁殖。

radio signal 广播信号

radio signal

☞ The *radio signal* was too weak to reach a mass audience. 广播信号太弱了，广大观众无法收听。

☞ It was an Italian inventor who created the first wireless device for sending out *radio signals* in 1895. 一位意大利发明家于 1895 年发明了第一台可发送广播信号的无线装置。

☞ broadcast signals

ragtime music 雷格泰姆音乐

☞ Paul preferred *ragtime music* to rock music. 与摇滚乐相比，保罗更喜欢雷格泰姆音乐。

🔍 这个词组造自托福经典加试题目中的一篇音乐方面的段落，重复率极高。

raise fees 提高费用

☞ A: Hey, did you hear that they're going to *raise* the dorm *fees* again.

B: Really? Am I glad I decide to move off campus?

A：嗨，你听说宿舍费又要涨了吗？

B：真的吗？那我是不是应该为决定要搬出学校而感到高兴呢？

raise one's pay/salary 涨工资

☞ Diana wants to ask her boss to *raise her pay*. 戴安娜想让老板给她涨工资。

reading assignment 阅读作业

☞ Since this is the topic in your *reading assignment* for next time, let me spend these last few minutes of class talking about it. 这是下次阅读作业的题目，我就用这堂课最后几分钟谈一下吧。

☞ A geology professor and a student are discussing a *reading assignment* about the ocean floor. 一位地理学教授和一个学生正在讨论有关海床的阅读作业。

reading list 阅读书目

☞ The *reading list* doesn't contain many interesting books. 这个阅读书目中的书都不是很有趣。

realistic movement 现实主义运动

☞ Stowe was an important forerunner to the *realistic movement* that became popular later in the 19th century. 斯托是 19 世纪后期流行的现实主义运动的重要先驱之一。

reapply for 再申请

☞ A: Oh my goodness! Your health services card is sitting right here on your file. It should've been sent out to you weeks ago. I hope you haven't had any need for it.

B: No, not yet. But it's nice to know I have it, so I needn't to *reapply for* a new one.

A：哦，天啊! 你的保健服务卡还在你文件上放着。应该几周前就寄给你的。希望你还没有用到。

B：是的，还没。但是很高兴知道我有这卡，我就不需要再申请了。

reasonable excuse 合理的借口

☞ If you would like to be absent in my class these days, please give me a *reasonable excuse*. 如果你想这些天不来上我的课，请给我一个合理的理由。

☞ good excuse

> 🔍 在托福听力中，"合理的借口"常用以上两种表达，而"糟糕的、荒唐的借口"常用 ridiculous excuse 或者 wild excuse。

reception office　接待处

☞ There is a vacancy for *reception office* in the company. 该公司有一个前台接待的职位空缺。

recharge batteries　给电池充电

☞ A: Can I *recharge* my cell phone *batteries* in the shopping mall?
B: Of course you can.
A：我能在这家购物中心给手机充电吗？
B：当然可以。

🔍 这里介绍一下各种电池的说法：
battery（cell）电池　　　　　　　　dry battery 干电池
storage battery 蓄电池

recommend sb. sth.　向某人推荐某物

☞ My roommate *recommended* me the red tie. 我室友向我推荐了这条红领带。

recreation center　娱乐中心

☞ I'm going over to the student *recreation center* to play some bridge. 我要去学生娱乐中心玩桥牌。

recreation room　娱乐室

☞ The *recreation room* isn't large enough for the party. 这个娱乐室用来举行聚会不够大。

☞ We can't have the party this week because the *recreation room* is being renovated. 我们这周不能聚会了，因为娱乐室正在被翻修。

recreation room

refer to　提到，谈到；参考，查阅；询问，查询

☞ These two great poems are believed to have been written some time between 800BC and 700BC, partly because the poems *refer to* the social conditions of that time, conditions that have been validated by the findings. 人们认为这两首伟大的诗篇大概写于公元前 800 年到公元前 700 年间的某个时期，部分原因是这些诗反映了当时的社会情况，并且被考古发现所证实。

reference book　参考书

☞ A: I think I'll add that information to my paper.
B: You really should check it out in your *reference book*.
A：我想把那个信息加进我的论文。
B：你最好在参考书中检查一下这条信息。

☞ I'll drop by the library to see if they have *reference books* on medicines. 我顺便去图书馆看看是否有与药物相关的参考书。

reflect back 反射回来

☞ This kind of material could *reflect back* the heat of burning fuel, so the fuel will burn much hotter and burn up more completely. 这种材料可以把燃料燃烧的热量反射回来，所以燃料就会燃烧得更热、更充分。

register trademark 注册商标

☞ In that country you must *register* your *trademark* with the local trademark office in order to protect your rights. 在那个国家，你必须去当地的商标管理处注册商标以保证你的权利。

> ℚ register 用作"注册"时后面多加 for, 如 register for the course, register for the class, register for the summer school。

registered capital 注册资本

☞ The food enterprise is a joint venture with its *registered capital* US$ 100,000. 这家食品企业是一个合资企业，注册资金为 10 万美元。

regulate spending 控制开支

☞ You all must learn to *regulate* your *spending* when you enter the college. 你们所有人在进入大学后必须学会控制自己的开支。

regulate the traffic 管制交通

☞ The department concerned decides to enact a new act to *regulate the traffic*. 相关部门决定颁布一项新法规来管制交通。

relate to 与…有关

☞ A: Have you decided what you are going to do over the summer break?

 B: Well, I've given it a thought, and I'd like to get a job in something *related to* marketing. But I haven't come up with anything definite yet.

 A：你决定暑假做什么了吗？

 B：嗯，我想过，我想找份营销方面的工作，但是还没想出具体要做什么。

☞ have to do with, be in connection with

release news 发布新闻

☞ The dean of the department, also the spokesman of the university, will be invited to *release news* on the new survey conducted by the students. 这个系的主任，同时也是这所大学的发言人，被邀请发布对学生做的新调查的消息。

relevant to 与…相关

☞ Your performance must be ***relevant to*** the audience and should help them understand the current situation. 你的表演必须是和观众息息相关的, 且能帮助他们理解当下的情况。

relevant working experience 相关工作经验

☞ The man who applies this position must have ***relevant working experience*** for more than five years. 申请这个职位的人必须有五年以上相关工作经验。

rely on 信任, 依赖, 指望

☞ A: I have to borrow enough money to buy a plane ticket. My archaeology class is taking a future trip to Alaska and I may never get another chance like this.

   B: Look, when push comes to show, the people you can ***rely on*** most are your family.

   A: 我必须借足够的钱买张飞机票。我们考古学课程要安排去阿拉斯加旅行, 我可能再也不会有这种机会了。

   B: 看吧, 当有急需的时候, 你最可以信赖的还是家人。

☞ depend on

remarkable recovery 显著恢复

☞ In the 1970s, the peregrine falcons almost disappeared as a result of the contamination of the food chain by the DDT in pesticide. The presence of the poison in their systems resulted in eggs too weak to support the incubating chicks. Their ***remarkable recovery*** is a result of the ban of DDT as a pesticide. 在20世纪70年代, 由于农药中的DDT污染了食物链, 游隼几乎都消失了。这种毒药出现在它们的系统中, 导致其蛋壳过于脆弱而不能孵化雏隼。后来游隼得以显著恢复是由于禁止农药中再使用DDT。

remind...of 提醒某人某事

☞ A: I don't imagine you have any interest in attending that lecture on sculpture.

   B: I do, now that you've ***reminded*** me ***of*** it.

   A: 我没想到你会对参加关于雕塑的讲座感兴趣。

   B: 我感兴趣, 既然你已经提醒我了。

☞ A: Hello!

   B: Hello! This is Dr. Grey's office. We're calling to ***remind*** you ***of*** your 4:15 appointment for your annual checkup tomorrow.

   A: Oh, thanks. It's a good thing you called. I thought it was 4:15 today.

   A: 你好!

   B: 您好! 这里是格雷医生办公室。我打电话来是提醒您预约了明天4点15分做年度体检。

   A: 哦, 谢谢你的提醒。我当成是今天的4点15了。

☞ Good morning, class. Before we begin today, I would like to address an issue that one of you *reminded* me *of* after the last lecture. 同学们，早上好。今天开始讲课前，我想讲一个问题，是上次讲座结束后你们当中的一个人提醒我的。

remote sense technology 遥感技术

☞ *Remote sense technology* has evolved into an important research tool for the natural sciences over the recent years. 近些年里，遥感技术在自然科学领域已演变成一个重要的研究工具。

🔍 该词经常出现在考古学场景中，要多加关注。

remove impurities from 从…中去除杂质

☞ The first step of the experiment is *removing impurities from* methanol. 这个实验的第一步是去除甲醇中的杂质。

representative of …的代表

☞ Next week we'll be looking at *the Gold Digger of 1933*, a piece that is very *representative of* the escapist trend in the films released during the Depression. 下周我们要看《1933年的淘金者》，这是一部在经济大萧条时期上映的有关逃避主义风潮的经典影片。

require...to 要求某人做

☞ A: I don't know why the university *requires* freshmen *to* live in dorms for a whole year!
　　B: Cheer up. You'll be able to live off-campus next year if you want!
　　A：我不知道为什么学校要求大一新生要在宿舍住一整年!
　　B：高兴点，如果你想的话，明年就可以搬出学校了!

☞ Using bicycles *requires* you *to* use both your arms and legs. 骑自行车需要你同时使用胳膊和腿。

☞ demand...to

required course 必修课

☞ A: I'm really disappointed; there are a couple of *required courses* I have to take before I can take the history class I'm interested in.
　　B: Don't be disappointed yet. You may be able to get special permission from the professor.
　　A：我真是失望透了，在我能选感兴趣的历史课前，还要上几门必修课。
　　B：先别失望，也许你可以从教授那里得到特许。

☞ A: Are you going to graduate this spring?
　　B: I still have two more *required courses*. Luckily, they are both being given this summer, so I don't have to wait until fall.

A：你是在今年春天毕业吗？

B：我还有两门必修课。不过幸运的是，课程都安排在夏天，所以就不用等到秋天了。

☞ compulsory course

🔍 selected course/optional course 选修课。另外，在美国的大学中，即使是必修课，学生也可以根据自己的时间来选择修读时间。换句话说，学生只要是修够专业课程的学分，其他选课很大程度上就是自主了。

research excavation 发掘研究

☞ The new *research excavation* will be one of the most exciting research projects this year. 这项新的发掘研究将是本年度最激动人心的研究项目之一。

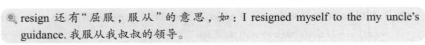

research excavation

research paper 研究论文

☞ A: Do you think I could use your computer to type my *research paper*?

B: If you don't mind waiting a couple of hours.

A：我能用你的计算机打我的研究论文吗？

B：如果你不介意等几个小时的话。

resemble telomeres 类端粒

☞ *Resemble telomeres* is capable of restoring cells to splitting. 类端粒可以使细胞恢复分裂能力。

reserved parking 预留停车位

☞ A: The sign says this is *reserved parking* only and your student parking sticker has expired, too.

B: I was just running in to turn in a paper, officer. I haven't been here for more than five minutes.

A：这个标牌上说这是预留停车位，而且你的学生停车许可证也过期了。

B：长官，我只是进去交论文，我到这儿还没有五分钟。

resign from 从⋯辞职

☞ Jeffrey intends to *resign from* his part-time position this semester. 杰弗里打算这个学期辞掉他的兼职职位。

resign one's seat/post/position 辞职

☞ Through careful consideration, I want to *resign* the current *post*. 经过慎重考虑，我打算辞掉现在的工作。

🔍 resign 还有"屈服，服从"的意思，如：I resigned myself to the my uncle's guidance. 我服从我叔叔的领导。

resistance genes 抗性基因

☞ The role of commensals in transmitting *resistance genes* is becoming a concern to the scientific field. 共生物在传递抗性基因过程中的角色正日益为科学领域所关注。

resistance to 抵制，抵抗

☞ My professor's *resistance to* the new construction proposal was perceived by us. 我们察觉到教授反对新的建筑议案。

respect for 对···尊重

☞ Frank Lloyd Wright was the greatest American architect of the 20th century who had great *respect for* the materials he used. 弗兰克·劳埃德·赖特是 20 世纪最伟大的美国建筑家，他非常尊重自己所使用的建筑材料。

respond to 回答，响应

☞ Today, we are going to talk about a special way some plants *respond to* being invaded by pests. 今天我们要讲的是，一些植物对于侵略它们的害虫所做出的特殊反应方式。

retreat from 从···撤退；逃避

☞ The soldiers should not *retreat from* their commitment. 士兵们不应该逃避他们的义务。

return address 寄信人地址

☞ A: Look! I got a letter from my cousin Jeff in Alaska.

B: Can I get the *return address* from the envelope?

A：看，我收到住在阿拉斯加堂(或表)哥/弟杰夫的来信了。

B：我可以从信封上得知寄信人的地址吗？

🔍 邮编可以说 post code 或 zip code。

review the material 复习资料

☞ A: So, have you finished *reviewing* all *the material* for the psychology exam?

B: Just about, but I still have details upon a few facts I'm not sure of.

A：你复习完心理学考试的所有内容了吗？

B：差不多了，但是我仍然对一些方面的细节不确定。

right away 立即，马上

☞ A: Nancy just got that special tennis racket she ordered through the mail.

B: Finally, that was a long time she had to wait. I'd bet she'd go out using it *right away*.

A：南希刚刚收到邮购来的特制网球拍。

B：终于到了，她等了很久啊，我打赌她会马上就用的。

☞ The doctor will give the man a new prescription *right away*. 医生要马上为这名男士开新药方。

☞ A: Sam won't be able to play in the basketball game this week.

B: Yah, he hurt his knee pretty badly a while back. I don't know why he didn't quit *right away*.

A：山姆这周不会打篮球赛了。

B：嗯，他的膝盖不久前受了严重的伤。我不知道他那时候为什么不马上退出。

☞ at once, immediately

ring off 挂断电话

☞ Due to the heavy schedule, I had to *ring off* at that time. 由于时间安排得很满，那时我必须挂掉电话。

ring up 打电话

☞ I will *ring up* now to see if my father is at home. 我现在就打个电话看看我爸爸在不在家。

rock and roll 摇滚乐

☞ The teacher had used *rock and roll* to demonstrate the principles of physics. 这名教师曾用摇滚乐来讲解物理原理。

roll up 卷起；到达；袅袅上升

☞ The scrolls of Buddhist manuscripts were very fragile, found *rolled up* in clay pots. 佛经手稿经卷很容易损坏，该经卷被发现时是卷起来放在泥罐里的。

rotten meat 腐烂的肉

☞ The *rotten meat* and the onion have stunk up the whole fridge. 腐肉和洋葱把整个冰箱都弄得很臭。

rule of thumb 经验法则，经验估计

☞ As a *rule of thumb*, you can cook lettuce for only two minutes. 凭经验而论，煮生菜只需要两分钟。

run away 逃跑，逃遁

☞ Do not let your anger *run away* in offices. 在办公室里，不要发脾气。

run behind 在…后面跑；落后于

run behind

A: The subway is ***running behind*** schedule, and traffic is backed up for blocks. I don't know if we'll make the 7:15 show.

B: It's a beautiful night. Let's try to get there on foot. And if we don't make it, let's just have dinner near the theater.

A：地铁晚点了，而且好几个街区都在堵车。我不知道我们能否赶上 7 点 15 的表演。

B：今天夜景很美，我们走着去吧。如果没赶上，我们就在剧院附近吃晚餐吧。

run counter to 违反，与…背道而驰

It may seem to ***run counter to*** common sense to say that introducing water into an area can cause it to become more like a desert. 把水引入某地会使该地更像沙漠，这种说法似乎与常识相悖。

NOTES

Unit 17

---

run down　跑下，往下跑；浏览，快读

☞ A: I think I'll **run down** to the bookstore and get a few things.

　　B: But aren't we going to meet Shirley at the student center? She is expecting us at 4. And it's almost that now.

　　A：我想我要跑去书店买点东西。

　　B：但我们不是要去学生中心跟雪莉见面吗？她四点在那里等我们。现在马上就到时间了。

🔍 down 在英语中除了有向下的意思外，通常还指"由郊区、城市的住宅区去向市区、商业区"，即向着城市中心的方向，比如我们用 down town 来指"市中心"。

　　与 run 相关的短语还有：run on 继续，run into sb. 偶遇某人，run out 用尽，耗尽。

---

run for　竞选

☞ A: James, I don't know if you know this. But I'm prepared to **run for** class president and I'm wondering if I can count on your vote?

　　B: Oh, maybe if you asked me sooner. But my roommate's running too and I've already promised him he had my support.

　　A：詹姆斯，我不知道你是否知道这件事。我准备竞选班长，我想我能否算上你的一票？

　　B：哦，你早点说的话也许可以。但是，我的室友也参加竞选，我已经答应支持他了。

🔍 在国外，学生干部也是由竞选选出的，参加竞选的人需要自己进行拉票、策划、宣传等一系列事情，很培养学生的能力。

---

run out of　用完，耗尽

☞ A: The view is spectacular. Could you take a picture of me with the mountains in the background?

　　B: I'm afraid I just **ran out of** film.

　　A：景色太美了，你能以山为背景给我照张相吗？

　　B：恐怕我的胶卷用完了。

☞ A: I can't believe that you missed the class again. Didn't professor Odell say something to you that last time?

B: Well, this time is different. I had a good excuse. My car *ran out of* gas.

A：我不能相信你又缺课了。难道上次奥德尔教授没和你说什么吗？

B：嗯，这次不一样，我有正当理由。我的汽车没油了。

☞ exhaust, deplete, use up

🔍 注意本短语中相邻两个单词会发生连读现象。

rush hour　高峰期

☞ A: Why don't we drive downtown now?

B: Wouldn't it be better to wait till after *rush hour*?

A：我们为什么不现在开车去城里呢？

B：等到过了高峰期不是更好些吗？

☞ A: Why are you leaving so early? The movie doesn't start till seven.

B: I don't want to be at the traffic there. It's a nightmare on the express way during *rush hour*.

A：你为什么这么早出发呢？电影七点才开演呢。

B：我可不想在车上待那么久。高峰时期待在高速公路上简直就是一场噩梦。

☞ peak time

rush out of　从…奔出来

☞ Several students said to the police that they saw two thieves *rush out of* the supermarket and run towards a car. 几名学生对警察说，他们看见两个小偷从超市跑出来，然后奔向一辆小轿车。

sacrificial ceremony　祭祀仪式

☞ A grand *sacrificial ceremony* will take place in this county this weekend. 这周末一场盛大的祭祀活动要在这个小镇举行。

sales coordinator　销售协调员

☞ Mark, a *sales coordinator* of this airline company, is selling air tickets at the company branch in Britain. 马克是这家航空公司的销售协调员，他正在该公司的伦敦分公司销售机票。

sales representative　销售代表

☞ Jerry served as a fertilizer *sales representative* this summer. 今年夏天，杰里做了化肥销售代表。

sample survey　抽样调查

☞ *Sample survey* plays a very important role in modern society that allows us to collect data in short time. 在当今社会，抽样调查起着很重要的作用，它能让我们在短时间内收集数据。

Sanitation Department　卫生部

☞ A: How do I get one of those green buckets?

　B: Oh, just call up the *Sanitation Department*. They'll deliver a bucket at no charge.

　A：我怎么才能领到一个那样的绿桶呢？

　B：哦，只要给卫生部门打个电话就行，他们会免费给你送一个的。

save...for　为…保留；为…储存，积攒(钱物等)

☞ Is it better to enjoy your money when you earn it or is it better to *save* your money *for* some time in the future? 是挣钱就花掉好呢，还是攒起来以备将来之用好呢？

save face　挽回脸面

☞ The two actors had done some charities over the past three months to *save face* in the scandal. 这两名演员在过去三个月中做慈善来挽回在丑闻中丢失的面子。

save up　存钱

☞ A: By walking through spring break, I managed to *save up* the US $500 for the trip to Canada this summer. How are you coming along?

　B: I'm still a way's off.

　A：整个春假我都四处奔走，终于攒够了夏天去加拿大旅行的 500 美元，你呢？

　B：我还差一些。

saving account　储蓄账户

☞ A: I'd like to enroll in the free seminar you advertised in newspaper, the one on managing your personal finances.

　B: Okay. Now the ad did say that you have to have a *saving account* at our bank to be eligible. Do you have one here?

　A：我想参加你们在报纸上登广告的那个自由研讨会，内容是关于个人理财的。

　B：好，广告上还说必须有我们银行的储蓄账户才有资格参加。您有吗？

sb. is only a phone call away　随时打电话都可以找到某人

☞ A: You were right about the puzzle you lent me last week. It really is a challenge. I want to try to get it myself though. So I'm going to work on it a little longer.

　B: Well, if you get really stuck, remember I'm *only a phone call away*.

　A：你说得对，你上周借我的那个拼图真是个挑战。但是我还想自己把它拼出来，所以我想再多研究一段时间。

　B：嗯，如果你实在搞不定了，记得打电话随时可找到我噢。

scarce mineral 稀缺矿物

☞ The manufacturing process uses up many *scarce minerals*. 这个生产过程用掉很多稀有矿物质。

scarce mineral

science auditorium 科学礼堂

☞ A: You wanna go to a lecture tonight over in the *science auditorium*? It's some guy who spent a year living in Antarctica.

B: No kidding! I'm doing a report on Antarctica for my geography class. Maybe I can get some good information to add to it.

A：你想去参加今晚在科学礼堂举行的讲座吗？演讲人是一个在南极洲生活了一年的人。

B：是真的吗！我正在写地理学课上关于南极洲的一个报告，也许我可以得到些有用的信息加到报告里。

science fiction fare 科幻节目

☞ A: Do you know about the *science fiction fair* on Saturday?

B: Of course, I wouldn't miss it for the world.

A：你知道周六那个科幻小说展览吗？

B：当然，无论如何我都不会错过的。

🔍 science fiction 科幻小说　　　　thriller 恐怖小说
detective novel 推理小说　　　　fantasy novel 魔幻小说

scientific discovery 科学发现

☞ This morning I want to tell you about a recent *scientific discovery* dealing with the relation between plants and animals. 今早，我要给你们讲一个最近的科学发现，关于植物和动物之间的关系。

scientific instrument 科学器械

☞ The researchers made the measurement with *scientific instrument*. 这些研究人员用科学器械来进行测量。

scientific study 科学研究

☞ The bunch of people are going for a field trip to conduct a *scientific study*. 这群人要去实地考察，做一个科学研究。

scrape off 削掉，刮去

☞ A: Oh, oh, I've burned your toast. I'll put in a couple of more slices.

B: No, don't waste the bread. Just *scrape off* the burnt part; it will be fine.

A：哦，哦，我把你的吐司烤糊了，我会再给你烤几片的。

B：不用了，别浪费面包了，把烤糊的地方削掉就好了。

scrape through   擦过，勉强通过，挤过

☞ Fat Danny are trying her best to *scrape through* the narrow aisle in the church. 胖丹尼用尽全力想挤过教堂里的窄小过道。

sculpture exhibit   雕塑展览

☞ A: I heard that the turn-out for the opening of the new *sculpture exhibit* was kind of disappointing.

B: I guess a lot of other people feel the way I do about modern art.

A：我听说新雕塑展览开幕有些令人失望。

B：我猜这就是很多人和我一样对现代艺术的感觉。

sea view   海景

☞ The manager made a reservation for a *sea view* room. 经理预订了一间海景房。

seasonal change   季节性改变

☞ Swallows migrate according to *seasonal change*. 燕子随着季节的变化而迁徙。

seed reproduction   种子繁殖

☞ Joe's final paper is written about studies on *seed reproduction* technique of tomato. 乔的期末论文写的是西红柿的种子繁殖技术。

send for   派人去请；召唤；申请，订购

☞ A: What's the matter, sir?

B: Can you do me a favor to *send for* a doctor right now?

A: Of course.

A：先生，有什么事？

B：你能马上帮我请一位医生吗？

A：当然可以。

send in   呈报，提交

☞ People from the television station have requested the viewers to *send in* their suggestions. 来自电视台的人要求观众提交他们的建议。

send out   发送，派遣

☞ The couple planned to *send out* all the invitations. 这对夫妇准备把所有的请帖都发出去。

☞ A: Gloria, are you going to *send out* invitations to the dance?

B: No. I got Dan to do it.

A：格洛丽亚，你要去送舞会的请帖吗？

B：不，我让丹去做了。

send out a questionnaire   散发问卷

☞ A: I just don't know if you should call everyone to collect the data or just *send out a questionnaire*. But you'd better make a decision soon.

B: I know. There's only one month till the election.

A：我还不知道你是应该打电话给每个人收集数据还是只分发一个调查问卷。但是你最好尽快做一个决定。

B：我知道，离选举还有一个月的时间了。

send out signals 发出信号

☞ Each of the satellites is constantly *sending out signals,* and each signal contains important information that can be used to determine the longitude, latitude and elevation at any point on the earth's surface. 每个卫星都持续发出信号，每个信号都包含着重要的信息，这些信息可以用来决定地球表面任何一点的经度、纬度和海拔高度。

sensory organ 感觉器官

☞ A grasshopper has two *sensory organs* located at the end of its abdomen. 蝗虫腹部末端有两个感觉器官。

separate from 从⋯分离

☞ Rodeos at agricultural fairs became so popular that ranchers and business people began to organize rodeos as independent events, *separate from* fairs. 骑术竞技表演在农贸集市上很受欢迎，所以大农场主和商人开始将这种表演从集市中分离出来，独立举办。

☞ Now we've been talking about the revolutionary period in the United States history when the colonies wanted to *separate from* England. 我们已经讲过了美国历史中殖民地想要从英国的统治中分离出来的革命时期。

🔍 注意 separate 和 divide 都是分开的意思，但是两个词是有所区别的，divide 表示把一个整体分成几部分，而 separate 是把整体中的某一部分分离出来。

set a record 创纪录，破纪录

☞ A: The concert *set a record* for attendance.

B: I understand there wasn't an empty seat in the house.

A：这场演唱会的上座率创纪录了。

B：我明白，屋中已经没空位了。

set sb./sth. up 安顿；安排；竖立，架起；建立，创立

set a record

☞ A: Michelle, this is Jeff, our new reporter. Would you have some time today to show him around? You know introducing to the others make him feel at home.

B: I'll be happy to. Then after lunch I can *set him up* at his desk so he can get to work.

A：米歇尔，这是杰夫，我们的新记者，你今天有时间带他到处转转吗？你知道的，把他介绍给其他人，让他感觉自在一些。

B：我很乐意，那么午饭后我就给他安排座位，这样他就可以开始工作了。

☞ A: The conference on career planning is only a month away, but there are still a few things that our organizing committee needs to work out.

B: Then it's clear that we'd better meet again and soon. Would you mind *setting it up*?

A：还有一个月就要开关于职业规划的会议了，但是我们组织委员会还有一些事情要做。

B：很明显，我们最好尽快再开一次会。你来安排一下好吗？

☞ A: Haven't you noticed the tents that had already been *set up*?

B: Yes, I have. What are they for?

A：你难道没注意到那些帐篷已经搭起来了吗？

B：是啊，注意到了，它们是用来做什么的呢？

☞ In Canada, the first wood pulp mill was *set up* in 1866 and it was immediately successful. 在加拿大，第一所木浆厂于 1866 年成立并且马上就成功了。

---

set sth. apart 使…分离

☞ The section was *set apart* for the exclusive use of reading. 这部分被分离出来是专门用来阅读的。

☞ dissociate from

---

set the alarm clock 设置闹钟

☞ Do *set the alarm clock* before you go to bed. 在你上床睡觉前一定要设置闹钟。

---

settle down 平静；定居，过安定的生活

☞ A: My neighbor comes home every night around 10 with his car windows rolled down and radio blaring. It stops as soon as he turns the car off. But by then Brian and Lisa are wide awake.

B: Oh, no.

A: Oh, Yes. Sometimes it takes us till midnight just to get them *settle down* again.

A：我的邻居每天都深夜 10 点左右回家，车窗开着，收音机开得很大声。等他把车熄火后，声音才会停下来，但是那时候布赖恩和莉萨就都醒了。

B：哦，不会吧。

A：哦，是的。有时，我们得到半夜才能把他们再哄入睡。

---

severe winter 严冬

☞ A: The forecast is for a *severe winter*. Are you prepared?

B: Hardly. I'm waiting for the next sale to get a down jacket.

A：天气预报说今年我们会有个严冬，你准备好了吗？

B：没有，我在等下一次大减价时买件羽绒服。

---

share sth. with 与…分享

☞ We are fortunate that Joe's consented to come to *share* some of his experiences *with* us. 我们很幸运地请到乔来和我们一起分享他的一些经验。

☞ I'd like to **share with** you today my experience with a new approach to building a house. 今天，我想和你们一起分享关于我采用新方法建造房子的经验。

sharpen sth.　使…锋利

☞ A: I'm having trouble slicing the bread with this knife.

B: Oh. Sorry about that. I haven't gotten around to **sharpening** it yet.

A：我用这把刀切面包有些困难。

B：哦，抱歉，我忘了磨刀了。

🔍 削铅笔: sharpen the pencil

shed out　散发，散布

☞ The huge impact created a vapor that **shed out** into space and eventually condensed as the moon. 巨大的冲击力形成了水汽，水汽散发于太空中最终凝结形成月球。

shift to　转移到；转换为

☞ When got stuck in writing a story, just **shift to** something else, like doing some work for one of other courses. 当写小说没有思路的时候，就换点其他的事情做，比如做其他科目的作业。

shipbuilding industry　造船业

☞ The lecture mainly talks about the development of the **shipbuilding industry** in New England. 这次讲座主要讲了新英格兰造船业的发展。

show (sb.) around　带领…参观

☞ A: Michelle, this is Jeff, our new reporter. Would you have some time today to **show him around**. You know introducing to the others make him feel at home.

B: I'll be happy to. Then after lunch I can set him up at his desk so he can get to work.

A：米歇尔，这是杰夫，我们的新记者，你今天有时间带他到处转转吗？你知道的，把他介绍给其他人，让他感觉自在一些。

B：我很乐意，那么午饭后我就给他安排座位，这样他就可以开始工作了。

show off　展示；使夺目；卖弄

☞ All the sponsors for the grand game are **showing off** their corporate social responsibility through various activities. 这次盛会的所有赞助商都在通过各种活动来展示他们企业的社会责任。

show up　出现，露面

☞ A: Oh, hi, I hate to tell you but we're done with lunch and dessert is on its way. We decided you weren't going to **show up**.

B: I can understand that. I've never seen such traffic. I am glad you didn't wait.

A：哦，嗨，我真不想告诉你我们已经吃完午饭了，马上就上甜点了。我们都以为你不会来了。

B：我能理解，我从没见过这么差的交通状况。我很高兴你们没有等我。

☞ A: What's keeping Kevin? He said last night he'd meet us here by 2 o'clock and it's already 2:30.

B: It's so typical of him, isn't it? Just watch, he's going to *show up* in 5 minutes with some wild excuse.

A：凯尔文又怎么了？他昨晚说今天两点钟在这里和我们见面，但是现在都两点半了。

B：他一向如此，不是吗？看着吧，他会在五分钟之内出现，并编一些不着边际的理由。

☞ appear

---

shuffle deck   洗牌

☞ A: When you are the dummy, what do you do while the cards are being played?

B: Anything you want. Sit there and study, *shuffle* another *deck*, get snacks for everyone. I like to stand behind my partner and watch.

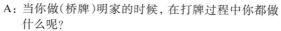

A：当你做（桥牌）明家的时候，在打牌过程中你都做什么呢？

B：做任何你想做的事，坐在那里研究，洗牌，给每个人弄点心。我喜欢站在我搭档的后面看。

---

sign a petition   签请愿书

☞ A: We're organizing a rally on Thursday afternoon to get the administration to reconsider the parking lot plan.

B: Well, I have a class on Thursday afternoon.

A: But, maybe you could *sign this petition*? We're going to submit it to the administration to demonstrate how the students feel about this.

B: Sure, let me get a pen and I'll sign it.

A：我们会在周四下午组织一次集会让管理处重新考虑停车场计划。

B：哦，我周四下午有课。

A：但是，你能签一下这个请愿书吗？我们要把它呈交给管理处去告诉他们学生是如何看待这件事的。

B：当然可以，我找支笔，这就签。

---

sign up   登记；注册

☞ A: Do you want to *sign up* for professor. Wilson's class? I heard he got his doctorate when he was 19.

B: Really?

A：你想报名上威尔逊教授的课吗？我听说他 19 岁就取得了博士学位。

B：真的吗？

☞ A: I wish I knew how to swim.

B: Why not *sign up* for the lessons offered by the Physical Education Department?

A：我希望自己会游泳。

B：为什么不报名上体育教育系开的课呢？

🔍 托福考试中，sign up 后常接介词 for，注意听 for 后面的内容。

skip a lecture 逃掉讲座

☞ George decides to *skip the lecture* given by the new professor. 乔治准备逃掉新教授的讲座。

slam on 猛击

☞ John has to *slam on* the brake to avoid an accident. 约翰不得不猛踩刹车来避免发生车祸。

slave trade 奴隶贸易

☞ On 2 March 1807 Thomas Jefferson signed a bill abolishing the *slave trade* to take effect on 1 January 1808. 在 1807 年 3 月 2 日，托马斯·杰弗逊颁布了一项废除奴隶交易的制度，该法案在 1808 年 1 月生效。

sleeping schedule 睡眠时间表

☞ A: They say the exercise is good for you, but I don't know. I mean dragging myself out of bed six-day and every day to go to the gym is reeking head on my *sleeping schedule*.

B: Sure, but who says you need to go every day?

A：人们说锻炼有好处，但是我不知道。我的意思是说，每周六天都要强迫自己早起，而且每天都要去健身房，这与我的睡眠时间冲突。

B：的确，可是谁说你每天都要去？

slice the bread 把面包切片

☞ Please *slice the bread* thin for the best toast. 请将面包切薄一点，这样烤得最好。

slip one's mind 忘记

☞ A: Donna, you said you'd take this package to accounting yesterday.

B: Oh, no. It must have *slipped my mind*.

A：唐纳，你昨天说过你要把这个包裹带去算账。

B：哦，天啊。我一定是忘了。

☞ A: Nobody told me that Bill was ill in hospital.

B: Sorry. I meant to give you a call when I found out, but it *slipped my mind*.

A：没有人告诉我比尔住院了。

B：对不起，我知道后想给你打电话来着，但是我忘记了。

☞ A: Jane, didn't you get my messages? I left two on your answering machine.

B: Ah? Sorry, Tom. I've been meaning to get back in touch with you. It just *slipped my mind*.

A：简，你难道没收到我的信息吗？我在你的电话答录机上留了两条。

B：啊？抱歉，汤姆。我想着回来联系你的，可是我忘了。

slip out of　从…脱落，滑落；被泄漏，不慎说出

☞ Please just give me several seconds to *slip out of* the wet clothes and I'll join the card game. 只给我几秒钟的时间脱掉这些湿衣服，然后和你们一起打牌。

slog through　步履艰难地行进；顽强地行进

☞ A: I'm the only one in class who didn't sign up for the biology trip. *Slogging through* a swamp in the rain can't get fun.

B: Nope. But I've got the feeling your classmates will come back knowing some things you won't know.

A：我是班里唯一一个没有报名参加生物学旅行的。在雨天的沼泽中艰难行进可没什么意思。

B：不是这样的。我觉得你的同学回来后会学到很多你不知道的知识。

slow reader　阅读速度很慢的人

☞ A: Sorry, but I can't go and have a cup of coffee with you now. I've only done half the readings for the philosophy class tomorrow.

B: And I thought I was a *slow reader*.

A：对不起，我现在不能和你去喝咖啡，明天哲学课的阅读我只读了一半。

B：我原以为我的阅读速度很慢呢。

so far　迄今

☞ *So far*, I'm really enjoying this course given by the professor. 目前为止，我真的很喜欢这位教授的课。

☞ A: And how many people have made pledges for you?

B: Eleven *so far*.

A：有多少人向你保证呢？

B：迄今为止有 11 个。

☞ A: Our basketball team's won every game *so far*.

B: Isn't that because of the new coach?

A：迄今为止，我们篮球队获得全胜。

B：是因为那个新教练吗？

☞ A: *So far* the clubs are about three hundred dollars in the red, and we still have four months to go before membership renewal.

B: Well, we may have to raise our dues.

A：到目前为止，俱乐部赤字约 300 美元。距会员资格更新还有四个月。

B：嗯，我们可能得提高会员费。

so the story goes 据传说

☞ Smith, *so the story goes*, was about to be executed when twelve-year-old Poke Hunters lay her head on top of his. 据传说，史密斯正要被处死时，12 岁的普克·亨特斯把自己的头置于其之上。

soak up the sun 晒日光浴

soak up the sun

☞ You may *soak up the sun* on the sand beaches or go shopping during the summer holiday. 你可以在暑假期间去沙滩晒日光浴或是购物。

soap bubble 肥皂泡

☞ Almost everyone likes to play *soap bubble* at childhood. 几乎每个人在小时候都喜欢玩肥皂泡。

soccer team 足球队

☞ A: I pretty much decide that I want to play on the *soccer team* next semester.

B: You are certainly good enough, but well, would you just tell me about how you really need to concentrate on improving your grades next semester?

A：我基本上决定了下学期参加足球队。

B：你当然有这个资格参加，但是你能先告诉我你下学期如何提高考试分数吗？

🔍 在美国的大学校园里，课外活动相当丰富。放学后(after class)，学生可以参加各种俱乐部，如戏剧俱乐部(drama club)、棒球俱乐部(baseball club)、橄榄球俱乐部(rugby club)等。

Ⓝⓞⓣⓔⓢ

Unit 18

social awareness 社会意识

☞ A: Look at all the pollution going into the air from those factories. Do you think
    they'll ever get that under control?

  B: With the new laws and *social awareness*, we'll turn things around.

  A：看一看从那些工厂排放到空气中的所有污染物，你认为它们会得到控
    制吗?

  B：随着新法律的出台和社会意识的提高，我们会使情况得到改善的。

social benefits 社会效益

☞ I do not know what kind of *social benefits* we can have through this round of
  promotion campaign. 我不知道通过这轮促销，我们可以得到什么样的社会
  效益。

social recognition 社会认同

☞ *Social recognition* is important for the evolution of an enterprise. 社会认同对一个
  企业的发展来说很重要。

soda machine 汽水机

☞ There were no big *soda machine* at any corner of the station or even drinking
  fountains. 车站的各个角落都没有大的汽水机，甚至都没有饮用水。

solar calendar 阳历

☞ In the *solar calendar*, May the first is International Labor Day. 阳历 5 月 1 日是国
  际劳动节。

solar eclipse 日食

☞ These students got up on the roof to watch the *solar eclipse*. 这些学生都爬上房顶
  看日食。

🔍 月食: lunar eclipse

solar power 太阳能

☞ We can use *solar power* to make electricity. 我们可以用太阳能发电。

☞ solar energy

🔍 表示"能源"的短语还有: nuclear energy 核能, wind power 风能。

216

solar system 太阳系

☞ Is the earth's moon larger than other moons or satellites in the *solar system*?
地球的卫星比太阳系中的其他卫星都要大吗?

🔍 太阳系包括八大行星, 依次是水星(Mercury)、金星(Venus)、地球(Earth)、火星（Mars)、木星（Jupiter)、土星（Saturn)、天王星（Uranus）和海王星（Neptune)。

sort of 有几分, 有那么点儿

☞ A: That chocolate cake looks delicious. Are you going to have some with me?

B: Well, that was a huge meal we just had, and I was *sort of* watching my calorie and ..., but what a healthy birthday only comes once a year.

A: 那个巧克力蛋糕看起来很好吃, 要和我一起吃一点吗?

B: 哦, 我们刚刚吃了一顿大餐, 我最近有点儿注意自己摄入的卡路里和···, 但是一年只有一次的生日怎么能只考虑到健康呢。

sound like 听起来像

☞ A: It's the third time this week my roommate had a party in our room. This is really starting to affect my class work. I wonder if I should talk to someone at the housing office about changing rooms.

B: *Sounds like* you've got a legitimate reason. You two are just not compatible at all.

A: 我的室友又在宿舍开派对, 这已经是本周的第三次了。这真的开始影响我做作业了。我在想我是否该和住宿部的人说说换个房间。

B: 听起来你的理由很合理。你们两个完全合不来。

spare time 空闲时间

☞ There is enough *spare time* to fix the projector. 有足够的空闲时间来修理这个投影仪。

special order 特别订货; 特别指令

☞ John was accused of violating the *special order* policy of the company. 约翰被指控违反了公司的特别订货政策。

special permission 特许

☞ A: I'm really disappointed; there are a couple of required courses I have to take before I can take the history class I'm interested in.

B: Don't be disappointed yet. You may be able to get *special permission* from the professor.

A: 我真是失望透了, 在我能选感兴趣的历史课前, 还要上几门必修课。

B: 先别失望, 也许你可以从教授那里得到特许。

spend budget 用掉预算

☞ A: I really need to make some extra money. I've practically *spent* my entire *budget* for the semester.

B: You should check out the new cafeteria. I think there're a few openings left in the evening.

A：我真的需要多挣一些钱了。我已经把整个学期的预算都花完了。

B：你可以去看看新开的那家餐厅，我想那里有些晚班的职位还空着。

🔍 注意 spend 和 budget 连读时会发生吞音现象，spend 的最后一个音 / d / 只完成发音位置，不发出声音。

spend...(in) doing 花…时间做

☞ I *spend* a lot of time tending to my garden. 我花大量时间照料我的花园。

🔍 托福听力中经常会出现在某地度假，如 spend my vocation in New York 在纽约度假。

spray cans 喷雾罐

☞ I remember reading something about DME. It's mostly used in *spray cans*, right? 我记得以前读过关于二甲醚的文章，它们大多数都装在喷雾罐里，对吗？

spread fertilizer 施肥

☞ These farmers *spread fertilizer* over the field at this time every year. 每年的这个时候，这些农民都在这块地上施肥。

spread over 遍布，覆盖

☞ The plastic beads are *spread over* an increasingly wide interval. 这些塑料珠子以一个比一个宽的间距散布开来。

spread up 分散

☞ A: How many people will be at the family reunion party?

B: Around sixty. My family is big and *spread up*, but we're pretty close.

A：有多少人会参加家庭聚会？

B：大概 60 人，我的家庭虽然庞大而且居住分散，但是关系很亲密。

spring break 春季休假

☞ A: Have you finalized your plans for *spring break* yet?

B: Well, I could visit some friends in Florida, or go to my roommate's home. It's a tough choice.

A：你定下来春季休假计划了吗？

B：嗯，我可以去佛罗里达州看朋友，或者去我室友的家里。这挺难决定。

☞ We will take a climbing trip during *spring break*. 我们将在春季休假时去爬山。

🔍 暑假可以表示为 summer break，寒假为 winter break。

stage setting 舞台布景

☞ The *stage setting* has a certain effect on an opera. 舞台布景对歌剧有一定的影响。

🔍 常考短语还有：stage effect 舞台效果

stage setting

stand a chance 很可能，有希望

☞ A: I've been trying to solve this puzzle for hours, but I just can't seem to get it.

　B: Well, if you can't, I won't *stand a chance*.

　A：我努力地解这道难题已经有几个小时了，但是我还是弄不明白。

　B：哦，如果你都不能解出来的话，我就更没希望了。

standard weight 标准重量

☞ A: How was the *standard weight* used?

　B: Well, the people in our department use it to check the scales all over the country.

　A：标准重量是如何被运用的？

　B：嗯，我们部门的人用它来衡量全国范围的重要尺度。

start out 出发，动身；着手进行

☞ A: What time should we *start out*?

　B: About seven from the hotel.

　A：我们大约几点出发？

　B：大约七点从酒店走。

☞ set off

start with 以…开始

☞ Let me *start with* some statistics. Did you know that 90% of the coast in this country is eroding? On the gulf of Mexico for instance, erosion averages 4 to 5 feet per year. 让我们以一些数据开始吧。你知道这个国家里 90%的海岸正在遭受侵蚀吗？拿墨西哥湾海岸为例吧，平均每年要被侵蚀四到五英尺。

☞ A: Hey Teresa! Thanks for agreeing to help me review all this history material.

　B: No problem, Bob. So do you want to *start with* the stuff missed yesterday? They are part about urban problems in the colonial period?

　A: Yeah, that'll be great.

　A：嘿，特雷莎！谢谢你同意帮我复习所有这些历史材料。

　B：不客气，鲍勃。那么你想从昨天落下的部分开始吗？一部分是关于殖民时期的城市问题？

　A：是的，太好了。

☞ begin with

statistical calculation 统计计算

☞ ***Statistical calculations*** should be done by hand. 统计计算应由人工进行。

statistical data 统计数据

☞ The latest ***statistical data*** shows that a qualified doctor can save more than 1,000 people's lives all his life long. 最新的统计数据表明，一个称职的医生在他的一生中可以挽救 1000 多人的生命。

statistics course 统计学课程

☞ Martin hopes to take a ***statistics course*** soon. 马丁希望很快就能上统计学课程。

stay awake 保持清醒

☞ We always ***stay awake*** for the midnight news program. 我们经常熬夜看午夜的新闻节目。

stay open 开门营业

☞ A: I thought the libraries ***stayed open*** till midnight during the weekend.

B: Well, their hours are shorter during the winter.

A：我还以为图书馆在周末会开到午夜呢。

B：嗯，在冬天的时候营业时间会缩短。

☞ keep open

🔍 托福考试中经常考到 stay 的一个的含义"保持"，其他词组还有：stay closed 关门，stay healthy 保持健康。

stay up 熬夜

☞ I have to ***stay up*** to finish my chemistry. 我得熬夜做完化学作业。

☞ A: Debra says she is going to ***stay up*** all night studying for her exam tomorrow morning.

B: Wouldn't she be better off getting a good night sleep so she will feel fresh in the morning?

A：德布拉说为了明早的考试，她今晚要通宵学习。

B：好好睡一觉会不会更有帮助呢？这样她明早就会感觉很清醒。

stick around 待在…附近

☞ A: Leaving the party so soon? We're just getting ready to cut the cake.

B: Sorry, I can't ***stick around***.

A：这么快就离开晚宴？我们正要切蛋糕呢。

B：抱歉，我不能待在这儿了。

stick with 坚持，继续做

☞ A: I started reading that book you loaned me, but I'm having a tough time keeping up with the main characters. It's hard to remember them all.

B: Yeah, I know. The first part isn't easy. All I can say is to **stick with** it. Once you get halfway through you won't want to put it down.

A：我开始读你借给我的那本书了，但是很难分清里面的主要人物。要记住所有人物很难。

B：是的，我知道，开始的部分确实不容易。我能说的就是坚持下去，一旦你读到一半，就不想放下了。

☞ A: I wonder what this new flavor of ice cream tastes like?

B: I tried it last week. If I were you, I would **stick with** an old favorite.

A：我想知道这种新口味的冰激凌吃起来怎么样？

B：我上周吃过了。如果我是你，还会吃以前喜欢的口味。

☞ A: I'm thinking about dropping my swimming class. I am just not catching on.

B: **Stick with** it. I did and I learned how to swim, eventually.

A：我正在考虑退掉游泳课。我有点跟不上了。

B：坚持下去。我坚持了，最后学会了游泳。

☞ insist on

stir up 搅动；激起，煽动

☞ A: Turbidity currents? Oh, yeah! When sediment like sand or mud gets **stirred up** and mixes with water?

B: Good!

A：浑浊流？哦，对！那是当沙子或泥之类的沉积物被搅动并和水混合后所产生的吗？

B：正确！

stock exchange 证券交易所

☞ In addition to being a place where business deals are made, a **stock exchange** collects statistics, publishes price quotations, and sets rules and standards for trading. 除了是生意成交的地方外，证券交易所还收集信息，发布价格行情，并为交易制定规则和标准。

stock holder 股东，股票持有人

☞ Bill became the first **stock holder** of the firm. 比尔成为了这家公司的第一大股东。

🔍 "股市"用英语说就是 stock market，"董事会"是 board of directors。

stop at 在…停留

☞ A: Look we're almost out of gas. We'd better **stop at** the next gas station. We have enough to make to the campus.

B: If we stop now, we'll be late for class.

A：看，我们的汽油快用完了，我们最好在下个加油站停一下，这样我们就能开到校园了。

B：如果我们现在停下，上课就会迟到的。

☞ stop over

straighten up　整理，清理；(使)挺直

☞ A: I am going to *straighten up* my desk now.

B: It's about time.

A：我现在要整理一下我的桌子。

B：是该整理了。

☞ clean up, clear up, tidy up

straighten up

strategic objective　战略目标

☞ The bunch of people have showed a bunch of *strategic objectives* to start this program. 那群人展示了开展这个项目的一系列战略目标。

strong flavor　口味重

☞ The kind of cookie has a *strong flavor* of onion. 这种饼干有浓重的洋葱味。

structure program　程序结构

☞ Ben was awarded 1,000 dollars for his *structure program* block. 本因设计了结构程序模块而获得了 1000 美元奖金。

struggle with　与…做斗争

☞ A: Do you have any idea why David wants to see me tomorrow? Is he having problems with his accounting project?

B: Yeah, he's been *struggling with* it from day on and I'm told you're an expert on that stuff.

A：你知道戴维为什么明天想见我吗？他的会计项目出了问题吗？

B：是的。他费力弄了一天也没结果，听说你是这方面的专家。

student center　学生中心

☞ Before we get to the *student center*, I'd like to show you Smith Hall. 在我们去学生中心前，我想带你看看史密斯礼堂。

student loan　学生贷款

☞ You could still apply for a *student loan* or sign up for a work-study program. 你仍旧可以申请学生贷款或者是参加一个勤工俭学项目。

☞ A: I thought there was still time for me to apply for *student loan*. But someone just told me that the closing date was last Wednesday.

B: Are you sure? I thought we still had another month. Wait, I've got a brochure right here. Last Wednesday was the opening date.

A：我以为还有时间去申请学生贷款呢，可是有人刚刚告诉我截止日期是上周三。

B：你确定吗？我以为我们还有一个月的时间呢。等一下，我正好有本手册。啊，上周三是开始日期啊。

student service　学生服务

☞ Students have access to some resources by logging into the **Student Service** Centre. 学生们可以通过登录"学生服务中心"使用某些资源。

🔍 学生会是 Student Union，有时缩写为 ST。

subdued color　柔和的颜色

☞ **Subdued colors** are frequently used in studies and bedrooms. 柔和的颜色常用于书房和卧室。

🔍 相关短语有：

warm color 暖色　　　　　　　　dark color 深色

subject to　取决于…；受…支配；使服从；使遭受

☞ In certain states clothes are **subject to** tax. 在某些州，衣服交易是要交税的。

☞ The Roman Empire **subjected** most of Europe **to** its rule. 罗马帝国把欧洲多数地区都置于自己的统治之下。

🔍 subject 作形容词时，be subject to 意为"易遭受…的；取决于；服从于"；作动词时，subject sb./sth. to sth. 意为"使某人或某物服从于/遭受"。

submit to　递交，提交；屈服，投降

☞ The female student didn't **submit** the thesis proposal **to** her professor on time. 那名女学生没有按时将论文开题报告交给她的教授。

suffer from　患（病）；遭受…的痛苦

☞ If our bodies are not exposed to ultraviolet rays from the sun we cannot convert vitamin D to its active form, and thus cannot make use of any of the calcium that we have consumed in our food. Eventually we would **suffer from** a calcium deficiency and have weak bones. 如果我们的身体不接触来自太阳的紫外线，我们就不能把维生素 D 转化成其活跃形式，这样我们就不能利用我们食物中所摄取的钙，最后就会患钙缺失以及骨质疏松。

summer break/holiday 暑假

☞ A: If I can keep up the pace I'll graduate in just three years.

B: That might be true, but I never want to give up my *summer breaks*.

A：如果我能以这个速度学习的话，我会在三年内毕业。

B：可能是吧，但是我绝对不会放弃我的暑假。

sun mass 太阳质量

☞ The *sun mass* is a standard way to express mass in astronomy, used to describe the masses of other stars and galaxies. 太阳质量在天文学上是质量的一个标准，用于描述其他恒星和星系的质量。

sun wind 太阳风

☞ Scientists forecast that a *sun wind* will break out next year. 科学家预测太阳风将于明年爆发。

supply...for 为…提供

☞ The company *supplies* printers *for* several schools in the city. 该公司为这个城市的一些学校提供打印机。

supply of 供应，补给

☞ There is an important precondition that must exist before you have advertising, and that's a large *supply of* consumer goods, that is, things to sell. 在你做广告之前，有个非常重要的前提条件，那就是有大量的消费品供应，即要出售的东西。

☞ Advertising really came into its own and became a central part of doing business, during the industry revolution. Suddenly there was a much greater *supply of* things to sell. 在工业革命期间，广告逐渐兴起，并成为了商业中的重要部分。一夜之间突然有了大量需要销售的东西。

☞ People who're dieting need a variety of foods to assure a constant *supply of* nutrients their bodies need. 节食的人需要吃多种类的食物，以保证他们身体所需营养得到持续供应。

support one's argument 支持某人的论点

☞ To *support their argument*, Unitarians stress the consistency of the character portrayed in the poetry. 为了支持他们的论点，一神论者强调诗歌中描述的人物要一致。

survey method 测量方法

☞ The elevation of Mount Everest was determined many years ago using traditional *surveying methods*. 珠穆朗玛峰的海拔高度是在很多年前用传统的测量方法测定的。

survive on 靠…维持生计

☞ Most of the children were abandoned, left to *survive on* their own effort. 这些孩子中大部分都是被抛弃的，要靠自己的努力生存。

swale erosion 洼地侵蚀

☞ The canyon is the result of *swale erosion*. 峡谷是洼地侵蚀的结果。

switch hours with 与…调时间

☞ A: You don't like evening classes?

B: No, that's not the point. I work in the cafeteria every evening. I need the money to pay my tuition.

A: Can you ask someone that works to *switch hours with* you? Maybe you could just switch a couple of evenings since the course probably only meets two times a week.

B: I wish I could.

A: 你不喜欢上夜课吗？

B: 不，不是那么回事。我每晚在餐厅工作，我需要挣钱付学费。

A: 你能和别人调一下时间吗？或许你只要调一两次夜班就可以了，因为这门课可能一周只有两次课。

B: 但愿可以吧。

switch to 切换到，转到

☞ A: What is that you are listening to? That beat's so strong that I can't concentrate on my work.

B: No problem. I can *switch* over *to* something lighter.

A: 你在听什么？节奏感太强了，我没法专心工作。

B: 没问题。我换一个轻柔一点的。

☞ A: Didn't I see you going into the administration building this afternoon?

B: I needed to *switch* my computer class *to* the ten o'clock section.

A: 我今天下午不是看到你去行政楼了吗？

B: 我要把我的计算机课调到 10 点。

take a drastic step 采取果断措施

☞ *A drastic step* should be *taken* immediately to control the disease. 我们应该采取果断措施来控制疾病。

take/have a look at 看一眼

☞ A: Could you *take a look at* my printer? It doesn't seem to be working.

B: I can't offer to set up this new one. Just give me a few minutes, OK?

A：你能看一下我的打印机吗？好像坏了。

B：这是新的，我不会修，给我几分钟好吗？

☞ A: You are going shopping? Can't you wait until you finish your story?

B: I am going there for my story. My detective solves a jewelry store robbery, so I want to ***take a look at*** how the jewelry cases are arranged, where the security cameras are located, that sort of thing.

A：你要去购物吗？你就不能等到写完你的小说再去吗？

B：我就是为我的小说去的。故事中的侦探破获了一个珠宝店抢劫案，所以我想去看看珠宝盒是怎样摆放的，以及摄像头的安装位置这一类的事。

☞ A: Hey Jean, can you ***take a look at*** this copy machine? I can't turn it on.

B: I am actually in the middle of something. How about in a couple of minutes?

A：嗨，琼，你能看一下这台复印机吗？我启动不了它。

B：我正在做别的事情。等一会好吗？

---

take a nap 打盹

☞ A: I can't concentrate on this final report any longer. Maybe I should ***take a nap*** before we continue.

B: They say the physical activity makes you more alert.

A：我无法专心做这份期末报告了。或许我应该小憩一会儿我们再继续。

B：有人说运动可以使人精神点。

---

take a stand 采取某种立场

☞ If the candidate wants more support he should have to ***take a stand*** on the current issue of petroleum. 如果这位候选人想得到更多的支持，就必须在当下的石油问题上做出表态。

☞ clarify a position

---

take a while 占用一段时间

☞ A: How did you ever manage to get through all 1000 pages of that new spy thriller?

B: It ***took a while***. But once I had started it, I couldn't put it down.

A：你怎么读完那部新的、关于间谍的 1000 页恐怖小说的？

B：花了我一段时间。但是我一开始读，就对它爱不释手了。

☞ A: Can you believe I just had to pay 30 bucks for a haircut in Santerbale?

B: You should try the salon where I go. It's only 15, but it ***takes a while*** to get an appointment.

A：你能相信吗？我刚刚在桑特贝尔剪头发花了 30 元！

B：你应该去我去的那个沙龙试试。那里只需 15 元，但是你得花点时间预约。

🔍 while 作连词时，意为"当…的时候；然而；尽管"。但是托福考试中通常考其名词词性，意为"一会儿"，如 after a while 意为"一会儿之后"。

226

take advantage of 利用；占…的便宜；捉弄，欺骗

☞ A: Do you want to go running down by the lake after psychology class? I really like to *take advantage of* the beautiful weather this afternoon.

　B: Well, normally I begin to gather with my study group then, but I guess I can skip that just this once.

　A：上完心理学课后你想在湖边跑步吗？我真的想好好享受一下今天下午这么美好的天气。

　B：哦，通常我都要在下午和学习小组成员集合，但是我觉得这次可以不去了。

take apart 拆卸

☞ The boy *took apart* the clock, but couldn't put it together. 那个小男孩把闹钟给拆开了，但是却不能重新组装起来。

take away 带走，拿走；消除，使消失

☞ Shelly drank a whole bottle of water to *take away* the bitter taste of the medicine. 谢丽喝了整整一瓶水来去除药物的苦味。

take care of 照顾，照料

☞ His sister might agree to *take care of* the cat. 他的妹妹答应照看这只猫了。

☞ A: You said you wanted to borrow my camera for Professor. Wilson's assignment. Well, here it is.

　B: I know this is precious to you, and I'll *take* good *care of* it. I hate using other people's things, especially expensive equipment like this.

　A：你说你想借我的相机做威尔逊教授的作业。嗯，给你。

　B：我知道这相机对你来说很珍贵，我会好好保管的。我讨厌用别人的东西，尤其像这么贵重的设备。

N O T E S

Unit 19

take it easy 别着急，别紧张，放松些

☞ Now that I finally turned in my thesis, I plan to *take it easy* for a while. 现在我终于把论文交上去了，我打算放松一阵子。

take off 脱下；拿走；起飞

☞ A: Do you mind if I *take off* my jacket?
B: Of course not, make yourself at home.
A：你介意我脱了衣服吗？
B：当然不会，请随便。

take over 接管，接办

☞ A: Can you *take over* for me here? I have a client coming to see me.
B: Well, I also have my hands full.
A：你能在这儿替我一会吗？我有一个客户要来。
B：嗯，我现在也很忙。

take photographs/pictures 拍照

☞ That camera ought to *take* very sharp *photographs*. 那台相机应该照得出很清晰的相片。

☞ It's difficult to *take photographs* indoors. 在室内照相很难。

take photographs

take place 发生；进行，举行

☞ The trade of grain and cotton *took place* at the coast, or near navigable rivers, because it was so expensive to transport goods over the roads that existed. 谷物和棉花的交易出现在沿海地区，或者适于航行的河流附近，因为当时的道路运输太贵了。

☞ An auction will *take place* on Saturday afternoon, and there will be some real treasures for sale then. 周六下午有一个拍卖会，到时会有一些真正的宝物待售。

☞ happen, occur

take/bring sth. back to 把…还回

☞ The man should *take* the stereo *back to* the store. 那个男人应该把音响还给商店。

☞ A: Hey, Bill, it's said that the art exhibition in the student centre is great. Would you like to go with me?
B: Yeah. But I'm going to *take* this book *back to* the library now.

A：嗨，比尔，据说学生中心的艺术展览很棒，想和我一起去看看吗？

B：想啊，可是我现在要去图书馆还书。

take sth. inside 把…带入内部

☞ A: I'm sorry. But you can't *take* your camera *inside*. You'll have to leave it here and pick it up after the concert.

B: Well, I guess it's too late to take it back to the car. Please be careful with it. It belongs to my roommate. She'll never forgive me if anything happens to it.

A：对不起，您不能带相机入内。您可以把它放在这里，音乐会结束后再来拿走。

B：哦，我想现在把它放回车里太晚了。请保管好它。这是我室友的，如果出了什么问题，她是不会原谅我的。

take up 开始从事；占去，占据；拿起，接收

☞ Robert wants to *take up* drawing. 罗伯特想开始画画。

☞ The device does not *take up* much place in kitchen. 这个装置在厨房中不占很大的地方。

take...for granted 想当然，认为…理所当然

☞ These people were responsible for many fundamental inventions and innovations that the modern world *takes for granted*. 这些人创造了很多现代社会认为理所当然应该存在的基础发明和革新。

☞ We *take for granted* some of the other inventions that enabled people to live and work in skyscrapers. 其他一些让人在摩天大楼里生活和工作的发明，我们认为都是理所当然存在的。

take...for instance/example 以…为例

☞ When the British were building cities in American colonies, they had to figure out how to make the cities run smoothly, right? Like...*take* traffic *for instance*. 当英国人在美洲殖民地建立城市时，他们需要考虑如何使城市顺利运转，对不对？像…，先以交通为例吧。

take...into account 把…考虑在内

☞ The design of the house should *take* these features of the property *into account*. 房子的设计应该把家具的这些特点也考虑在内。

talent show 才艺表演，才能展示

☞ A: Weren't you the person who said that not many students would sigh up for the *talent show*?

B: Yeah, I was really off the mark on that prediction.

A：难道你不是那个称不会有太多学生报名参加才艺表演的人吗？

B：是呀，我的预测真是错了。

tape recorder 录音机

☞ A: We got the **_tape recorder_** repaired last week.

B: Oh, so it could be repaired.

A：我们上周把录音机送去修了。

B：哦，那么它可能已经修好了。

☞ A: Oh, I'm sorry, I just realized that I forgot to bring the **_tape recorder_** you lent me. I left it back in my dorm.

B: That's all right. I won't need it until tonight. As long as I've got it by then.

A：哦，对不起，我刚刚意识到我忘了把你借给我的录音机带来了，我把它忘在我的宿舍了。

B：没关系的，今天白天我都不用，只要晚上之前还给我就可以。

target areas for 确定…的区域/范围

☞ A: About this survey on the quality of life in the dorm, I feel sort of awkward because, well, I'm not really comfortable here. Are you sure you want me to fill out this survey form?

B: It's people like you who can help us **_target areas for_** improvement.

A：关于这份宿舍生活质量的调查，我感到有些尴尬，因为，呃，我在这里住的很不舒服。你确定要我填这份调查表吗？

B：正是像你这样的人才能够帮我们找到应该提高的方面。

taste much better 尝起来更好

☞ A: I'm still not sure which brand of ice cream I should buy.

B: Oh, not that one. It's cheaper but these other brands **_taste much better_**.

A：我还是不确定应该买哪一个牌子的冰激凌。

B：哦，不是那个，虽然那个便宜但是其他牌子的味道要更好些。

team work 团队合作

☞ Good understanding of **_team work_** is critical for one's career success. 对团队合作有一个好的理解是一个人职业成功的关键。

🔍 团队精神可以表达为 team spirit。诚实（honesty）和勤奋（hard-working）在工作中也很重要。

technical innovation 技术革新

☞ This **_technical innovation_** will save us much time in housework. 这项技术革新会为我们在家务活上节省很多时间。

tedious debate 单调乏味的辩论

☞ The **_tedious debates_** made us doze. 那场乏味的辩论让我们都打瞌睡了。

tedious fellow　令人生厌的家伙

☞ My former roommate is an exceedingly *tedious fellow*. 我以前的室友真的是一个十足讨厌的家伙。

telephone communication　电话通信；电话沟通

☞ *Telephone communication* between the two cities restored after three days. 三天后，两个城市间的电话通信恢复了。

temperature regulation　温度调节

☞ The human body takes an active role in *temperature regulation*. 人体在体温调节方面发挥着积极的作用。

tend to do　倾向做

☞ A: I'm amazed that you still haven't gotten to know your neighbors.
B: They *tend to* keep to themselves.
A：我很惊讶你还不认识你的邻居。
B：他们不太和外人来往。

☞ People who use computers *tend to* stare at the monitor and blink less often than they normally would. That leads to dry irritated eyes. 常用电脑的人经常盯着显示器，比正常情况下眨眼的次数少，这样就会导致眼睛干涩。

tendency to do　做…的趋势

☞ We have been looking at the fear from a biology perspective, and some one asked whether the *tendency to* be fearful is genetic. 我们一直从生物学视角来看恐惧，有些人问是否恐惧也是遗传的。

tendency towards　…的倾向，…的趋势

☞ While a *tendency towards* anxiety and fear may well be an inherited trait, the specific form that the fear takes has more to do with the individual's environment. 恐惧和焦虑的倾向是天生的特点，而恐惧呈现出的具体形式则和其个人所处的环境有关。

test tube　试管

☞ A: Are you going to keep your part-time job next semester at the biology laboratory or you are going try for a different laboratory this time?
B: Actually neither. One semester as a lab assistant is enough; washing *test tubes* can get old pretty fast.
A：你下学期打算继续在生物实验室做兼职还是打算去不同的实验室？
B：事实上两个都不了。做一学期的实验室助理就受够了，清洗试管会让人老得很快。

the accuracy of scales 精确范围，精确尺度

☞ Industries depend on our government agency to monitor *the accuracy of scales* so that when people buy and sell their products there is one standard. 各行业依靠政府机构来监测尺度的精确度，以便他们在买卖产品时有相同标准。

the advent of …的到来

☞ The early form of advertising going back many hundreds of years with a simple sign there were shop doors that told you whether the shop was a bakery, a butcher shop or what you could get, then was *the advent of* the printing crest. 广告的早期形式可以追溯到几百年以前，那时的广告只是商店门口简单的标牌，告诉你这是一家面包店还是肉店，或者你能从该商店购买到什么物品。之后才迎来了印刷广告的顶峰时期。

the brick exterior 砖面

☞ What makes Chicago's Home Insurance Building important is that it had true skyscraper construction with an internal metal skeleton that carried the weight of *the brick exterior*. 芝加哥家庭保险大厦之所以重要是因为它有真正的摩天大楼结构，其内部是一个金属框架，支撑外部砖面的重量。

the distribution of …的分配

☞ The picture shows *the distribution of* different species of amphibians. 这幅图展示了不同种类两栖动物的分布情况。

the dominant/greatest power in the world 世界头号强国

☞ Once, Britain is *the dominant power in the world*. 英国曾经是世界头号强国。

the early stage of civilization 文明的最初阶段

☞ Today, the professor introduced a person who belongs to *the early stage of civilization*. 今天，教授给我们讲了一个生活在文明初始阶段的人。

the extension of …的扩大

☞ A: You are the group that's opposing *the extension of* the parking lot next to the Main Hall, right?

B: That's us. We just feel that it's important to save some of the natural beauty of the campus.

A：你们就是反对在主楼附近扩建停车场的人吗？

B：是我们。我们觉得保护校园里的自然景色很重要。

the Faculty of Law 法学院

☞ *The Faculty of Law* in our University was founded in 1996. Although we are a young faculty, we still have a rapid development. 我们大学的法学院于 1996 年建成。尽管我们是一个年轻的团队，但是我们的发展迅速。

the Faculty of Law

the inspection of　…的检查

☞ The federal government at that time is responsible for *the inspection of* new homes built on western lands. 那个时候的联邦政府负责监督建在西部的新房屋。

the interplay between ...　…的相互作用

☞ It's important to read the assigned poems aloud, so you can develop an appreciation of the sounds of the poetry: the rhymes, the rhythm, the repetition of words or sounds, and to get a sense of *the interplay between* the sounds of the words and their meaning. This is really critical as we move into modern poetry. 大声朗读所指定的诗是很重要的，这样可以培养你们对诗歌音律的鉴赏力：韵、节奏、词和音节的重复，同时对单词的读音与其意义间的相互作用有所感知。这对我们进入现代诗部分的学习非常重要。

the origins of civilization　文明的起源

☞ *The origins of civilization* should be related to the origins of cultural achievements. 文明的起源应该和文化成就的根源相关联。

the presence of　…的出现/出席

☞ *The presence of* the poison in the food chain resulted in eggs too weak to support the incubating chicks. 这种毒药出现在食物链中，导致蛋壳过于脆弱而不能孵化雏鸟。

the process of　…的过程

☞ Some salt leaves the ocean through *the process of* evaporation. 一些盐通过蒸发过程从海洋中析出。

the quality of one's handwriting　某人的书写质量

☞ The professor is discussing penmanship: *the quality of one's handwriting*. 那名教授正在讨论书法：一个人书写的质量。

the student action coalition　学生运动联盟

☞ I'm going door to door tonight to tell people about *the student action coalition*. 我今晚打算挨个门告诉大家有关学生运动联盟的事。

the symbol of　…的标志

☞ Where did the term Piggy Bank come from? Today the simple piggy bank is seen everywhere as *the symbol of* saving and frugality, for putting away funds for a rainy day, or building a nest egg for life's sudden money needs, such as paying college expenses, buying a home, or financing retirement. "存钱罐"这个词是怎么来的？如今，这个简单的存钱罐被视为是省钱和节约的象征，是用来把钱存起来以备不时之需的，或者是为生活中忽然需用钱时建立储蓄金，比如支付大学学费、买房子或是养老。

the volume of the music　音乐的音量

☞ Please turn down *the volume of the music*. 请把音乐的音量调小一点。

the younger/older generation　年轻/老一代

☞ *The older generation* doesn't like this kind of movie. 老一代人不喜欢这种电影。

thorny bumps　带刺的凸起

☞ Starfish are not really fish. They belong to the family of echinoderms which are spiny skinned sea animal, that is, their skin is covered with *thorny bumps*. 海星并不是真正的鱼，它们属于棘皮类动物，是皮肤上长满刺的海洋动物，也就是说，它们的皮肤上覆盖着带刺的凸起。

threat of disease　疾病的威胁

☞ For about 20 years the movement of people and goods was mostly from Maine to Quebec, and then the trend reversed as thousands of Canadians immigrated to Maine to escape poor crops, the lack of jobs and *the threat of disease*. 大概 20 年的时间里，人和货物的迁移大都是从缅因州到魁北克的，随后情况发生了逆转，成千上万的加拿大人为了逃避庄稼歉收、失业以及疾病的威胁而移民到缅因州。

throw out　扔掉；赶走；不予考虑

☞ A: Quick, bring some paper towels. I drop the bag with the eggs.
　 B: Paper towels? You may as well just *throw out* everything in the bag.
　 A：快点！递给我些手纸，我把一袋子鸡蛋掉到地上了。
　 B：手纸？你还不如把袋子里的东西都扔了。

throw up　猛地举起或抛起

☞ When an earthquake occurs under water, it *throws up* tremendous amounts of mud or sand that becomes suspended in a layer of water near the bottom of the ocean. 当地震发生在水下的时候，它就会抛起大量的泥沙，这些泥沙会在海底附近形成一层悬浮物。

tide sb. over　帮助某人度过难关

☞ A: Could I borrow a twenty to *tide me over* till payday next Thursday?
　 B: You are in luck. I've just cashed the check.
　 A：你能借我 20 美元撑到下周四发工资的日子吗？
　 B：你真幸运，我刚刚兑现了支票。

tie up　占用（电话）；忙于，被占用

☞ A: Dick, please don't *tie up* the phone. I need to make a call.
　 B: I'll be off in a minute.
　 A：迪克，请不要占着电话，我要打个电话。
　 B：一分钟就好。

☞ A: Professor, have you graded my term paper yet?
　 B: To tell you the truth, I've been *tied up* in committee meetings all week.
　 A：教授，您给我的学期论文评分了吗？
　 B：老实说，我这一周都在忙委员会议，抽不开身。

☞ A: Hi, I'd like to see the manager of the store. I'm applying for a job.

B: She's going to be **tied up** in meetings all day today and tomorrow.

A：嗨，我想见一下这家店的老板，我想申请一份工作。

B：今天和明天两天她都要忙着开会。

to be honest 实话实说

☞ **To be honest**, I didn't think much of the play. 说实话，我并不是很看好这部戏。

to some degree 从某种程度上来说

☞ Some studies done with mice indicate that mammals do inherit fearfulness **to some degree**. 从在老鼠身上做的试验可以看出，哺乳动物在某种程度上确实遗传恐惧感。

to tell you the truth 实话告诉你

☞ A: The drama club is holding auditions for their annual play; it's musical. What do you think?

B: **To tell you the truth**, I don't really act all things, but thanks for thinking of me.

A：戏剧俱乐部正在为一年一度的戏剧举行试镜，是部音乐剧。你认为怎么样？

B：老实说，我真的什么都演不了，不过谢谢你想到我。

too... to... 太…而不能

☞ A: Did you bring your blue and yellow sweater for me to wear at the game today? You know I like to wear school colors at these games.

B: Oh, I know I've forgotten something and it's **too** fatigue **to** get back. Will my yellow scarf do?

A：你的那件蓝黄相间的毛衣带来了吗？我今天比赛要穿。你知道我想在这些比赛中穿代表学校颜色的服装。

B：哦，我就知道我忘了什么东西，可回去拿太麻烦了。戴我的黄围巾行吗？

top priority 最优先考虑的事

☞ A: I know this jack is a little old and faint but I got some other things to take care of before the interview.

B: If you want my opinion, a new suit should be a **top priority**.

A：我知道这件夹克有点旧了而且有些褪色，但是在面试之前我还有一些其他事情要做。

B：如果你想听我的建议的话，一套新西装是最好的选择。

trade places with 与…交换职位

☞ A lot of people would like to **trade places with** you. 很多人都想跟你交换工作岗位。

traditional view 传统观点

☞ The professor said the more **traditional view** was that the ocean water came from volcanoes. 教授称更为传统的一种说法是海水从火山而来。

traffic laws 交通法

☞ The colonists passed **traffic laws** to prevent traffic from being interfered with by pigs. 殖民者颁布了相关交通法以防止交通被猪妨碍。

🔍 与"交通"相关的常考短语还有：

traffic policeman 交警　　　　　　　　traffic jam 交通堵塞

transfer to 迁移至，转移至；调往

☞ A: You are not planning to **transfer to** a different University next year, are you?
　 B: If I were, you'd be the first to know.
　 A：你没有打算明年转到另一所大学，对不对？
　 B：如果我有此打算，我会第一个通知你。

☞ A: I hear that your brother is planning to **transfer to** another university.
　 B: Not if I can talk him out of it. And believe me, I'm trying.
　 A：我听说你弟弟打算转到另一所大学。
　 B：如果我能说服他，他就不会转了。相信我，我要试试。

NOTES

Unit 20

transmit to　向…传送

☞ These organs of a grasshopper sense of change in air pressure which might be produced by an enemy approaching, and impulses ***transmitted to*** the legs. 在得知敌人靠近时，蝗虫身上的这些器官就会感知到气压变化以及传递到腿上的刺激。

trash can　垃圾桶

☞ Instead of seeing the usual brown trash cans all over the campus, from now on you'll see four different colors of ***trash cans***. 从今以后，你在整个校园都看不到普通的棕色垃圾桶了，取而代之的是四种不同颜色的垃圾桶。

☞ garbage bin, garbage can

travel on　乘…旅行

travel on

☞ Private companies built the roads, and collected fees from all vehicles ***travelling on*** them. 私人公司修建了道路，并对行驶在这些道路上的所有车辆收费。

🔍 该词组后面接交通工具，如：
travel on foot 徒步旅行　　　　travel on a train/ship/plane 乘火车/船/飞机旅行

trial period　试用阶段

☞ Jefferson was taken on for a one-month ***trial period*** before being accepted as a permanent staff in the club. 在成为这家俱乐部的正式员工之前，杰斐逊要经过一个月的试用期。

☞ probation period

🔍 "某人在试用期内" 用介词 on, 如：The boss will take you on a three-month period. 老板会让你先经过三个月的试用期。

trickle down　滴下来

☞ Caves are normally created by carbonic acid that ***trickles down*** from above. 通常情况下，岩洞是由自上滴下的碳酸腐蚀形成的。

tropical environment　热带环境

☞ These plants have only partially adapted to their *tropical environment*. 这些植物仅仅部分地适应了热带环境。

try to　尝试做

☞ A: The subway is running behind schedule, and traffic is backed up for blocks. I don't know if we'll make the 7:15 show.

B: It's a beautiful night. Let's *try to* get there on foot. And if we don't make it, let's just have dinner near the theater.

A：地铁晚点了，而且好几个街区都在堵车。我不知道我们能否赶上 7 点 15 的表演。

B：今天夜景很美，我们走着去吧。如果没赶上，我们就在剧院附近吃晚餐吧。

☞ A: I'd like to *try to* sell some of my textbooks from last semester.

B: You and a few hundred other people.

A：我想要卖上学期的一些课本。

B：你和其他几百人都是这么想的。

☞ A: I'm taking this great course, the psychology of language. It's so interesting. You are a psychology major. You should sign up for it.

B: Actually I *tried to* do that. But they told me I need to have taken a linguistic first.

A：我要选这门了不起的课程，语言心理学。这课太有意思了。你是心理专业的学生，应该报名参加的。

B：事实上我试过了。但是他们跟我说要先修语言学才行。

☞ attempt to

tuition payment　学费

☞ A: Please tell me I haven't missed the deadline for *tuition payment*.

B: I'm afraid you are about a week late.

A：希望我还没错过交学费的最后期限。

B：恐怕你已经晚了一周。

turbidity current　浊流

☞ It's true that deep down on the ocean floor we won't have the same kinds of currents we find in shallower parts. But we do find what we call *turbidity currents*. 确实，在海床上我们没有遇到在浅海区域发现的同样的水流，但是我们却在那里发现了所谓的浊流。

turn face up　亮牌

☞ The cards of one of the four players are *turned face up*. That player is called the dummy. 四个选手中的其中一个亮牌，这个选手就叫做(桥牌)明手。

Bridge(桥牌)是托福听力中的一个高频话题。下面介绍一些与桥牌有关的词汇：

Club 梅花   Diamond 方块
Heart 红心   Spade 黑桃
Double 加倍   Redouble 再加倍
Pass 不叫牌

turn out　结果是，被证明是

☞ A: You didn't think the concert **turned out** this great, did you?

 B: I sure didn't. I heard this band once before and didn't think they were all that hot.

 A：你没有想到这场演唱会的效果会这么好，是吗？

 B：确实没有，我以前听说过这个乐队一次，但是没想到他们这么火爆。

☞ A: This course wasn't supposed to be hard.

 B: But it sure **turned out** to be, didn't it?

 A：这门课程不应该这么难。

 B：但结果它确实是难，不是吗？

☞ This idea **turned out** to be closer to the truth. 这个想法被证明更接近真理。

turn over a new leaf　重新开始；改过自新

☞ A: You know Frank's appearance seems to be neater these days. I wonder why.

 B: Maybe he just decided it was time to **turn over a new leaf**.

 A：知道吧，弗兰克这几天似乎把自己收拾得更利索了，我想知道原因。

 B：或许他觉得是该"洗心革面"的时候了。

turn sb. down　拒绝某人

☞ A: I'm working on a short story that I'd like to get published in the *Campus Literary Review*. You've done that, haven't you? Didn't I see a poem of yours in last month's issue?

 B: Yes, I was so excited to finally see my work in print. It was my third submission. You just have to keep trying if they **turn you down**.

 A：我正在写一篇短篇故事，我想在《校园文学评论》上发表。你已经发表过了，是吧？上个月的期刊上我看有你一首诗吧？

 B：是的，看到自己的作品终于发表了真的很高兴。那是我第三次投稿了，如果他们拒绝你的话，你一定要坚持。

☞ reject

ultraviolet radiation　紫外线辐射

☞ The wings of the birds are easily damaged by the **ultraviolet radiation**. 这种鸟类的翅膀很容易被紫外线辐射伤害。

相关词汇：ultraviolet rays 紫外线

under construction 在施工，在建设中

☞ The portal website of the country is still **under construction**. 这个国家的门户网站仍在建设之中。

under pressure 处于压力之下

☞ A: Could you work **under pressure**?

B: Pressure always gives us an impetus. We'll be lazy if there's no pressure.

A：你能在压力下工作吗？

B：压力会激励我们，如果没有压力的话，我们就会变得懒惰。

under the circumstances 在…情况下

☞ A: Dr. Jones, I was wondering if you would consider giving me an extension on my paper. I just got back on campus yesterday from hospital.

B: Well, **under the circumstances** I can't see how I can deny your request.

A：琼斯博士，我想知道您能否考虑再宽限我几天写论文。我昨天刚出院回到学校。

B：好吧，这种情况下我都不知道如何拒绝你。

☞ in such a case, in this instance

under the protection of 在…的保护下

under the protection of

☞ The artists don't have to file any documents and **under the protection of** the Copyright Law, any recreation of their original work such as prints are also covered by the artists copyright. 艺术家不用把文件归档，在版权法的保护下，任何对他们原创作品——比如画作的再创作，都在艺术版权的保护范围之内。

up in the air 未定的，悬而不决的

☞ A: Thank heaven. It's Friday. Are you doing anything special this weekend?

B: Good question. To tell you the truth, my brother might be coming over and so everything is **up in the air** right now.

A：谢天谢地，终于到星期五了，你这周末有什么特别的事情要做吗？

B：问得好，实话告诉你，我弟弟可能会来，所以现在所有事情都还没定呢。

☞ unsettled

> 🔍托福考试中经常考到与 up 相关的口语用法，还有 It's up to sb.意为"由某人决定"。另外，go up in the air 是"怒火冲天"的意思，hands up in the air 意为"挥舞双手"。

upward motion 向上的运动

☞ Aristotle considered an object's downward or **upward motion** to be a result of the dominant nature of the object. 亚里士多德认为，一个物体是向上还是向下运动取决于这个物体的主导性质。

vacuum cleaner 真空吸尘器

☞ A: My parents are coming to see our apartment this weekend.

B: Looks as if I'd better lend you my **vacuum cleaner** then.

A：我父母这周末要来看我们的公寓。

B：看样子到时候我最好把我的真空吸尘器借给你。

☞ At that time, electric power was available for lamps, sewing machines, irons, and even **vacuum cleaners**. 那时候，灯、缝纫机、熨斗甚至真空吸尘器都可以用电了。

🔍 托福听力常考电器名称：

furnace 加热器，炉子   air conditioner 空调

microwave oven 微波炉   dryer 烘干机

oven 烤箱   dishwasher 洗碗机

vary the volume 调整音量

☞ Tina never **vary the volume** when she listens to music. 蒂娜听音乐的时候从来都不调音量。

☞ adjust the volume

🔍 调大或调小音量为 increase the volume 和 decrease the volume。

vegetative reproduction 营养繁殖

☞ **Vegetative reproduction** is a type of asexual reproduction for plants. 对于植物来说，营养繁殖是一种无性繁殖。

vehicle maintenance 车辆的保养

☞ A: Where can I find a **vehicle maintenance** place?

B: Just behind the building.

A：我在哪里能找到车辆保养的地方？

B：就在大厦的后面。

vertical movement 垂直运动

☞ There are both horizontal and **vertical movements** in air. 大气中存在垂直运动和水平运动。

vertical wind　垂直风向

☞ A statistical analysis shows that **vertical wind** shear has an effect on tropical cyclone development. 一项数据分析显示垂直风切变对热带气旋的形成有影响。

visualize sb. doing sth.　设想某人做某事

☞ I just **visualize** a bunch of cash coming in the boxes. 我幻想着能有几箱子现金到我身边。

volunteer work　志愿工作

☞ A: What are you doing?

　B: I always do **volunteer work** on the first Saturday of every month.

　A：你在做什么?

　B：我经常在每个月的第一个星期六做志愿工作。

vote for　为…投票

☞ The woman should ask his roommate to **vote for** her. 这个女人应该让她的室友为她投票。

☞ ballot for

walking hibernation　(北极熊的)冬眠

☞ When the polar bears are in **walking hibernation** phase, they only make a little efforts to catch prey. 当北极熊处在冬眠期时，它们只用很少的力气去捉捕猎物。

☞ dormancy

🔍 该词组曾在托福考试中出现过，因为北极熊的冬眠并不像其他动物一样需要睡整个冬天，它还是会出来寻找食物等，所以它的冬眠叫"walking hibernation"。

warm up　(使)做准备活动，(使)热身；(使)变暖

☞ A: Are you ready to go jogging?

　B: Almost. I have to **warm up** first.

　A：你准备好慢跑了吗?

　B：差不多了，我得先热热身。

☞ The weather will **warm up** soon. 天气很快就会变暖。

wash up　洗手洗脸；洗餐具；冲洗

☞ A: My fingers are sticky from that candy bar. Do you mind if I use the restroom to **wash up** before we leave?

　B: Sure. I'll be over at the bus stop.

　A：我的手摸过糖块之后变得粘糊糊的。在我们离开之前我能用这个洗手间洗一下吗?

　B：当然可以，我会在公交车站等你。

water molecule 水分子

☞ The research indicates that most of the **water molecules** from the comet would have burned up as they fell through the atmosphere. 研究表明，彗星上的大部分水分子在通过大气层坠落时就已经燃烧殆尽了。

🔍 hydrogen atom 氢原子　　　　　　oxygen atom 氧原子

wave field 波场

☞ Investigating the **wave field** has been of increasing significance. 研究波场的重要性日益增加。

wear a suit 穿西服

wear a suit

☞ A: I'm thinking of **wearing a** new **suit** to James' wedding.

B: I just hope that my old suit still fits. You know how I feel about shopping.

A：我正在考虑穿新西服去参加詹姆斯的婚礼。

B：我希望我那件旧西服还合身，你知道我很烦购物的。

wear out 使筋疲力尽；穿破，磨损

☞ A: You look **worn out**. Are you feeling under the weather?

B: Not at all. But I have been putting in some wrong errors in the chemistry lab.

A：你看起来很疲惫，感觉不舒服吗？

B：没有。我在化学实验室犯了些错误。

🔍 wear 的过去式 wore 和过去分词 worn 都不规则，特别是过去分词在听力中会与后面的 out 有连读，要多加注意。

weather report 天气预报

☞ A: Do you hear? The **weather report** says we'll gonna get at least foot of snow tomorrow.

B: That much? That's incredible! I can't wait to go outside to play in it.

A：你听见了吗？天气预报说我们这儿明天会有至少一英尺的降雪。

B：那么多吗？真是不可思议啊！我都等不及要到外面去玩雪了。

☞ A: These summer days are getting to be more than I can take. It was even too hot to go to the pool yesterday.

B: Hold on. According to the **weather report** we should have some relief by the end of the week.

A：这几个夏日热得已经让我受不了了。昨天热得都不能去游泳池。

B：再坚持一下，天气预报说这个周末天气情况会有所缓解。

243

☞ A: Did you hear the *weather report* for today?

  B: The pollution's going to be so bad. They recommend staying indoors.

  A：你听今天的天气预报了吗？

  B：污染情况会很严重，建议我们最好待在室内。

weather variations   天气变化

☞ *Weather variations* in the desert is the main topic in today's tutorial. 沙漠里的天气变化是今天辅导课的重要话题之一。

What's up?   怎么了？

☞ A: Hello, Larry. It's Carol Baldwin.

  B: Oh, hi, Carol. *What's up*?

  A: I was just looking at the TV section of the newspaper and I noticed that the dinosaur series I was telling you about is going to be rebroadcast this week, starting tonight.

  A：你好，拉里，我是卡萝尔·鲍德温。

  B：哦，嗨，卡萝尔，怎么了？

  A：我刚看了报纸的电视栏，注意到我告诉你的恐龙系列片要在这周重播了，从今天晚上开始。

☞ A: Stan, do you have a minute?

  B: Oh, hi, Cathy. Sure. *What's up*?

  A: Well. I've been meaning to talk to you about the situation in the office.

  B: I'm not in there very often. It's so noisy that I can't work.

  A：斯坦，你能抽出一分钟来吗？

  B：哦，嗨，凯茜。当然可以，怎么了？

  A：嗯，我想和你说一下办公室的情况。

  B：我不是经常在那儿，那儿太吵了，以至于我不能工作。

☞ What's the matter?

wildlife habitat   野生动物栖息地

☞ The forest fire nearly destroyed the *wildlife habitat*. 那场森林大火差点就把野生动物栖息地给毁了。

wipe out   抹掉，擦去，除去；消灭，毁灭

☞ We must make effort to *wipe out* the memory of the terrible events. 我们必须努力抹去那些可怕事件给我们留下的记忆。

wireless device   无线电装置

☞ It was an Italian inventor who created the first *wireless device* for sending out radio signals in 1895. 于 1895 年发明第一台可发送广播信号的无线装置的是一位意大利发明家。

with details of   关于…的细节

☞ We enclose a brochure *with details of* our company. 随信附上一份关于我们公司详细情况的小册子。

with/in reference to   关于

☞ *In reference to* your advertisement in the newspaper, I believe that I have the qualification to do this job. 鉴于您在报纸上登的广告，我相信我能胜任这份工作。

wonder if   想知道是否

☞ A: I *wonder if* a job like this can be handled by Alex.

B: Well, if he can't handle it, no one can.

A：我在想象这种工作亚历克斯能否处理。

B：哦，如果他不能，就没人可以了。

☞ A: I've been running a mile every afternoon for the past month, but I still haven't been able to lose more than a pound or two. I *wonder if* it's worth it.

B: Oh, don't give up now. It always seems hard when you are just starting out.

A：我在过去的一个月里每天下午都跑一英里，但是我减掉的体重也不过一两磅。我在想这么做值不值得。

B：噢，别现在就放弃，万事开头难嘛。

☞ A: Tom and I are having a party next week. We *wonder if* you and Joe would be free to join us.

B: Sounds great. But I'd better talk to Joe before we say yes.

A：我和汤姆下周要开个派对。我们想问你和乔有没有时间来。

B：听起来很棒啊。但是我最好还是先问问乔。

wood fiber   木纤维

☞ The scientific research aims at the composition of this kind of *wood fiber*. 该科学研究的是这种木纤维的成分。

work a part-time job   做兼职

☞ A: You know, I really think you should run for class president. Everybody knows you and likes you. And you got some great ideas.

B: Thanks. I have thought about it. I'm taking six classes and *working a part-time job*. That's about all I can handle right now.

A：知道吗，我真的认为你应该竞选班长。每个人都认识你、喜欢你，并且你有很多很好的想法。

B：谢谢。我想过这件事。我现在在修着六门课程同时还做兼职。这些是我目前力所能及的了。

work extra hours　加班

☞ A: This is the second time this month that my boss's asked me to **work extra hours**. I am glad to get a bigger paycheck, but I just don't want her to give me such a heavy schedule.

　　B: Better watch your step. A lot of people would like to trade places with you.

　　A：在这个月里，这是老板第二次让我加班了。我很高兴可以得到更多的报酬，但是我不想她将我的工作日程安排得这么紧张。

　　B：你最好小心行事。很多人想跟你换位子呢。

☞ work overtime

work on　从事于，致力于

☞ A: I wonder who'd be willing to **work on** this committee.

　　B: Well, you know more about it than anyone.

　　A：我想知道谁愿意在这个委员会工作。

　　B：哦，你比任何人都清楚。

☞ A: Don't you think the professor is giving us too many projects to **work on**?

　　B: Well, I would like to have some free time once in a while.

　　A：难道你不认为教授给我们太多项目做了吗？

　　B：哦，我想偶尔能有些空闲时间。

work out　想出，制定出；解决；计算出；理解，弄懂

☞ A: The conference on career planning is only a month away, but there are still a few things that our organizing committee needs to **work out**.

　　B: Then it's clear that we'd better meet again and soon. Would you mind setting it up?

　　A：还有一个月就要开关于职业规划的会议了，但是我们组委会还有一些事情要做。

　　B：很明显，我们最好尽快再开一次会。你来安排一下好吗？

🔍 注意两词连读 /'wɜːrkˌaʊt/。

would like to　愿意做

☞ A: We've got an hour before our next class, **would** you **like to** get something to eat here?

　　B: I can join you for a quick sandwich, but I need to run some errands afterward.

　　A：距下节课上课还有一个小时，你想不想在这里吃点东西？

　　B：我可以和你一起随便吃个三明治，但是随后我还有些其他的事情要做。

☞ A: I was just about to go to the art exhibit. **Would** you **like to** go over there with me?

　　B: I made plans with Susan to go tomorrow afternoon.

　　A：我正要去看艺术展览呢，你想跟我一起去吗？

　　B：我计划明天下午和苏珊一起去。

☞ A: John, **I'd like to** talk to you about the way you come late every day. It disrupts the class.

B: I'm sorry professor. I didn't realize I was bothering anyone. I will watch from now on.

A：约翰，我想和你谈谈，你每天迟到扰乱了课堂秩序。

B：教授，我很抱歉。我没有意识到自己打扰到了大家，从现在开始，我会注意的。

wrap up   完成；专心致志于，沉浸在；裹住

☞ A: Do you think we can **wrap up** this report by five?

B: Have you looked at the clock recently?

A：你认为我们在五点前可以完成这个报告吗？

B：难道你刚刚没看表吗？

☞ A: Are you ready to start studying for the test yet or are you to **wrap up** in that TV show?

B: Ask me again in about half an hour.

A：你准备开始复习考试还是继续沉浸在那个电视节目中呢？

B：半个小时后再说吧。

🔍 注意 wrap 和 up 组成短语时会发生连读现象 /ˈræpˌʌp/。

Xinhua News Agency   新华社

☞ The **Xinhua News Agency** says the reconstruction work started last week. 新华社报道，重建工作已于上周开始。

---

yell at   向…大喊大叫

☞ A: Can you believe the bus driver just **yelled at** me like that?

B: And just what did you think would happen when you spill the coffee all over the floor?

A：你能相信那个公交车司机竟然那样对我大喊大叫吗？

B：只要想一下你把咖啡溅得满地都是时会发生什么吧？

☞ shout at

---

yield to   屈服，服从

☞ The little boy does not want to **yield to** his father's advice. 这个小男孩不想听从他爸爸的建议。

☞ give in, submit to

You bet   的确，当然

☞ A: Are you still planning to go to the concert?

B: **You bet** I am.

A：你仍旧计划去演唱会吗？

B：当然。

☞ A: Are you looking forward to your move in April?

B: **You bet** I am. The rooms here are too small and there is no storage space.

A：你盼着四月份搬家吗？

B：当然了，这里的房间太小了，而且没有储物间。

☞ A: I'm going to Chicago on business and somebody said you were the right person to talk to about what I can do there for fun.

B: *You bet* I am. I hope you've got at least a month.

A：我要去芝加哥出差了，有人说你可以告诉我那儿有什么娱乐的好地方。

B：当然啊，我希望你能在那里至少待一个月。

☞ A: Hey, congratulations on winning the essay contest. That thousand-dollar prize money should really come in handy.

B: *You bet*! I've already put it aside to cover the increase my landlord just announced for next year.

A：嘿，恭喜你在散文比赛中获胜。那三千元美元的奖励来得太容易了。

B：当然！我已把钱存起来了，用来付房东刚说的要在明年涨的那部分房租。

☞ You know it.

You can say that again. 你说的没错。

☞ A: You didn't care for the movie, did you?

B: *You can say that again*.

A：你不喜欢这部电影，不是吗？

B：你说的没错。

☞ A: So I hear you're really happy with your new car. I bet it's a lot better than the last one you got stuck with, the one you bought from Cathy?

B: *You can say that again*. I'm sure I've made a good choice this time.

A：我听说你很满意你的新车。我猜它一定比你上次那辆麻烦不断的车好吧？就是你从凯茜手里买的那辆。

B：你说的没错，我肯定这次的选择是对的。

You got that right. 你说对了。

☞ A: I noticed you haven't been getting along well with your roommate lately.

B: *You got that right*. And it's going to be a long time before I feel comfortable with him again.

A：我注意到你最近和你的室友相处得不是很好。

B：你说对了。而且我和他很长一段时间内都不会和好了。

----

zebra crossing 斑马线

☞ We should take the *zebra crossing* or underpass to cross the road. 我们在过马路的时候要走斑马线或地下通道。

☞ pedestrian crossing

🔍 其他常用交通词汇：

intersection / crossroad 十字路口　　　　　T-junction 丁字路口

pavement / sidewalk 人行道

248